THE MIGRANT DIARIES

THE MIGRANT DIARIES

Lynne Jones

Refuge Press, New York, 2020

ISBN#13: 978-0-8232-9699-6 (Hard Cover)
ISBN#13: 978-0-8232-9698-9 (Paperback)
ISBN#13: 978-0-8232-9700-9 (ePub)
ISBN#13: 978-0-8232-9701-6 (WebPDF)

Cover and book design: Mauro Sarri
Cover image: Abdullah (age 9)

Printed in the United States of America.

This book is dedicated to
all those forced to leave the place they call home.

Acknowledgements

Some of the material in these Diaries was first published in *Outside the Asylum: A Memoir of War Disaster and Humanitarian Psychiatry* published by Weidenfeld & Nicolson in 2017. I would like to thank them for permission to reuse it. I would like to thank the Lancet and Elsevier for permission to reuse material that appeared in Borderlands, published in July 2017. I am also grateful to the FXB Center for Health and Human Rights at Harvard University for publishing some of these diaries on their website. Thank you to the Rights and Opportunities Foundation for continuously supporting my work in the migrant crises in Europe and Central America. Many other people have helped me in numerous ways. Thanks to Ahmad Alsalmo; Hiba Alsalmo; Giorgos Anastoulis; Mahmoud Alhossary; Bushra Al Khayat; Dalia Al Sharkawi; Yara Amparo López López; Giorgos Anastoulis; Luis Arriola Vega; Bashar Ayob; Yanira Chica; Maureen Jane Condon; Ed Cotton; Enrique Coraza de los Santos; Mark Cousins; Sebastian Dempf; Caia Fallowfield; Rowan Farrell; Soori Gharedaghi; Cindy Gonzalez Malo; Benoit Grancier; Maddie Harris; Ben Harrison; Housam Jackaly; Daniela Krišová; Eivor Lægreid; Hannah Lindner; Broeder Johannes Maertens; Shizuka Maruta; Elizabet Monzón Gálvez; Tracey Myers; Mohsen Naeem; Dina Prior; Luke Pye; Tom Radcliffe; Phoebe Ramsay; Alex Reyna; Don Rito; Cristina Robledo Cossio; Nour Shehada; Sarah Story; Panagiotis Tzannetakis; Jeffrey Utter; Heather Wurtz. Thanks also to the volunteers and staff in all of the following organisations: L'Auberge des Migrants, France; Refugee Women's Centre, France; Danish Refugee Council, Greece; Drop in the Ocean, Greece; International Medical Corps, Greece; AccoglieRete, Italy; Caritas, Italy; Terre des Hommes, Italy; Comité Estratégico de Ayuda Humanitaria, Mexico; Help Refugees, UK, France and Greece; Indigo Volunteers, UK. I would also like to thank the many friends who wish their names to be anonymous, particularly the individuals, children and their families who chose to share their stories. I continue to learn and to be inspired by their courage and grace under pressure. More children's stories, pictures, and film can be found on the website: migrantchildstorytelling.org. I should emphasize that these are personal diaries, and any mistakes or inaccuracies in the relating of events are my own.

Thanks to Brendan Cahill, at Refuge Press, for his enthusiasm for this book and Johanna Lawton for scrupulous editing and Mauro Sarri for design.

Finally, special thanks to my husband Asmamaw, my companion in so many of these journeys and a constant support in my work.

Table of Contents

Introduction

The full horror of the human tragedy unfolding on the shores of Europe was brought home on Wednesday, as images of the lifeless body of a young boy—one of at least 12 Syrians who drowned attempting to reach the Greek island of Kos—encapsulated the extraordinary risks refugees are taking to reach the west.

—Guardian, 2 September 2015

Reacting to yesterday's news that almost 150 people have drowned in the Mediterranean and around the same number have been returned to Libya by the Libyan Coastguard, where they risk indefinite detention, Massimo Moratti, Research Director for Europe at Amnesty International, said: "This high number represents a new low for European leaders. They have done everything they can to pull up the drawbridge to Europe; withdrawing Search and Rescue Operations; criminalising NGO rescue boats; cooperating with the Libyan coastguard, and yet people are still risking their lives to come to Europe."

—Amnesty International, 26 July 2019

"Twelve people have died while Malta and Europe were watching. We should never forget that these deaths are the direct result of Malta's and Europe's non-assistance policies, and their clear intention to let people die at sea. These deaths could and should have been prevented." The survivors are all still in detention cells, including the toddler and baby, at Tripoli's Tariq al-Sikka, where, according to lawyers and charities, they have no access to medical treatment, or sufficient food and water.

—Guardian, 19 May 2020

Three-year-old Alan Kurdi's death captured Europe's imagination in the Autumn of 2015. The media coverage led to an outpouring of support for those seeking refuge in Europe. Germany had already opened its borders, and, over the course of that year, allowed over

13

one million people to enter.

I started working with migrants arriving in Northern France that same Autumn of 2015. After some twenty years of establishing mental health programmes in emergencies across the globe, including East and West Africa, Central America, and the Middle East; the emergency now appeared to be on my own doorstep. Since then, I have continued to work in different 'hotspots' in France, Italy, Greece, and in Mexico—where a similar crisis plays out on the US border.

Over these five years, I have watched as the initial welcome and compassion shifted to indifference, and sometimes overt hostility towards all those seeking refuge, driven by negative media stereotypes and a European and US leadership that either embraces, or is intimidated by, the racism of the far right. Meanwhile, the conflicts and desperate circumstances that drive this flight have become background noise to domestic preoccupations.

I kept these diaries, publishing some as online blogs, because I wanted to show what it's like to be caught up on the front lines of the migrant crises in Europe and Central America, either as a person in flight, or as a volunteer.

Why diaries? I love diaries, both as a reader and a writer. For a reader, diaries provide a sense of immediacy, explaining how things happened at that moment in time—what people felt, thought, said and did. As a writer, this is what I strive to capture, so that my readers can time travel in history. The diary format provides an honest, completely personal account. It provides continuity in the present tense, which allows readers to accompany me and directly witness how people and situations change and evolve, rather than have them summarised through retrospective analysis, with hindsight thrown in for good measure.

I have tried to throw a spotlight on the human dimension of the migrant crisis allowing particular people and places to come to life. I wanted to increase our understanding of who migrants are, what forces them to take such extraordinary risks in travel and put up with so much uncertainty and ill-treatment.

Secondly, I wanted to document the emergence of a new kind of humanitarianism that challenges the professional models that have framed my own working life. The large international agencies, both UN and NGO, with the exception of Medecins Sans Frontieres (MSF) and Medecins Du Monde (MDM), were for the most part, largely absent in the earlier part of this crisis. Two groups stepped into the void. One was the migrants themselves. In the absence of outside support, they started taking care of themselves, often in astonishingly creative ways. The other was unpaid volunteers who arrived from all over the world, many with no previous humanitarian experience. Over the course of time, both groups have come together to create new ways of working that, in many respects, appear more egalitarian and empowering than old models.

I also wanted to describe what it was like to try to provide mental health and psychosocial support in these situations, and how my own practice evolved and developed over time. Working in these settings challenged my stereotypes of how we cope with stress and what fosters resilience. One of the most rewarding aspects was how often I witnessed, and was told, how helping others had helped people to help themselves.

Another aspect of this resilience came through creativity. Alpha, an artist from Mauritania, who opened an art school in the Calais Jungle told me:

— *If you want to survive, do art. Work hard at it, and every time you are drinking poison if you do art, you will lose all the pain in your life.*

Wherever I went, I saw migrants creating artwork and beauty around them, out of whatever was available: stuffed toys, plastic bottles, tear gas canisters. I wanted to encourage this. With colleagues and friends, we created a story telling project to provide an opportunity for children to tell stories about any aspect of their lives, in any form they wanted. The work is shown in exhibits and online. Some of the children's stories (and pictures) are included in this book. In this way children can talk directly to the reader, sharing what is important to them, unmediated by myself.

I have struggled with the issue of what term to use—migrant, asylum seeker, or refugee—and have used all three over the years. I started out feeling that the term migrant was so heavily stigmatised that it was better to avoid it. Al Jazeera took a similar position in 2015 arguing that:

"The umbrella term migrant is no longer fit for purpose when it comes to describing the horror unfolding in the Mediterranean. It has evolved from its dictionary definitions into a tool that dehumanises and distances, a blunt pejorative. [...] Migrant is a word that strips suffering people of voice. Substituting refugee for it is—in the smallest way—an attempt to give some back."[1]

In fact, the term refugee has a strict legal definition. According to the 1951 UN Convention on Refugees: "A refugee is an individual who 'owing to well-founded fear of being persecuted for reasons of race, religion, nationality, membership of a particular social group or political opinion' fled the country of their nationality." They have defined rights under that Convention; one of the most fundamental principles being that refugees should not be expelled or returned to situations where their life or freedom would be under threat.[2]

The term 'migrant' is not defined under international law and is used in varying ways. For example, it's used as a term to describe those who choose to leave their own country for economic reasons or to study. The problem with making a clear distinction between migrants who choose to leave their home countries for 'economic' reasons and refugees 'forced' to flee because of fear of persecution or war, is that it ignores the complex reasons forcing people, particularly children, to flee difficulties and/or poverty at home, the complete lack of normal standards of protection for many children living in countries which are not at war, and the growing impact of climate degradation. What would you do if you were abused or prostituted by your own family? How would you react if all your family's cattle were killed by disease? Where would you go if drought or floods made life impossible at home?

The International Organisation for Migration uses the term 'migrant' to describe any person "who moves away from his or her place of usual residence, whether within a country or across an international border, temporarily or permanently, and for a variety of reasons."[3]

The Office of the United Nations High Commissioner for Human Rights (OHCHR) describes an international migrant as "any person who is outside a State of which they are a citizen or national, or, in the case of a stateless person, their State of birth or habitual residence."[4] Thus, refugees fleeing war or persecution are one form of forced migration. There are "important overlaps in the challenges and vulnerabilities faced by people who move along the same routes, use the same forms of transport, and are similarly exposed to human rights violations, abuse and xenophobia. Moreover, today, and notwithstanding the gradual expansion of refugee protection, many people are compelled to leave their homes for reasons that do not fall within the refugee definitions, such as the adverse impacts of climate change including slow-onset processes or flight from food insecurity." The OHCHR also points out that all migrants of any category are entitled to the protections of international law, which includes not being returned to situations where their life is endangered.

Taking all these definitions and considerations into account, although initially, I used the term refugee, from late 2016 I started to use the term 'migrant' as an all-encompassing term that includes refugees and asylum seekers, when the status of those in the group I was describing was mixed or unknown.[5] I hope these diaries and stories will make clear that all of those I encountered were fleeing to survive, and are equally deserving of our concern and protection. I also hope that in giving the term life through the voices of all the migrants I met, I could challenge the negative stereotypes attached to the word.

In the last five years of working in these settings I have met some of the bravest, most creative, resilient, and extraordinary people of all ages. Of course, there was violence and crime, as there is in all communities. But it is the ability to cope and survive in the most dehumanising conditions, the compassion and concern for each other, and the courage and dreams that have inspired me, that I hope I have accurately reflected here.

Note on the text. All migrant names and some personal details have been changed to protect identity. Some individuals (Housam, Stella, Daniel and Cosimo, Mahmoud and Aboolfazl) have given permission for their names to be used.

All pictures, unless individually credited, are by the author. The picture credits by children from the storytelling project are taken from *https:///migrantchildstorytelling.org/the-pictures* and use pseudonyms chosen by the children.

2015

London

Amsterdam

Brussels

Calais

Paris

Calais

France, October—November 2015

The Jungle, Sunday 18 October

How stupid can you be?

I pull up on the muddy track that provides one point of access to the camp. On one side there is a 'restaurant' constructed from heavy plastic tarpaulin and wood. On the other is a field of tents stretching to an embankment with an 8-metre metal fence topped with barbed wire. This protects the endless queue of container lorries, on their way to the cross-channel ferry, from the rabble in the field below. It is midday; there is no one around. A thin African boy walks up to me and asks if I have shoes. He is wearing flip-flops.

– *Actually, I do,* I say pulling open the boot.

I have six pairs in the back of my car, donated by my neighbours in the half hour before I left home. Immediately some dozen young men are around me, pushing and grabbing at the boots in the vehicle. They quickly work out that none fit and hand them back, but one man is shouting at me:

– *Your phone, your phone, it's taken!*

Someone has reached in and grabbed it from the front. Well at least they left my bag with passport and purse. The other men look sad and shake their heads. The thief has disappeared into the cluster of sodden tents. A couple run to try and find him, but he has disappeared.

– *Welcome to the Jungle.*

A young man in a woollen cap and duffle coat comes up:

– *Hello, I'm Toby. First rule—don't distribute from the back of your car.* You might think I would know that after some twenty five years working in refugee camps.

I am here to meet Tom and Shizuka who have been coming to the camp regularly since August and have set up 'Help Calais', a crowd funding platform that has already raised more than £60,000 to help various projects in the camp. When I asked on social media if they

21

The Jungle, Calais, October 2015

needed some help, they said: *please come over.*

I drive back into Calais to find a WIFI connection for my computer and cancel my mobile SIM. I don't mind losing an old smartphone, but I can't afford to fund endless telephone calls to the Middle East or wherever. On the way back, I pass three bewildered looking young men standing on a roundabout. Two are clearly Ethiopian and one says he's Afghan. They just got to Calais and want to find the Jungle. I suddenly feel like an old hand: *Get in.*

We drive back along Route des Gravelines, passing a procession of refugees, mostly men and boys all walking in the camp direction after a night spent trying to get on trains or lorries in order to get across the Channel.

The Ethiopians are from Dire Dawa. They are delighted to hear my husband comes from neighbouring Harar and that I know the town well. The Afghan boy cannot speak any English and stares solemnly out the window. I take them to the Pink Caravan where Toby lives and from which he does some distribution. There is a sign up saying, "tents are for newcomers only." Toby says he will get them sorted.

I spend the rest of the day trailing Tom. He is a Buddhist priest who gave up a career in acting to become a mental health outreach worker in Lewisham. Now he applies his casework skills to the Jungle. He and Shizuka spent the morning helping a heavily pregnant woman relocate from a filthy tent in a satellite camp to a better one nearer the medical tent run by Medecins Du Monde. He wants me to meet Riyad, who we find at Jungle Books.

This is a small, brightly painted wooden construction filled with do-nated books, dictionaries and language training materials. It was set up by Bahirun, one of the Afghan refugees, and Mary, a volunteer. Three young men are sitting reading inside. Next door, there is a larg-er meeting room with a wood-burning stove. Riyad is a tall, thin, sad looking man who greets me with a gentle courtesy. He left his home, shop, wife and child in Sudan when the regular arrests, beatings and extortionate demands for money, that were meted out for his failure to support the government, became unbearable. He simply wants to make a better life for his family. He speaks fluent English and cannot imagine how he would adapt to any other culture. That's why he will try to cross over to the UK.

Mustafa, who is sitting here with us, is taking a different route. He is a sociology student who was driven out of Darfur by the continuing conflict. His home has been completely destroyed. He had hoped to get to Britain, but after one night at the Tunnel Terminal, watching the police and dogs, seeing the injuries suffered by fellow migrants, and hearing about the regular deaths that occurred, he decided— *it's not worth my life.* Possibly between one and three people die in the Tunnel every week. It is impossible to get accurate figures, but everyone knows that a 16-year-old Afghan refugee died a week ago. His body was spread over 400 meters of rail track. Mustafa has applied for asylum in France, been fingerprinted, and told to wait in the Jungle.

Bizarrely, although the French Authorities regard the settlement as illegal, they still use it as a holding area for their own asylum seekers, without providing any assistance for them. Later in the evening I meet two more Sudanese who have both waited almost a year among these sand dunes for their asylum applications to be processed. They are now off to start new lives in Paris and Lyon. Riyad cannot bear the thought of remaining in France, not just because of the appalling conditions in the camp, but because of the way he is treated in town.

– *People spit at you; they won't speak to you or serve you in shops.*

One man tells me about injuring his leg and being told by the police that he would only be taken to the hospital if he agreed to be fingerprinted here. He refused and crawled back to camp to get treatment from Medecins Du Monde. A few weeks ago, a refugee was attacked by local people, stripped, beaten and left for dead. He managed to make it back to the camp, naked, but no one helped him along the way.

– *We are human beings, we have not committed any crime, we just hope for a better life.*

It is a refrain I will hear again and again over the next few days. People will endure the dirt, cold and squalor here in the hope of reaching a country, which they believe will treat them with respect and dignity, as well as giving them the minimum necessities to start their lives. Warnings that life for asylum seekers and refugees in the UK is not a bed of roses, fall on deaf ears.

The Jungle, Monday 19 October

I have made friends with two Afghan boys—12-year-old Abdul and his 11-year-old friend Hassan. Abdul is in jeans cut just below the knee and a thin jacket. Hassan is similarly inadequately dressed. They were both at school in their home province of Kunduz in Afghanistan, when their village was shelled, and everyone ran away and got separated. Neither has any idea where their parents are, or if they are alive. They have been travelling together for the last two months. – *A good man helped us. We walked, took cars, a train. We took a big ship from Turkey to Greece. I want to go to England. I have an uncle there, in Manchester.*

They have been here two days living in a half-collapsed tent. Abdul hasn't eaten today, so I take him to the 'Ashram' tent, one of a number serving free hot food. He tries the porridge but hates it, so he eats some biscuits instead. There is a French Charity trying to help unaccompanied children. They visit regularly and offer them care and support and school in St. Omer, as well as help in the process of applying for French asylum. Abdul begs me not to alert them. He is determined to go to England and find his relatives. He thinks he will try tonight. I ask him to give himself a few days to at least orient himself and eat some proper food.

—You could even learn better English and get more information about the asylum process.

This catches his interest. After leaving Abdul at the library, looking at grammar books and dictionaries, and discussing English with a volunteer, I have tea with a Kurdish father and his 8-year-old daughter Samira, in what is called the 'family camp.' They both tried the Tunnel last night but got turned back by police with pepper spray and dogs before they even got to the fence. The idea of this little girl trying to jump onto a train fills me with horror. The father tells me this is no life here. They fled from Mosul when ISIS attacked—no life

25

there either. Around me, other families are cooking over open fires. Smoke rises in the sunlight. Children play with donated scooters, an infant charges around unsteadily, watched by his mother, a baby cries. This family camp has only been here a few weeks, springing up in the Kurdish area on the Southern edge of the Jungle, it looks pleasant enough now, but what will happen when temperatures drop and rain puts out the fires around which people warm themselves?

I think I have come to grips with the geography of this place. People have mostly camped out next to neighbours of similar ethnicity. There is an Afghan area near the bridge with a large number of established shops and restaurants; a Syrian area on the dunes in the centre; and an Ethiopian and Eritrean area around the Ethiopian Orthodox church whose walled compound emblazons "St. Michael Jungle Church." It's constructed out of wood and plastic, carpeted and lit with candles inside, and decorated with paintings.

The Sudanese area is along the Eastern border beside a sandy road called Chemin de Dunes. Many of their shelters are large and well-constructed, built around immaculately swept and organised compounds.

I looked up the history of this site. Asylum seekers and migrants have been camping unofficially in Calais since Sarkozy closed the Red Cross reception centre in 2002, provoking riots. Since then, an ever-growing number of new arrivals have established new encampments in various locations, only to have them bulldozed after a period of time.

This particular 'Jungle,' created on a landfill site that may well contain various forms of toxic waste, has existed since Spring of this year when there were thought to be approximately 1500 people living here. The estimated population is now around 6000–7000. The majority are young men, but there are growing numbers of women and children. Some of these are staying in the Jules Ferry Centre on the Northern border of the dunes, where a French Charity called La Vie Actif provides accommodation for them, along with a very limited number of hot showers and a soup kitchen for the wider community.

I tramp about in an amazed rage. How is it possible that on the borders of a north European town, there are some 6000 people living in conditions worse than those I have encountered with Somali refugees on the Ethiopian border, Pakistanis after a devastating earthquake, or Darfuris in the deserts of Northern Chad—one of the poorest countries in the world? I pick my way through rivers of mud and between piles of uncollected garbage, try to help a teenage boy get water out of a blocked faucet—water that is apparently positive for E coli—hold my breath while making use of portacabin loos that no one has cleaned for days, and step over human excrement lying six inches from tent doorways where children play. I can't answer my question, but I do begin to see that something else is going on.

In between the muddy footpaths and bursting bin bags, people are building a community. Mosques are being constructed to shelter newcomers at night and create quiet clean warm space for anyone. Some of the Help Calais crowd funding has gone to building an information centre which will explain people's rights and the asylum process. There is a Women and Children's Centre, where ex-firewoman Liz and other volunteers provide a warm refuge. And there is an extraordinary flowering of creativity: a theatre space in a Dome, where I sit and watch grown men work delightedly with pastels and paper, while outside paintings cover the plastic walls of the tents.

One of my favourite places is a bright blue painted house on the boundary of Chemin de Dunes with a thatched roof and chair perched above it, and stunning pictures on the walls. Alpha was one of the first people to build a shelter in the area. He shows me pictures of himself gathering reeds for the thatch. Alpha left Mauritania, *because in that country, black people are slaves.* He had been moving around the continent for some ten years without papers before coming to the Jungle. He never trained as an artist, but he had been in jail in Greece when he heard that his mother had died, he was prostrate and could not stop weeping. That night a voice in his ears told him:
– *If you want to survive, do art. Work hard at it, and every time you are drinking poison if you do art, you will lose all the pain in your life. I opened my eyes and I could not see anyone, so I knew it was a message from God. So, I have to create. I just take everything and create.*

Everything he touches is turned into art; moulded plastic bottles form a sculpture in the garden. Next door he has an art school open to all.

Meanwhile, in the Jungle Books Library, English and French and other classes are held every day. This week Gil Galasso, a famous Maitre D' from the Basque area, is running a certified course in the 'Art of the Table.' I sit watching Galasso, in immaculate blazer and pressed trousers, show four young Sudanese how to make cocktails, match the right wine with cheese, and hold multiple plates. They all hope it will help them find jobs in France. Galasso's own family migrated to France from Italy in the thirties to escape hunger and find work, just like his students.

The Jungle, Tuesday 20 October

At the Bed and Breakfast this morning I met an Iranian refugee with a blind daughter. He needed children's clothes, so we took him to the warehouse run by L'Auberge Migrant, a long-established Calais Charity. The warehouse is enormous and piled ceiling high with donations mostly from Britain. Much is useful: warm clothing, tents and sleeping bags, shoes and bicycles, all desperately needed. But I am curious as to the thinking of those who give away smart handbags, high-heeled shoes and dirty underwear. Distributions are getting organised, with van runs to different parts of the camp every day.

Back at the camp, I play chess at Jungle Books with Abdul and Hassan. They did not go to the Tunnel last night. They said they took my advice to learn more, but they are almost certainly going tonight.

It's a wet, chilly, misty morning—a hint of things to come. I walk across the camp to the Dome. Musicians Against Borders have brought musical instruments, and a crowd of Sudanese boys are banging drums and playing guitars. I ask my new Sudanese friend, Adam, to come and join us. Adam sings us an English pop song in a high tenor voice. He invited me into his tent as I was passing yesterday. He is 16 and left Darfur because of the fighting.

– I wanted a safe country where I could get an education.

He spent three months getting to Libya where he worked on a building site for another three months to get the 1000 dollars he needed to take a boat with 450 others. In Italy, he got on a train, hid from the police and made it to France. He has an uncle in the North of Britain. He tried jumping onto the channel tunnel train some 19 times, but he got arrested a week ago and was put in jail. When he came up in front of a judge, they told him he was free to go, as he was only 16. So, he is back here.

In the afternoon there is a Volunteers Meeting. They too are getting organised. Eva has turned up with a chart, drawn onto two large pieces of cardboard. She has mapped all the sectors: sanitation, food, shelter, health care, arts, and education, as well as which groups are trying to address which needs in different parts of the camp. It is the *Who, What, Where, When* chart beloved by humanitarian communities in emergencies. These volunteers—many of whom have never done anything like this before in their lives—have worked it out for themselves. They have also worked out that they need some kind of security guidelines and a code of conduct: no volunteers consuming alcohol or drugs on the site, for example: *Volunteers getting shitfaced is completely inappropriate*—someone says. There is a lively discussion on how female volunteers should dress. Tifa, who is Iranian and works in the Women and Children's Centre, stands up in baggy jeans and a loose long-sleeved top. Her long dark hair is neatly tied.

– *This is the appropriate way for us to dress here. No miniskirts, no tight jeans, no long loose hair and we have to be careful about touching and hugging. It is not appropriate. For many people here, these things are provocations and misunderstood, and we are not the ones who suffer the consequences, it is the women who live with these men. I understand what the men are saying and it's not polite.*

A woman from No Borders disagrees:

–*They are coming to Europe; they will be living amongst women like us. This is a chance to educate them.*

– *This is not the place to start, in a vulnerable community where 90% are young men. There will be time for that. Right now, our job is to protect any women living here from harassment.*

– What about rape alarms?

– No woman refugee would use a rape alarm. It would be shameful to for them to do so.

Distribution is also a contentious subject. Mass distributions from the warehouse are efficient and safe, but do they reach the most vulnerable? Smaller distributions are needed, under the control of the communities themselves, but how can we avoid stuff getting onto the black market? What about containers on site and allowing refugee leaders to distribute directly? And what about people who turn up at night? Where should they go?

There is a call for better coordination with the French NGO's who have been working with the migrant community for fifteen years; the sudden mass influx of British volunteers has taken everyone by surprise. Notice boards in prominent locations are planned to help the 'weekend warriors' (kind people who drive across the Channel for a day to drop off donations) orient themselves and avoid getting their mobiles stolen.

*– This is all very good—*a tall, thin young man speaks up—*and humanitarianism is essential for people's day-to-day needs, but what they want is to get to the UK and nothing we have discussed here addresses that…Blankets won't solve the problem of police violence. Fascist rallies are planned in Calais.*

I don't completely agree. It's clear to me, and to the French Authorities, that the existence of the camp itself is politically threatening, it challenges the whole organised asylum process and exposes its weaknesses. In fact, this camp has much more in common with the Occupy movements or Greenham Common Women's Peace Camp,[6] than any humanitarian operation in which I have been involved. For one thing, the volunteers have been much more successful at breaking down the usual barrier between givers and receivers. At many points in the meeting, I have no idea whether it is a volunteer or refugee voicing a view, and when Tom, who is chairing, announces: *If anyone wants to help and volunteer, they may. A volunteer is someone who helps other people. There is no distinction in this respect between volunteer and refugee—*no one disagrees.

The question is where are the big agencies? Alongside MDM, MSF is here. They have been laying down rubble in the mud for the last few days and dealing with toilets and garbage. They tell me they are planning a hospital outside the camp boundaries, but the other big NGOs, and UNHCR and UNICEF, are noticeably absent.

— *It's completely political*—Ben, volunteering in his gap year between Eton and Yale, tells me. He is fluent in French and goes to their coordination meetings. *The French authorities don't want anything that attracts more migrants, but they don't want it to be so awful it creates a scandal. Possibly in some way we are playing straight into their hands just preventing things tipping over the edge.*

— *You're saying it might be better if there were a mass outbreak of disease or people froze to death?*

— *Of course not, but how do we actually get people out of this situation?*

— *Argue for HMG to come here and sort out asylum claims jointly with the French. That's what the UN is asking them to do.*

— *It will never happen. The French don't want this place to be a magnet for refugees all over Europe.*

— *They are already coming.*

One of the first films I saw as a child was Dickens' 'A Tale of Two Cities.' There was an unforgettable scene where a child is killed under the carriage wheels of a French aristocrat. I remember wondering how could people live right next door to abject suffering and poverty and remain unmoved—how did you drive by it and over it? The consequences of such indifference were clear, the downtrodden took matters into their own hands. They pulled down the walls and gates and executed both the indifferent and those who were not indifferent but had not done much to change things. Now the downtrodden are at our own gates. All they want is to come in.

It's dark and late. We sit round Raul's fire. He and a handful of Kurdish friends share a large tent near the south entrance. We are always welcomed with tea. Raul is 25 and was studying literature in Mosul. He had spoken eloquently at the meeting. It was the first time he did such a thing and he is rightly very proud of himself.

The Jungle, Calais, October 2015

The Jungle, Wednesday 21 October

Some people at the volunteer meeting asked me to do a session on volunteer self-care. I turn up at 10am at the Ashram tent. Scott undoes the marquee door tape and lets me in. The volunteers are already preparing breakfast, although, at this time, most camp residents are still asleep, having tramped three hours to the tunnel entrance, spent two to three hours climbing fences, evading police and dogs, and another three hours walking back during the night.

Scott tells me he just came for the day originally, but then he got asked to lay a floor in this tent. Then they started cooking a few meals for volunteers, then it sort of grew, and now they cook twice daily for hundreds of migrants. He stayed and organises. Outside it's raining a light drizzle, but as the weather worsens, these communal spaces will become vital. That's if the French allow the camp to stand. Rumours abound. Yesterday's local paper had a two-page spread on how the mayor was calling in the Army to help deal with security. L'Auberge was quoted as suggesting the French army should learn a lesson from the Germans and help build good facilities.

And apparently there is a plan for a new camp. But it will only house the most vulnerable 1500, will have fences and security around it, and will mean the eviction of at least 400 camped out in the planned space. Besides, how many will want to move into a new camp if they are not allowed out of it?

Meanwhile, the Jungle has petty crime, a black market, drugs, alcohol, and violence, as in any community. I was having a coffee with Bahirun in his restaurant in the Afghan area, when he was called, because a young Sudanese man had gone to the MDM tent with a knife. Bahirun got some other Sudanese to mediate and went and sorted it out without any casualties. It is remarkable how quickly fights here can be deescalated.

Bahirun has spent five years in Europe. He actually got asylum in Italy (after waiting three years), but there was no work. Then he spent a number of years in Norway until they told him there were no problems in Afghanistan, and he should go back.

– *I would love to go back. All I want to do is help my people. It's impossible at the moment. And this is your fault. You made the problems in my country, not me. Look around you—here are Pashtun, Tajik, Uzbek, we all get on, but in Afghanistan, there are more than forty two countries with their guns, making things worse.*

He came to Calais in July to try and get to the UK to find work. He was in the hospital for three weeks because of a beating. But now, he has stopped trying to cross the Channel and puts his energy into helping his fellow countrymen.

— At the Voice of Refugees meeting last week, I was discussing 'how not to die.' It's essential they know that if you walk to the tunnel for three hours and your clothes are wet and you are tired, you will go under a train and you will die. If people really want to help, they should provide a bus so that at least people are warm and dry before they make the attempt!

— I doubt the French would allow it—bussing refugees to the tunnel...

— Then people will go on dying. Bahirun is not completely happy with volunteers. *Some are only here for themselves. We know who needs clothes and shoes.*

— I think that is why they plan to have people like you distribute.

Bahirun tells me he has a plan of his own, to open a more expensive restaurant with good food, where volunteers will eat, especially the 'weekend warriors.' And he will encourage them to buy attractive cards marked up in a particular way. Then he will ask them to visit different areas of the camp and see who really needs help. They should give the card to a vulnerable person who can then return to the restaurant for a free meal. Bahirun has worked out a neat system of assessing needs and providing food to the most vulnerable, while using the time and energy of random volunteers. Brilliant.

I leave Bahirun and go look for Samira and her father, as I promised a visit. But their neighbour says they did not come back from the train yesterday. Perhaps they have made it? Or taken another route? Or got hurt or detained? I don't want to think about that. I go and visit Liz at the red and orange Women and Children's Centre. Three teenage Afghan boys have come in and she is sorting out some stuff for them. One of them has cut his hand and lost his shoes trying to climb the Tunnel fence last night. We clean him up and find him shoes. One of them wants a bicycle, and Liz promises to try and find one in the warehouse.

— *It's not about the product*—she explains. *I don't mind if it's a bicycle or a woolly hat. If I can use the donations to encourage them to come and spend some time here, that's less time with the Hashish smokers and other unsavoury types.*

Liz has created one of the most comfortable spaces in the Camp. While we are sitting there, a tearful Sudanese woman comes in. Liz puts the kettle on the small gas ring. Last night, it was a heavily pregnant Kurdish woman, just days away from giving birth. Her husband had already paid $7000 to a lorry driver to take her to the UK, and then discovered it was a scam and the lorry was going South.

— *Liz saved us as well*—Susan, a volunteer, tells me. She explains that she was working as a hotel manager.

— *I had guests screaming at me that they did not get a good night's sleep because the beds were lumpy. I had to do something more useful.*

When the migrant crisis hit the news in August, she started an NGO called Drive to Humanity, and drove to Calais with Tifa and two others, and a van full of donations.

— *Except we hadn't a clue how to distribute stuff or what to do. We decided we might as well start collecting rubbish with bin bags. We were all fighting amongst ourselves and crying. Then Liz came over and gave us a hug and asked if we wanted to help her.* They have been helping her ever since.

The Jungle, Thursday 22 October

When I walk into the Camp in the morning, someone asks me to go and see a sick four-year-old who arrived last night. They are a Kurdish family camped inside the Ashram restaurant. In fact, the four-year-old is running around munching biscuits with no evidence of fever or distress, so I prescribe porridge.

A team have come from Brighton who plan to bring a school bus across. They ask me to introduce them to some children who might benefit from such a project, so I take them to meet Abdul and Hassan, who now live in a caravan with another boy in the family area. Abdul is as friendly as always, if a bit dopey. He explains politely why school is not for him:

– *I have to get to England. I spend all night trying. It takes many hours to walk there, many hours to try and reach a train, and if I fail, many hours to walk back. In the day I have to sleep, so I have no time for school.*

I leave them to their assessment and head across the camp. The Jungle has changed dramatically in the last four days. The information centre is now a roofed and plastic-covered solid structure. MSF have cobbled the muddiest roads and cleaned some of the toilets. There is a whole batch of new caravans and new structures. Outside the Dome, a truck is distributing long thin pieces of wood, and a large number of refugees of all ethnicities are engaged in building simple shelters. Inside the Dome, another music session is going on. An Afghan sings and drums with astonishing beauty, while another plays guitar. Meanwhile, Sudanese boys sit clapping as one of them walks across shyly, picks up another drum, and joins in. Once again, I am struck by our capacity in extremis to both cooperate and create beauty. Why not build on these virtues?

On my way back across the camp I meet another young Kurd who asks me to stop and chat. I think one of the most useful things volunteers do is just hang out and listen wherever and whenever. He wants me to see the broken tent in which he lives. I look at the wet soggy tunnel and tell him I am sure we can find something better, but he tells me not to worry about it, as he is out every night trying to get on a train. The words pour out.

– *I was a history student in Mosul until ISIS came. Then I went to Turkey, but I was not a refugee so everything costs money. So, I worked illegally in a factory, but you earn nothing. So, I took a boat. If you agree to be captain it's free, although of course you risk a seven-year jail sentence— but we made it to Greece. Then Macedonia, then Hungary—they put us on a bus for Austria, and the Austrians are lovely people, wonderful! They gave us money and food and put us on a bus for Germany, where we were in a Camp for three days. But I don't speak any German, and in England there is work…*

If governments wanted a selection process for identifying the most resilient and able candidates for entry into their countries, one possible way might be to ask refugees to find their own way across either Eurasia and the Middle East, or Sub-Saharan Africa, risk drowning in the Mediterranean, and then place them in a toxic waste dump on minimal hand-outs, before offering further life threatening challenges in the form of avoiding electrocution while jumping onto trains, or freezing or suffocating in the back of a lorry. Indeed, I am amazed these journeys have not yet been franchised as some kind of reality TV show in which the public votes for whom they want to come in.

As you see, I don't use the word migrant. In my five days here I have not met anyone who is not fleeing a war we started or failed to stop, a genocide we have failed to end, or human rights abuses to which we have turned a blind eye. Yet, what shines through is intelligence, courage, concern for one another, and a deep admiration for Britain. I would welcome any of the people I have met—Riyad, Raul, Bahirun, Abdul or Hassan—as my neighbours.

The Jungle confronts us all with a very simple question: will we share the resources of this one world equitably, or will those of us with more firepower build ever higher fences to protect ourselves from those 'marauding swarms' trying to escape the poverty, violence and injustice that we are complicit in creating?

There are consequences to locking ourselves in a fortress. While I was sitting in Bahirun's restaurant the other day, I got talking to Tawab, one of the boys helping out. He was 19 and had left Afghanistan when he was ten. His parents had been killed when the Taliban bombed his village. He ran away to avoid recruitment by them. After nine years of wandering in Europe, including 14 months in a camp in Italy, an arrival in the UK closely followed by deportation, and spending three months in a French detention centre, he has asked the French government to help him go back to Afghanistan.

– I want to go back and help my country, I don't care about money, I don't care about Europe. I did not see any human rights here. And when I get home, I will ask for ten minutes on Afghan TV, and I will tell them what I experienced here. And I will say yes, there are some good people, but when Americans and British come to our country, without passports

and with guns, we should kill them.

He sees the shock on my face.

– You don't know human rights, but you teach them in Afghanistan! Why do you think I left Afghanistan? Because if I had not, they would have forced me to join a group—it was the only way to survive. There are no human rights there, the government fucks people up. It's impossible to be a normal person in Afghanistan, the Taliban is everywhere and now we have ISIL. In Italy, I was in a camp for fourteen months, but what can I do with Asylum in Italy when there is no work, no housing, no benefits, and yes, I know it's the same in the UK, I know that now, that is why I am going back…

And tell me this? How can you come and work in my country, when I cannot work in yours? How can you come with a Kalashnikov and no passport when I am not allowed in yours? Your soldier, he is born in England, he comes to my country, he walks my roads and mountains and villages with his Kalashnikov, and we give him tea, we give him everything. I don't have a Kalashnikov. I am not like you. I am just a donkey—Afghan, Iraqi, Syrian, we are all kicked. You see me as a dog, but I am a human being and all humans are the same. We understand the law, just like you, we don't break laws.

So now, when I get home I will go on TV and tell people: when you get to Europe, they fuck you up, they beat you and put you in prison, they hate you, so if they come here, you have to kill them…

I cannot think of anything to say to make it better.

2016

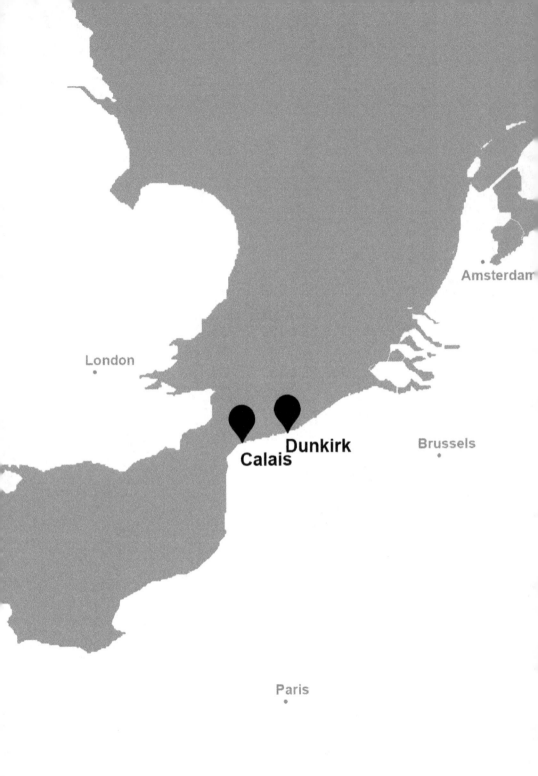

Calais, Dunkirk

France, February 2016

The Jungle, Saturday 6 February

It is not what I expected. After all the news reports about the erasure of part of the Jungle, I pictured something shattered and flattened. Instead, I walk straight into the opening ceremony for 'the secular school of Chemin des Dunes.' In an open space between four makeshift classrooms sits a play castle with a crocodile painted on it. Here, a cluster of French educators stand beside Zimako the refugee founder, while he makes a speech.

He rejects the word Jungle because of its associations with inhumanity and chaos:

– This place is the land of heroes who have crossed thousands of miles to find peace and escape the terror or the militias and terrorists. Change will come when we will all be together… our public space is open to all. It is a place of meeting, exchange, fraternity among people where everyone has the right to speak, a space of freedom.

Beyond the school, where the family camp was, there is now a wide, muddy Cordon Sanitaire between the Camp and the fenced motorway to the port. Inside banks of heaped earth, the squalid tent city has morphed into a shanty town. Huts of wood and plastic are closely packed along cobbled streets. Cafés, restaurants and shops jostle in the Afghan area. St. Michaels is still standing. Jungle Books has transformed from a small library into a network of rooms, where language classes in French and English go on all day long, next door to a new radio station.

The information centre now has comfortable chairs, a kettle, and racks of leaflets in every language: how to seek asylum in every European Country, what are your rights in detention, how to apply to join family in the UK. A first aid post stands opposite, opening when the MSF clinic outside the Camp is closed at weekends. I follow the cobbled road around a loop between yet more wooden and plastic shelters to an area of close packed caravans and discover a legal support centre in a beautiful wooden hut besides the Dome, where volunteer lawyers give free advice.

Coming back, I stumble across the new container camp. It is in the middle, next to Chemin du Dunes. There is a large fenced area with a ditch around it. Inside there is a grid of white containers stacked two stories high, currently completely empty and completely alienating. It's as if someone dropped a space station in the middle of a medieval marketplace. I hear my name being shouted. I turn and there is Adam from Darfur, in a white Peruvian woolly hat with earflaps running after me.

– Lynne! Lynne! Do you remember me?

– Of course I do! I am so pleased to see you and glad you are not injured or arrested. Where are you staying? I could not find your tent…

He takes me to the small new hut he shares with a friend. He has stopped trying the train. A British lawyer is helping him get to his uncle in the UK. As he is an unaccompanied 16-year-old, there is some possibility.[7] Meanwhile, he just sits in his hut and waits. He curls up on his bed and looks at me. The energy that was there three months ago has gone—this is not the young man who sang pop songs for us in the Dome.

– Do you do anything with your days?

He shakes his head.

– What about the Jungle Books where I took you?

He shrugs.

– And there is a new school, and a Darfuri school and English classes.

Again, a sad shrug.

– What do you dream of doing when you get to England?

– I want to study, I want to learn.

– Well, why not start here? It's free, there are teachers and books. If you don't like the idea of class, we could go to the library together and get some. What sort do you like?

– Ones that give me wisdom…

– OK … I think we can manage that. Let's meet and go together.

We make an appointment for Monday morning. A friend has arrived.

– He is already French—Adam tells me.

The friend has asylum in France. He came when he was 13 and went to the accommodation centre in St. Omer. *I just want to go to my uncle*—Adam says again.

Riyad has acquired a caravan. He invites me in. He is doing an interview with a visiting barrister, so I get to hear in forensic detail what's actually been happening in the last few months. He's been assaulted without provocation three times since I last saw him, most recently, two weeks ago when he was just walking into Calais. A policeman parked a car, jumped out, and came over spraying tear gas from a cannister into his eyes, and then started beating him until he fell to the ground. Then he yelled—*go back to the Jungle*—got in his car, and drove off. The other two occasions happened near the train station.

— *They just set on you with sticks, kicking you once you are down. I was kicked in the head and stomach and left vomiting.* He shows us a scar on his hand where he protected his head. *Two months ago, we were just walking to the camp when five of them jumped out and attacked us with sticks. We just ran.*

And now there are the attacks on the camp. The most recent one was a few days ago. A right-wing group started throwing gas cannisters into the Kurdish area. The enraged Kurds responded by throwing stones with slingshots. Then the police let loose with tear gas and rubber bullets. My friend Rowan's car was getting hit from both sides. Riyad says the tear gas and rubber bullet attacks are frequent and indiscriminate, occurring without provocation, and can go on for an hour or more.

— *They don't care. They chased a Sudanese guy a few weeks back. He ran out into the road, got hit by a truck, and was killed. The fascists are worse.* He thinks the right-wing groups and police are hand in glove. One night, while walking home he had saw a well-known fascist car and hid while two men holding knives searched for him with a torch. They talked on a radio. Three minutes later the police arrived and started searching too. They did not find him.

— *Fascists came into the camp three days ago. Four of us went to police to complain and they just said, 'go back to the Jungle.' They all wear police uniforms, but without markings... they are all the same, but these guys*

45

The Jungle, Calais, February 2016

are worse than the police. Three people are missing. They have disappeared without a trace. Twenty people are in hospital, but if you complain, they do nothing. If they see us being attacked, the police stick their thumbs up (Riyad demonstrates) *and give the guy a pat on the back: 'good job!' – And forget going to the hospital. They treat you like a bowl of shit. If you come from here, they leave you sitting there for eight hours, then send you away with nothing. I went with a cough and fever. They would not look at me. A friend went with a swollen hand, but as he was not seeking asylum in France, they said they could not see him. He returned with a volunteer and it turned out he had broken his arm. If you go with a volunteer, it might be OK. The ambulances won't come into the camp. I called them three times. Once for a woman about to deliver a baby, once for a man with a heart attack, another time a man was stabbed. Every time, we had to carry them out of the Jungle ourselves.*

Riyad stares down at his feet. He looks exhausted and very sad. He has tried the train thirteen times.

– And you ask me why I don't want to stay in France. He shakes his head. *I won't stay here.*

While we are talking, a man knocks on the door. He is a thin young Afghan in army fatigue trousers. He wants to talk to the Barrister. He was a British army translator. Everyone else he worked with already has asylum in the UK, including a friend who was in Calais.

– Some army guys helped them. But I was in Germany at the time. The barrister explains that there is no actual law, and it would have been easier if he had applied from Afghanistan.

– I could not stay, I was facing death threats.

She says she will try to get in touch with the army officer who helped, if he can give details. He does not have any, just a phone number for the friend of a friend. This is how it goes—tiny painful steps. But for most, these run straight into a brick wall. The barrister says the reality is that there is no legal route for adults from the Jungle to get to the UK, unless they have a husband or wife already there. Nothing else counts.

This discussion has left all of us tired and depressed. We decide to go and eat in the Kabul café. Tom and Shizuka have just arrived, and in the warmth and light with music on the DVD monitor, and plates of rice and chicken in front of us, it could be an evening out with friends anywhere. I feel completely at home.

The Jungle, Sunday 7 February

We wake to hail on the windows and local news that the fascists held their banned demonstration yesterday afternoon in town. Twenty of them were arrested.

We have our own encounter with the police this afternoon. Maia from L'Auberge wanted to mark the destruction of the Mosque and a Church last week and plant wildflower seeds in the wide muddy strip that makes our new cordon sanitaire. So, a motley little group of refugees and volunteers head out, clutching our plastic cups full of seeds.

We form a circle. Tom says a few words about remembering all the people who had come through, those who had stayed, and those who had not made it, and we have two minutes of silence. Meanwhile, the sunlight thinks it's in a Turner painting and lights up the mass of dark grey clouds piling up above the camp, and we all walk across the muddy fields, as our seeds swirl out of the plastic cups in small tornadoes. A cluster of policemen wander down from their spot on the motorway, and, after polite discussion with Maia, tell us we have ten minutes to turn around and walk back whence we came. We do as we are told, while three van loads of police with riot shields form a small cordon to walk behind us. Wildflower seeds, so difficult to deal with, they drift in the wind and spring up anywhere.

I head off to the Women and Children's tent where Domdom, a retired French computer engineer from Calais, has set up a cinema. A delighted group of small children are watching Kung Fu Panda, with subtitles in four languages. Unfortunately, four teenage boys are bored and unhappy. One holds a long thin piece of metal; another has a knife. They are not threatening anyone, but they keep messing with the computer to the point where Domdom has had enough and shuts it down, to the distress of the smaller ones watching. They are all unaccompanied boys that Liz has taken under her wing. When

49

she is there, they are contained and happy. She manages to provide affection and security, combined with clear boundaries, and they respect her. But when she is away, they run riot. When I suggest disarming them at the door, one of the volunteers snaps at me.

– *We have no exclusion policy and we have to look after the most vulnerable children.*

– *But the most vulnerable are not always the noisiest and most aggressive. These boys are needy in one way, but so are some of the quiet younger ones. It may not be possible to work with them all in one place.*

– *You don't work here day after day!*

Certainly true. I retreat. The good thing is that a Youth Centre is starting this week. Besides indoor activities, Jess, Ben, Johnny and Jake will be organising boxing, football and cricket matches in the muddy space created by the cordon sanitaire. Hopefully, it will be a more attractive place for these teenagers.

I have found Abdul. After the movie, he and his brother walk me back to his Caravan, untidy as the worst student bedsit, but at least dry and warm. Abdul also has a lawyer trying to track down his relatives in the UK, so he, too, has stopped trying to get onto trains. Just now, he was upset because someone stole his bicycle.

– *And too many people have died. People outside the camp are attacking us!*

The Jungle and Grand Synthe, Monday 8 February

I am determined to get Adam to school. I find him coming from Salaam carrying breakfast: a carton of milk and a bag with some bread, jam and butter, and we head off to Jungle Books. There is a new sign up: "Didn't make it to England? Keep calm and come to English lessons."

Adam tells me he is absolutely uninterested in stories. We select two horrible histories: one on mediaeval Britain and one on the 20th century—factually accurate and funny with pictures. Perfect.

We go to see Cath who runs the radio station at Jungle books to see if he might like to help make radio programmes. *Can I sing?* He asks when she questions what he would like to record. Sarah arrives, and after a quick chat establishing that he completed grade 7 of primary

50

school, tells him that he would be perfect for Class 2.

Adam says he has to deliver a charger to a friend and promises to come back. I am uncertain whether this is procrastination. I will just keep trying. Rowan and I head off to Dunkirk.

This camp is different. Just off the motorway into Grand Synthe, there is an upmarket housing development of detached villas with steep tiled roofs and dormer windows. It is surrounded by a forest: a nature reserve between highway and estate. I was admiring the living fence of trees that had been built to contain it, when I looked to ground level and saw that the woods were filled with scrappy tents held down by boulders with piles of rotting garbage and sodden clothes, which were intersected by deep rivers of mud—much worse than Calais.

Almost all Kurds,—Rowan explains—*they have given up trying through Calais.*

The only good news is that a new camp is being constructed by the local authorities, and after some tussles, apparently it will not be 'closed.' MSF insisted they would have nothing to do with a closed camp and won. Except, Maddie explains, the position next to a fenced off highway on one side and a heavily fenced area on the other makes it feel closed. Maddie is one of the key volunteers here. We find her standing on the single cobbled road, talking into a radio.

She is frantic because there is an Amber warning out for major winds coming at night, and she wants a contingency plan for families if tents blow down. The tents in the New Camp have already blown down. MSF has refused to let her use their warehouses in the worst case. In the meantime, she immediately dispatches me to the small school and asks me to call on a family she is worried about.

The school is in a wooden hut. When we arrive, Lydia is trying to lay down new planks of wood over the mud beside the boot racks, while stopping a 2-year-old from escaping. Inside, a handful of Kurdish boys and girls sit with another young volunteer.

Lydia is a nursery schoolteacher with multiple concerns: What to do with the slightly older, more hyperactive boys? How to find more long-term volunteers so that children can be divided into age-appropriate groups? She also wants ways to allow the children to be physically active in a small space. There, at least, I can help. I promise to do a movement session when we have more volunteers on Wednesday.

I get out my puppets, and everyone grabs one. The rat and turtle are fighting, as are the cat and lion. It's interesting how the default mode of action here is aggression. I stand on my head. Long ago, I discovered that this is an excellent way to get the attention and quieten a hyperactive group of small children who are all fighting with one another, having spent far too long cooped up in tiny shelters or cramped caravans. They all want to learn how to do it.

I head off to see the family. Hosein has lined his shelter with blankets, and he has a small stove. He tells me his story while his two small sons run in and out to play with the puppets. His wife and baby son were in one lorry. He and the two boys were in another. His lorry got stopped by the police. Her lorry made it to the UK. Now, the boys cry all the time asking—*where is our mother?* He is so stressed he cannot sleep. He shows me some paracetamol that MSF provided and shakes his head. It does not help. He does not know what to do.

– First of all, let's get the children into school every day so they have something to do and are more tired. Secondly, now that your wife is actually in the UK, you have a better chance of joining her, so rather than trying a lorry again, you need some legal advice as to what are the best options.

Once again, I think a legal training might have been more useful than a medical one. I promise to return with more information and to take the children to the school on Wednesday.

On my way out of the camp, a policeman stops me and asks me to open my rucksack. I pull out my tortoise, rat and cat. He waves me on. Sitting in my car, parked at the shopping centre, I can feel the wind strengthening. Meanwhile, a volunteer comes up to me and tells me there has been a knife fight at the end of the camp.

I go back to the camp. This time, a red haired 20-year-old policeman tells me that I cannot go back in unless I have a paper. I explain that I have no paper but have been here all day. I pull out the puppets again. Confronted with my sobbing cat, he relents.

Inside the camp, groups of men are standing around in tense crowds. A volunteer comes up and says—*All the volunteers should leave, as they are threatening us as well.* Who? It's unclear.

— Why not ask the police to intervene, as they are standing right there—be nice if they could be encouraged to play a protective role?

— They never help.

— There is no harm in asking.

— The problem is the traffickers—a large man with a turban tells me. *We don't like them. One of them is very dangerous. He attacked someone with a knife. Now the refugees have attacked them back.*

— So why not tell the police who this guy is?

— Too dangerous.

Maddie and the other volunteers echo this. They cannot be seen talking with the police, or they will be at risk as well.

A tall French man, Patrick, and I decide that, as we are just short-term visitors, we can take the risk. We explain what is going on to the policemen. Fully kitted, they go down to the end of the camp. I don't know if they resolved it. Having turned myself into a stool pigeon, I head back to Calais. The threatened storm has not materialised, but the winds are strong enough to make my car shake. I hope I have not made myself a persona non grata. When I come back, I will wear dark glasses and a different hat.

The Jungle, Tuesday 9 February

— Proximity to the crisis should not define responsibility, there has to be a sharing... The UN Special Rapporteur for International Migration, is saying on the World Service as I get up.

Turkey will, if push comes to shove, take 600,000 more refugees from Syria. The EU is asking them to barricade those same refugees and stop them travelling any further. Twenty more drowned on their way to Greece yesterday. Meanwhile, Cameron is trying to terrify the residents of Southern England with prospects of Calais-style encampments in the lovely South Downs if we leave the EU.

When I get to camp and park in front of one of the distribution points, there is a small riot going on. A thin Kurdish man has a long metal pole and is threatening one of the Sudanese. Large groups of people are separating them, and the man appears to calm down. But then, another young black guy comes and pushes to the front of the line, and I see the Kurd rile up again. I walk forward and link my arm through that of the young black man, smile and shake my head, and say—*no queue jumping, let's walk to the back.* He is so astonished that he goes without protest. Then I stand in the centre with my arms folded, looking extremely stern.

– *I am old enough to be the mother of most of you here, so no queue jumping! I am watching you.* Another Kurd is translating. Everyone laughs.

– *And by the way, if you all want to go to the UK, this is the time to learn our habits. We queue. We love queuing. We believe you have to be fair. First come, first served, form a line and NO QUEUE JUMPING. So now is your chance to learn to queue!*

More laughter. *I am watching you…*

Actually, I am not. I leave to go and see someone, but I come back in twenty minutes and they are all queuing quietly besides Riyad's caravan. He tells me there are no problems, and the black guy, who is still in his place, gives me a smile and a wave.

The volunteers running the new Baloo Youth Centre and some others from Jungle Books want to discuss problem children—one boy in particular is always fighting with everyone. He is very emotional and always sorry afterwards. Unsurprisingly, he is completely without parents or friends.

We all agree on the importance of keeping the Youth Centre safe; children cannot bring in any sticks or knives. There are enough male staff here to give the boys a lot of individual attention, so if G is breaking up the toys, one of them can both exclude him from the Centre, and stay with him at the same time so that he can be prevented from doing more damage, but also receive attention and care, and discuss what led to any outbursts. I call it 'accompanied exclusion.'

The Jungle, Wednesday 10 February

The migrant crisis appears to have stimulated a new kind of humanitarianism. These social spaces have all been created entirely by the refugees themselves, assisted by a network of independent volunteers and local French associations. The volunteers come from all over Europe: I have met Belgians, Germans, Swiss and Dutch, but the majority are British people who have heard about the crisis on the news, looked up a local support network on social media, and jumped on the train or the ferry and come for the day, the weekend or the entire duration.

Jess was working with vulnerable 16 to 25-year-olds in the UK and was due to start work in a children's home. She came for a week in October and decided not to return—she stayed and set up the Youth Centre along with Johnny and Ben T., who had both done Masters in Humanitarian Aid and wanted to put what they had learned in class, into practice. Sarah was teaching English abroad and working on migration and human rights issues with a law firm and various charities in Britain. She had planned to work for UNHCR in Ecuador before deciding that Calais was more important. She started off volunteering in the warehouse before teaching and organising in Jungle Books and helping to establish the legal centre. Rowan arrived with some second-hand computers for Jungle Books in the Autumn. He meant to stay for a few days, but ended up remaining for months, helping with any projects that needed him.

Almost all the longer-term volunteers I talk to have similar stories: a short spontaneous trip planned out of anger or disgust at their own government's response. The short visit morphs into a longer stay, as needs become apparent, jobs and career plans are abandoned, savings are used up, and yet, there is a growing commitment to staying until the situation is resolved in some way or another.

The volunteers live in caravans on site, stay at the youth hostel, share rented accommodation in town, or bike out to the caravan park. Some of the longer-term ones receive a small stipend to help with daily expenses from Help Refugees (the new name for Help Calais, which has also morphed into a bigger, more professional fund-raising organisation).

– The big difference between us and the professionals is that everyone is

here simply because they want to help the refugees and make sure they are OK—it's not a job—Ben tells me. No one is here because it's where they have been told to go, or because it's part of their career as a professional humanitarian.

Ben acknowledges that they are not always efficient.

– There is a revolving door of volunteers coming and going. New people arrive and say this is how you should do it, but if it's a poor idea and they don't command respect, within two weeks they burn out and are gone. The good thing is you cannot blag your way into doing stuff because you will be found out immediately. For example, you can turn up with a van and announce you want to reorganise distribution, but if you cannot get people to work with you, you will have nothing to do.

– What you are saying is that the good projects endure because they attract the good workers?

– Exactly. It's the work, not the qualifications, that matter. Look at Liz, she has taken on twelve psychologically disturbed young Afghans and actually does some good. When six children were sent into the French Care system, four immediately ran away. The French child protection expert told us that if they wanted to run away, that was their choice!

One could argue that professional humanitarians are better able to rapidly assess needs, work efficiently, and avoid duplication and danger. But, having watched the Pakistani Army and UNHCR argue over the best kind of heating stove to use in camps for the displaced after the 2005 earthquake in Pakistan, while those displaced took matters into their own hands, and lit open fires that burnt down tents, I am not sure this is true. Nor do the big NGOs have the flexibility to respond to the rapidly changing political situation.

L'Auberge Migrant now sends out 2500 hot meals to both Calais and Dunkirk every day. They also distribute raw ingredients to a further 1200 people, enabling them to cook for themselves. Their ability to do all this depends on the material and financial donations from all over Europe, as well as the manpower provided by a variably skilled, constantly changing, volunteer workforce.

In response to the threatened eviction, Ben, working with a team of volunteers and refugees, has engaged in the building and distribution of 1700 shelters to rehouse people in the northern half of the camp. Tents are no longer being given out from the back of a pink caravan, or people driving up with shelter material and building at random.

— *It's taken us a while to learn on the job. We've been through seven different designs. The simple wooden frame is made up in the warehouse and taken to the camp with pallets and plastic, where volunteer building crews and refugees construct it together.*

This continues to be another extraordinary aspect of the Jungle: the absence of the rigid boundaries between the helper and the helped. Some of the most impressive volunteers are refugees themselves, like Bahirun and Alpha. Yesterday, I met Nahida, a professor of pedagogy from Afghanistan, who teaches women and children in a small dome-like structure opposite the Caravan where she lives with her four children.

— *They built this dome for me*—Nahida told me. *I translate and I teach in the evenings and two afternoons. All the Sudanese people call me 'Mama,' they respect me, and we find words in common.*

Nahida trained teachers at Kabul University. Her marriage to a foreigner made her children stateless and the Taliban threatened her. Separated from her husband, she fled Afghanistan in search of a nationality for her children, giving up a good job and home and paying 40,000 dollars to people smugglers. The five of them had travelled by foot, horseback, boat, car and bus through Pakistan, Iran and the Balkans.

— *Why England?*

— *My brother is there, and twenty family members.*

— *I have tried the truck twice. Mary was crying, 'Don't take your children, something could happen.' You know, I grew up in a war, I lived in a war and grew old in a war. Sometimes I want to go back to Afghanistan. Muslim people believe it's up to God, but I know this Afghanistan is a football, the Russians come, the Americans come, the Taliban come, Daesh comes... There is a boy who comes to me who has seen the Taliban execute someone in his family with an axe, he cannot sleep.*

She looks at me in angry despair, and I think of my conversation with Tawab last year.

— All I want is for my children to have a nationality. How long can my children stay here without education? They are really intelligent. So how long?

I don't have an answer, but I tell her that the Jungle is lucky to have her help.

In Haiti, after the 2010 Earthquake, while the dispossessed clustered in makeshift camps on roundabouts and in garbage-filled canyons— not dissimilar to this one—the UN administered the aid effort from a compound at the airport that was closed to all but those with international NGO accreditation. Even local charities were entirely absent from the coordination meetings that were supposedly going to rebuild the lives of the devastated Haitians. That failure to empower local people to restore their own lives may have contributed to the homelessness and impoverishment that continues six years later. Here in Calais, I have not heard the word 'beneficiary' used once. Coordination meetings are open to all. Besides establishing and running restaurants, schools and libraries, refugees volunteer in the warehouse, work in the clean-up squads, translate for each other and the volunteers, organise, and assist in the distribution points across the camp.

Coordination with the French has improved since last year. There is now a weekly coordination meeting led by ACTED, a French NGO contracted by the French government to provide water and clear the rubbish. The main topic today is the three people who have disappeared and the apparent reluctance of the French police to investigate. The woman from ACTED explains that in order to address the issue, the police need statements from those who actually knew the missing persons. Bahirun makes another passionate, angry speech about how many times they have been to the police to make reports.

— This is not about tickets or distributions, it's about missing people, they should come to us. Why do we have to go there?

An older Afghan in a Pashtun hat starts speaking.

— We came from Afghanistan and Syria because it is dangerous. But it is dangerous here. Europe is dangerous. It is dangerous to go to the City, even the volunteers are scared. Why does no one care?

– Look—says a volunteer—*let's get the right group together, people who can do the identifying with translators, with transport. It is tedious, but we have to keep trying.*

Bahirun is asking what happened to the idea of a camp taxi to take someone to hospital at night. It needs a trusted volunteer who knows Calais. Meanwhile, fifteen beds have been arranged in a convalescence facility for men with traumatic injuries, but Bahirun wants to see more space for tired and sick people. The containers at Salaam are only for the women and children. Someone wants the ambulance extraction points explained. A Frenchman suggests that there should be a communication person in each community to spread correct information.

A psychotherapist comes up to me after the meeting. He is planning to pop over once a week from Britain and was wondering how I thought he could help. Perhaps he could do some psychological debriefing?[8]

– Umm, I am not sure debriefing is what is needed here.

– What do you recommend?

– Hanging out, sitting and listening to people wherever they are, whenever they want. Not forcing people to talk or sitting in a 'counselling tent'. Being as well-informed as possible about where everything is, including relevant asylum information, the nearest free food, activities. Actually, I think the most useful things I do are drive a car, carry a thermos flask of warm tea at all times, and be able to stand on my head.

I am not joking. Burnt out volunteers don't have time to come to sessions on self-care, but they do need lifts to get petrol for generators, travel between meetings in warehouse and camp, and then get back to wherever they are sleeping. A warm car is as good a place as any to ventilate about the latest idiotic suggestion made by a new volunteer or the behaviour of the CRS.

These lessons were reinforced this morning. I had driven over to Dunkirk early to meet Lydia at the school. Maddie had walked me in and sat on the bench outside. She was still exhausted, saying she needed a good weep really, so I poured out some hot tea and we had a natter. Apparently, the fight settled down. The problem is that

59

the refugees have a love-hate relationship with the people smugglers, which is now the main route to the UK. A few weeks ago, some Albanians turned up and started trying to muscle in on the Kurdish patch. It was that conflict that led to gun shots. The refugees were saying—*give us a break, we fled from all of this.*

Then I went to meet Lydia for the planned developmental movement session for children. (Thank you, Veronica Sherborne. The training I had from you in Bristol in developmental movement for children has helped me in so many places.) It's amazing at providing a way of moving and exercising in small, cramped shelters, and helping children feel and understand their bodies. It's good for building relationships and good for dealing with aggression. Best of all, it is fun. Two young Swiss volunteers turn up, and we practice rolling each other across the floor, being rocking boats or immovable rocks, making swings and jumps and tunnels with bodies for children to crawl through. Everyone was laughing and relaxed after forty minutes.

When Maddie heard I was driving back for the coordination meeting, she asked for a lift and used the whole journey to ventilate. It turns out, she has been a festival organiser for around ten years, which seems to provide an ideal skillset for working in Northern France.

Calais and Dunkirk, Thursday 18 February

The days run into each other, and it's hard to remember what I did on which day. The camps are an exercise in not doing the things you thought you were going to do and finding yourself doing something entirely different (but hopefully useful). It might be visiting a child with learning difficulties or one that is being overactive and aggressive. It might be group work with exhausted volunteers. Today, it was group play activities at the caravans the French government have provided as winter accommodation for the most vulnerable women and children. They get food vouchers, but there is no transport and no school, so the children are miserable and bored. One small boy is wailing inconsolably for no apparent reason.

So, we play my favourite games for bored children; 'Crossing the River' is great for using up energy. Mark out two lines about twenty feet apart. Line up all the children on one side. Stand in the river looking ferocious and waving your arms like a crocodile, dragon or water snake—whatever is culturally appropriate. Have additional adults play monitor to watch out for falls and scrapes and say 'go.' At that point, the children must run across the river without getting caught. Those caught turn into crocodiles and catch more children at the next crossing. It never fails. Children enjoy being crocodiles as much as they do crossing without being caught. I recommend following with quieter games like 'knots.' In this game, children must form a circle, put their hands in front of them, close their eyes and walk forwards until each hand has caught another hand. Then they open their eyes, and, keeping hold of the hands, untangle the knot in silence. The magic works here in Dunkirk. Two minutes into the session, the wailing boy is smiling and running.

Afterwards, there's a discussion group at the Women and Children's Centre at Grand Synthe. This is a large beautiful yurt-like structure, draped, carpeted and cushioned with a central stove and a tunnel entrance where you can deboot, swing your legs across a bench and enter without bringing mud onto the carpeted floor. Between 1pm and 6pm it's women and children only. At night, it's an emergency shelter for new arrivals.

It was built by Dylan, an Irish tree surgeon and carpenter. Prior to this, Dylan was squatting in Dublin, running an anarchist social centre. Incensed by what was happening in Syria, he had planned to go and help the Kurdish opposition in Rojava, but then decided he could be more useful helping the Kurdish community camped out in Dunkirk.

Today, the volunteers want to discuss why everyone gets angry, which naturally leads to talking about loss and stress reactions. Then, we move onto organisational difficulties and coping with burn out. I realise I need to develop a workshop specifically for this context.

What a difference weather makes. Today, bright sunlight lights up blossoms and the stuffed children's toys some people have hung in the trees around their tents. The camp has a gaudy appearance if you ignore the mud, pools and swamps.

The Camp at Grand Synthe Dunkirk, February 2016

I know how lucky I am to have a quiet sanctuary in which to sleep and write. Benoit runs a B&B in the centre of the old part of town, looking over the park. Most importantly, he is friendly to volunteers and is welcoming whenever I return.

The Jungle, Friday 19 February

The French Prefecture has served a formal notice of eviction on the inhabitants of the southern half of the camp. In the evening, refugees and volunteers pack together into the Jungle Books meeting room as Mary summarises the key points from the eviction order:

The refugees are accused of attacking the cars and property of residents nearby, of distracting the police forces from more urgent security needs in the fight against 'terrorism' in a state of emergency, and of living in unsafe, unsanitary conditions that lack human dignity.

Another stated reason is the "attacks on migrants by individual members of small radical groups around the 'La Lande' camp and the incitement to hatred and violence circulating on internet blogs by extreme left-wing and extreme right-wing groups." So, living in hellish conditions and being attacked by fascists are not arguments for protection, but for eviction!

The authorities state that the southern half of the camp only houses 800 to 1000 refugees—a number that can be accommodated in the new container camp. Others can go to the spaces they have available in accommodation centres around France.

But Help Refugees have done a census in the last week. The actual figures are 3500, which means there is insufficient provision for all those who need it, in particular for the unaccompanied minors. This is the basis for the legal action taken by the Jungle residents, supported by the Associations, contesting the eviction. They argue that no humane, dignified provision has been made for the majority of people living in the camp.

Fortunately, it seems likely that Ben's rebuilding programme should be able to rehouse all those affected in the northern part of the camp, in either a fixed structure or a caravan. But all social spaces are in the southern part: the Youth Centre, Jungle Books, and the Ethiopian Church.

But should people move into these new spaces in the northern half when their legal case to stop the eviction rests on residents remaining present in their homes in the southern half, while the arguments are pursued in court?

The legal action was discussed by all the communities at the coordination meeting last week:

— *The Sudanese people already decided 100% no one is going to move. We are prepared to die*—Riyad had said. Afghan, Eritrean and Kurdish representatives all agreed.

It is a paradoxical situation. No one actually wants to stay in the Jungle. As one refugee said—*it's shit*—but their experiences at the hands of French authorities have made most wary of any offer of protection from the French State. When three young Sudanese men dressed in bright red, warm anoraks, clean trousers and smart trainers turned up at the coordination meeting last week to explain what happened if you accepted accommodation in France, most of the refugees walked out, and those that stayed would not believe their accounts. Later that same evening at yet another meeting, the anger was palpable.

— *They say to seek asylum here, but eighty percent of those who do get rejected. They don't keep their promises. We are not on holiday. We came because there is war and conflict in our countries, and we all suffered losses.*

— *They destroyed Sangatte in 2004. They destroyed the first Jungle in 2008. I tried asylum in France. I have been trying for nine months. Nothing! Please go to court and explain what is happening to us. People have been killed; people have disappeared. I have taken children to those centres. They promise they will go to the UK soon, but it does not happen. So many of you come to help us, but nothing happens. We don't trust the French government. We are in deep trouble and they don't care about us. We came to save our lives, what are you doing? Please do something!*

And even if the authorities do provide sufficient accommodation, most refugees don't want to move into the Containers.

— *The children refuse, how can I force them?* Nahida asked me. *There is no kitchen, no water—it's just a container, and a container is for animals, not humans, and there is no school.*

One Afghan boy who moved in 20 days ago, told me it was miserable.

— It's twelve people to a room. There is nowhere to lock your things. The toilets and showers do not work. There is no drinking water. You have to get food outside at Salaam, and there is no social space of any kind.

So, forget education or physical activities. The gates are locked at night, and if you stay away more than 48 hours, you lose your place. His biggest concern is that they fingerprinted him on entrance, and he worries that will mean he can never go to the UK.

What the Containers and dispersal cannot offer is the dignity, humanity and interconnected community that refugees have created here, out of nothing. At its heart, a constant lively interchange is going on: it is a marketplace, an art show, a school, a library, and a café—all places where it is possible to learn or sit, meet and talk, or just relax. These spaces offer the chance to feel human, become dignified, and treat others with dignity. It is both filthy and intoxicating. Ben told me he knows of refugees who made it to the UK and returned because life in a lonely bedsit was bleak in comparison.

The Jungle, Saturday 20 February

There is music and drumming at the Ethiopian Church when I get to the camp. Men and women wrapped in the long white shawls come in and out making obeisance to the Cross. The dignity and beauty of other people's religious rituals is always moving, even for a non-believer. The building and ritual and warmth and light state: this is who we are. This is what matters. We are civilised and decent, respect us. Solomon who built the church, sits quietly on the bench at the side of the compound watching people come and go.

Then a Mercedes drives up and parks near the church. Two men get out and start handing out packages from the boot. A cluster of men immediately gather around, and a fight ensues. The combatants are quickly separated by other refugees, but the tension remains. I ask the men why they did not take the stuff to the warehouse.

— We've promised to put it directly into the hands of refugees.

— But, this way, it's only going into the hands of the biggest and strongest who live nearest the road.

The man shrugs and turns away, and I give up interfering.

What's remarkable is that, even in these times of extreme stress, there is still not too much violence or crime in the Jungle. Bahirun told me the other night that since the emergence of a community leadership, consisting of respected elders from each ethnic group, relationships within the camp are much better, communities can sort things out pretty quickly and there are fewer fights.

It would be wrong to idealise the situation. Sarah had her phone stolen from her at ten in the morning a few days ago. I know of two sexual assaults, and there are still tensions between ethnic groups.

— I have had Afghans threatening to burn down the shelters of the Eritrean women because they were getting built first—Ben told me. His solution was to take the Afghan making the threat along to an Eritrean part of the camp and offer him a lighter.

— Of course, he did not really want to do it. It was just frustration and bluster. Just imagine if you got a bunch of English, German, French and Dutch young men dumped in these conditions. They would be drunk in minutes and fighting in hours. These men have had incredibly traumatic experiences—many have been in the army or fled bombs falling on them. Many have never encountered cultures other than their own. Given all of this, it's miraculous that there is not more trouble. The only death was an accident in a drunken brawl when someone pulled a knife.

— This IS a jungle—Nahida said to me—*no trees, but a people jungle. There is no law, so how to live together without law? But refugees do want to help one another.*

She is right. People do form queues, they do come to meetings and listen attentively to get information which they share, and they do take care of themselves and one another.

The same with the volunteers, who somehow assimilate and see where they might help. Later in the day I meet a man wearing gloves and carrying a plastic bag. He has flown all the way from Canada to pick up rubbish.

— Why? I ask.

— Because this place is the most extraordinary thing on the planet.

The Jungle, Sunday 21 February

The response of the volunteers and refugees to the threat of eviction makes it clear that this is a solidarity movement, not a humanitarian operation. The threat has galvanised the community into action. There are nightly meetings in Jungle Books to share information and ideas. Some, like Sarah, work night and day, collecting testimonies from refugees and volunteers as to why eviction will be damaging to people's dignity. Other volunteers offer training in non-violence, first aid and legal rights if arrested.

Since Friday, I have been doing regular trainings in psychological first aid, both in the warehouse and in the Jungle. The freely downloadable handbook from the WHO website does not include forced eviction from a migrant shanty town in its examples of possibly stressful situations, but this is just as high stress as the conflict and disaster scenarios provided.[9]

I explain that the before and after periods are equally important: before, when people are extremely stressed about not knowing what is going to happen and how to prepare; and after, when, if worst case scenario arises and the bulldozers come, there may be arrests and confrontations. They are likely to be disorientated and confused, lacking information as to what they can do.

The message that we can all provide psychological support to one another in times of extreme stress, and that counselling tents, a degree in psychology, or training in 'debriefing' are not required, goes down well with both volunteers and refugees. The key actions of attending to people's basic needs, making sure they are safe, providing information and immediate comfort, connecting them to others who can take care of them, are what almost all the volunteers here do every day, so finding that these are endorsed as essential first steps to improving people's wellbeing is reassuring.

In the afternoon, a stream of celebrities including Jude Law, Tom Stoppard, Toby Jones and Juliet Stephenson, among others, arrives at the Dome to join the refugees in a performance of live music and letter reading. The volunteer lawyers are working flat out, as they do every day, in the legal centre next door. I bring a young Sudanese man for advice. As I expected, because he has no relatives in the UK, they advise him to claim asylum here. There is a queue of people waiting, and the lawyer tells me they are jealous because they are missing Jude Law, so I run over to ask Jamie Byng from Canongate if he will please bring the celebrities to the lawyers when they are done performing. He does, and the lawyers are as delighted as small children at Christmas, even though, as Jude Law points out, their work is more vital than his.

In the evening, there are about one hundred people gathered in the Jungle Books meeting room waiting for evening training—almost all refugees. They speak three languages. It's not particularly comfortable or warm, and, as usual, there is the low murmur of conversation. I stand on the small platform around the stove. We get people into language groups so that all translators can work simultaneously, and I see to my amazement that all these young men are listening intently. They are eager to know how to cope, help, and take care of themselves and others. They answer my questions and get the idea. Towards the end, one of them asks:

– *If there is an eviction, will you be here to look after us?*

– *Alas, no*—I explain—*I have to go back to the UK and then to Greece.*

– *So what will we do?*

– *You will support and take care of each other and there are many here to help.*

The Jungle, Monday 22 February

I wake up with a profound feeling of depression. I probably should not listen to the World Service in the morning. Further disintegrations in Syria. Fighting between US backed opposition groups. Migrants breaching the fence in Hungary, so they are extending it around Romania. Trump triumphs in the US on a rhetoric of excluding Muslims and building walls. I have a sense of descending into modern medievalism. Unless we radically rethink the way we live, we will become a world of walled kingdoms and endless hi-tech war, surrounded by the shanty towns and encampments of the dispossessed.

I am trying to tie up loose ends before I leave. Suddenly, everyone calls. Ben T. wants me at the Youth Centre to see two boys who have 'freaked out,' although they have calmed them down by the time I get there. Then, Laura asks me to come to the nursery to advise on a hyperactive infant. Again, I get there to find she is doing all the right things, and the child is cheerful and doing well.

I go around saying goodbye to friends. I have finally discovered why Adam's shelter has been locked every time I visited in the last ten days. A volunteer friend tells me he has accepted adoption by a French family. It had been offered before, but he turned it down when a lawyer told him there was a chance he might be able to join his uncle in the UK. But recently, he heard that the uncle had rejected him, so he had asked the family if they would consider him again, and they had said *yes*. I am so happy to hear this. At Alpha's beautifully painted house, some French people are measuring it up, preparing to move it to a museum—better to be a piece of artwork than a de-stroyed refugee home. Alpha shows me the bag of tear gas canisters he has just picked up and is going to make into something beautiful.

UNHCR is also here, along with a French Government official. The two women have come to assure young people that they will receive all necessary protection. In the ACTED tent they meet with some thirty boys whom Jess has dragged, somewhat reluctantly, from the Youth Centre.

— If you apply for asylum in France, we can promise you will be given food and accommodation, until the process is finished. We have buses going to Bordeaux and Perpignan—says the woman from UNHCR.

— We know people who have applied for asylum, and they don't get food and medicine—says a Sudanese boy.

— Perhaps there were mistakes. I don't know, I am not responsible.

— I work for the French government, and I can assure you, if you apply for asylum here, you will have all protections. If you know of specific cases, please tell me about them.

There is a discontented murmuring, and the UNHCR woman suddenly loses her temper.

— Do stop complaining! Just give me the names—be efficient!

There is a stunned silence, then a girl asks:

— *Are there spaces for three hundred children around France?*

— *I cannot say, as protection is the responsibility of the departments.*

From the look on her face, the UNHCR lady is clearly regretting attending the meeting. The French government official steps in:

— *We have centres for adults, but if we have to find spaces for children, we will. If you want to be protected, we will protect you.*

Silence, no one looks reassured.

— *I have been here five months with my family. It's the English who have helped. I have seen no one from the French government*—says another boy.

— *We will be here every day.* The French Government woman smiles.

— *The decision to evict has been put on hold*—the lawyer tells us at the packed evening meeting. The judge agreed with the Help Refugees' estimate of numbers and was concerned about the estimated three hundred unaccompanied children in the camp. Apparently, she is visiting tomorrow to assess the situation for herself.

The Jungle, Tuesday 23 February

It's my last day in the camp. I follow the judge in. As requested in last night's meeting, everyone is up early to greet her and make a visible display of the numbers living in the southern half. Families with immaculately dressed children stand outside the entrance to the secular school. One of the kitchens is serving fried eggs and onions to a long queue by the information centre. But the judge's diminutive figure is scarcely visible behind the gaggle of journalists and police around her. The speed with which she moves through, making only perfunctory stops in St. Michaels and the Women and Children's Centre, suggest the visit has more to do with public relations than genuine enquiry. The judge goes back to Lille to continue the court case.

I leave for the port.

Cornwall, Thursday 25 February

The judge has ruled that the southern part of the camp can be cleared, but that the social spaces must remain. The prefecture promises the process will be 'gradual.' *What does that mean?*

Cornwall, Monday 29 February

The police started clearing this morning. Some refused to move so then it was tear gas and stun guns. Apparently, some set fire to their tents, and there was rock throwing. I scroll through photos and videos on social media, feeling miserable and useless.

Just before I left, one of my Afghan friends showed me a note he had written out very carefully:

My only wish is to be in a safe place. I want to live in a place where I can find peace and study. I am very tired of this situation and it makes me cry. When I get on a truck, I feel happy, but when we get taken off, we become sad and give up. It is better just to die.

He is sixteen years old.

Ahmed's Story

Ahmed is Kurdish and comes from Kurdistan in Northern Iraq. He was sixteen years old when he told me this story in August 2016, when he was living in a refugee camp in Northern Greece.

We lived in a small village. My father ran a factory, and my mother was a housewife. I have three brothers and three sisters; I am the third eldest.

I cannot remember any happy times before the war. All I can recall is that, when I was eight or nine, the whole family went on a journey to see some place near the village. I was very happy that day. My best times were playing with friends there or walking around with family. It was a beautiful place.

I started school when I was six years old. I loved school because I wanted to improve and learn many things and not stay as a stupid boy. I liked science, Kurdish and English. I had just finished 6th grade at primary school. We had to leave Iraq. We left five months ago, because there was no more work for my father and because the Islamic state was very close, and we had to run away.

In our community, there was no fighting, but there was in others—against the Peshmerga. I don't like ISIS; I am very upset with them because they came to Iraq and Syria and destroyed the country. From the moment we heard of this so-called Islamic state, we knew they were seeking to harm us and destroy the country. Everything about them is about destruction and harming the country. They do nothing good for anyone. No one has been hurt in my family, but one family who lived near us was converted, and we became afraid of how they can manipulate minds. From the moment that family converted and went to join ISIS, no one knows what happened to them. The father was with ISIS from the beginning, but it was secret, then he came and took the whole family. That is how we knew.

We are Muslim. ISIS are not Muslim, because our Islam is not like that. They are carrying flags and saying Allah is great. They write Islamic verses on walls and then they burn the flags and the walls. This is not Islam. What they do to people—all that destruction—is not good.

We left Iraq in secrecy, going over the mountains to Turkey. It took twenty-four hours; we were in the mountains a whole day. We had no water, and there was snow up to our knees. We took a car to one point and then it was on foot. We were about twenty families together, and we all suffered together. At one moment, we lost our father. He was very tired and had fallen asleep while walking through some trees. We looked for hours, and we finally found him in the woods. He was exhausted. I was not afraid for myself, but I was worried for my little sisters, and I was worried about another Assyrian family with a little baby in the deep snow. They suffered a lot because, as we walked, they fell down every few steps in the snow.

We had four smugglers with us on the journey, and when we reached a river, they told us—*when you cross the river you are in Turkey.* The smugglers gave everyone two sticks to help them wade through the river. It was not difficult for me, but it was for others because the stream was very powerful. No one fell. I helped by carrying their bags from one side to the other.

After the river, we walked for four hours and reached an area full of soldiers who said—*let's put you all in vehicles and send you back to Iraq, you have no business here.* So we all got together and agreed to give the soldiers money and they let us through. Each person paid about fifty dollars. After the soldiers got the money, they gave us bananas and water. They let us rest in one room which they had been using. They allowed the women and girls to rest there for two hours then we had to go on. We walked for another two hours to a small village where there was an explosion. The explosion was in an empty shop, it destroyed the surroundings, but no one was hurt. We were not close, but we could see what was going on. No one could explain why. I was not afraid, but it was very loud.

Then we got on a bus for twenty-four hours and went to a town near the Sea. We stayed there in a hotel for four days. Every day, the

74

smuggler was telling us—*It's OK. I will take you out of here.* Finally, we left the hotel and the smuggler took us to the place where we got the rubber boat. Then it was two and a half hours on the sea. We were all frightened. The rubber boat was tipping and about to sink, when the strong waves came, but God saved us. The driver owned the boat. There were 110 people on it. It was very overcrowded. I could sit down. We bought life jackets for 10 euros each. I don't know if they were any good, but the smuggler said—*no lifebuoy rings*—because he wanted space. I have never been to sea. I saw it on TV. I cannot swim. Everyone was afraid and people fell asleep from fear.

When we reached our destination—the Island of Samos—the rubber boat stopped. Everyone got out, and we looked at the GPS to see where we were. Then, we walked another hour from the coast. We saw no one, no coastguards, no police, nothing. The boat owner had given us a number and told us to walk for an hour and then call that number. We were told to say we were stuck in the mountains and ask them to—*Please come and rescue us, as we have a man and a woman in a wheelchair.* So, after we called, the police came and took us to another island. We stayed in a place where there was a big camp of Afghan refugees. We stayed there two days and then they put us on a big ship for Athens. When we reached Athens, we rang another number that someone gave us on the boat, and a big bus came and moved us to Eko. We paid for that bus ourselves; it had nothing to do with the Greek government.

When we got to Eko, our father went to the border and signed a paper with all our names. He was going to come and get us, but at the last moment, the border closed. Father was number thirty on that paper, but, at that time, only sixteen were crossing. Then they closed it.

We did not leave. We thought we would stay and wait. We thought, OK, sixteen today, but tomorrow it will be our turn. But then we heard on the internet and TV that it was closed. We stayed a few more weeks, and then we came here. There was a protest. It was over four days—we all went in the road and closed it. My father and I participated in the protest. I had a paper in my hands on which I

75

had written: You must open the borders immediately. We closed the road, but then we saw cars going around us, so we closed that road also. But then people felt helpless. It was four days with no food, so they gave up.

Eko was better than here because at Eko Camp we had toilets with water, and the showers had hot and cold water (although we had to pay). Here, every time I go to the toilet, I suffer a lot because I must take water since the toilets are always dirty. And the food is no good here. We don't eat it. It's only edible on one day a week when they give us meat and rice. We buy everything and my mother cooks. We have a small electric oven inside the tent. It's better than nothing.

My father told us when we planned to leave Iraq, we were not allowed to tell anyone about our plans or that we were leaving. We planned to go to Germany. My brother is already there. Life here is very boring. I have nothing to do—I go out of the tent, I hang around, and I go back in the tent. There is nothing to do. This little school? (Ahmed makes a rude gesture with his hand.) We do a bit of football. I hope they could fix the ground for us in a field where we can play football, and I would like a school in which we can learn. We have no doctor here after 5pm, so we teach each other first aid. We have two paramedics from the Red Crescent in Syria among the refugees. We call it the 'open borders group' because we are stuck here and want the borders to open.

Would I go back to Iraq? Of course, if I knew my village was safe, I would go back. The Peshmerga are the only ones who can defeat Daesh, and they will finish them.

Refugees protest the closure of the Greek border with Macedonia, March 2016.

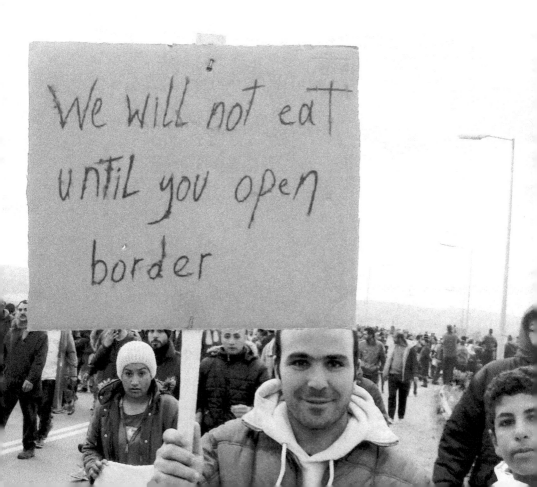

Island of Lesvos

Greece, March 2016

Molyvos, Monday 7 March

The Castle above Molyvos has very thick walls. The Byzantines kept out the Cretan Arabs; the Genoese kept out the Turks; the Ottomans kept out the Europeans. Each empire adding yet more bricks and mortar so that, today, Asmamaw and I can sit among the carefully maintained ruins and gaze down on the NATO ships patrolling the tiny stretch of water between this Greek island and Turkey. They are here to keep out yet another invasion—this one unarmed and desperate. The patrolling has lessened the flow slightly, but it has done nothing to decrease the dangers. Twenty-five migrants died today just off the tourist beaches of Turkey. Can you imagine the reaction if that was off Bournemouth or Torquay? Here it is, just a footnote to the more than four thousand who have drowned or gone missing this year, trying to make it to Europe. Those that do make it, are either picked up by the Greek Coastguard and taken into Mytilene, or, like the one hundred people that arrived early this morning onto the northern beaches, are welcomed by a motley crew of Greek and international volunteers.

Asmamaw and I have spent the weekend getting our bearings, driving the dirt road from Molyvos to Skala Sykamineas, between hillsides blooming with Broom and Ashphodel and a silky sea. Just below the Castle in Molyvos, there is the Hope Centre, set up by Eric and Rachel Kempson, a resident British couple who have spent most of a year rescuing people and decided to use donated funds to convert an unused hotel into a small friendly way station with rooms for families and changes of clothes. Further along, sitting in strategically placed chairs on the cliff's edge and armed with night vision binoculars, are two Norwegians and a Japanese man from Drop in the Ocean. The Japanese man has travelled for sixty hours at his own expense to spend three weeks 'helping out.' Down the road are the minibuses and ranked tents of the International Rescue

Lifejackets at the dump
near Molyvos
Lesvos, Greece, March 2016

Committee (IRC). Rumour has it that the guards and drivers are all from the neo-Nazi group, Golden Dawn—their antagonisms to migrants muted somewhat by the employment possibilities offered. Although, migrants are still a divisive issue in Molyvos. The medical tent near the Hope Centre has been burned down three times. Beyond IRC are the beach-side shelters created by the Lighthouse, well-constructed from tarpaulin and wood, and set among trees. Jen, an advertising executive from London who has used all her leave to volunteer, showed us around. There is separate warming, drying and changing space for men, women and children. There are sorted, donated clothes available, a kitchen for making hot food and even a small playground for children. Platanos, a mainly Greek anarchist collective, has a similar set-up, slightly further along the road, while in the village itself, the Spanish lifeguard volunteers, and the medics from Israid hang out at Goji café and wait to be called.

Moria Registration Camp, Tuesday 8 March

So this is how it goes: once your rubber dinghy has landed and you have been warmed up, fed, and given dry clothes by one of the groups mentioned above, you are then picked up by an IRC or UNHCR minibus to be taken across the island to the Moria registration centre in the olive clad hills near Mytilene. Unfortunately, Moria looks like a prison, with cellblocks and barbed wire topping double metal fences—because that is what it was. But this is where the Greek Government provides papers that allow you to spend a transitional period in Greece while you make your way first to Athens and then up to the North to cross into Macedonia and the Balkans, and onwards towards the dream of Germany. The transitional period varies: six months for Syrians, and one month for everyone else, but there is a chance of renewal or of applying for asylum in Greece.

Just outside the Prison is an informal tented camp. This is 'Better Days for Moria' (BDFM), set up by unpaid Greek and international volunteers who despaired at the conditions and understaffing inside Moria and their inability to get adequate services for people who needed them because of guns, barbed wire and bureaucracy. So, they rented land next door, set up kitchens, clothes and tent distribution. Currently, some 600-800 Pakistanis, Moroccans and Afghans live here in tents among the olive trees. With brightly painted coloured signs, an always open tea tent, a seemingly endless game of cricket going on in the one flat space, and a children's play tent and playground, it is much more welcoming than behind the barbed wire, where everyone is turfed out of their rooms at 7am to sit on the concrete walkways, come rain or shine. So, not surprisingly, many of the refugees walk over to use the facilities here. Now that the Macedonian border guards are only allowing entry to their country on the basis of what city you come from in Syria, both camps are overflowing.

Asmamaw and I are now officially registered as independent volunteers. You can do it in five minutes on the Northern Aegean Prefecture website or walk into their office as we did this morning. We also registered with the Greek Medical Association, so we have permission to volunteer at the Health post in BDFM. There are official MSF and MDM-run clinics inside Moria, but they are understaffed and overwhelmed, so many people come to Health Point. Jim, a retired GP from Scotland who has been working here a week, has been seeing 70 to 100 patients on every shift. Last night, he had to take a man with a two-week-old suppurating fracture to the hospital, deal with a person in status asthmaticus, and sort out medication for someone with uncontrolled epilepsy. There are supposedly two organised camps for vulnerable patients, but they are both full.

— *Mostly it's triviata, coughs, colds, aches and pains. You are just providing comfort, as GP's mostly do at home, reassuring them there is nothing more serious. But there's a lot of antenatal care needed and quite a few with serious illnesses: vascular damage from cold injuries, pneumonia, dehydration, feverish or hypothermic babies.*

There is also a scabies infestation. Ideally, we would like to refer these cases back to MSF, who have hot showers and a treatment protocol. The trouble is the Pakistanis, who make up most of the occupants of the informal camp, don't want to go to MSF because they are afraid that, if they go into Moria, they will be registered for deportation. There is no possibility of them transiting Greece. Unaccompanied

83

minors can register with UNHCR and go to school and be cared for in Athens, at least until they are 18. Adults can claim asylum in Greece if they can prove there was a threat to their life, but most can't do this, so they face deportation and a humiliating return to their families with nothing to show but overwhelming debt. At one of the meetings discussing their options, one of the Pakistani men lay down on the floor and said—*Well, why not just kill me now?*

Sofia, a volunteer translator who has come here from Islamabad, has got to know many of them. She thinks a particularly vulnerable group has been targeted by smugglers.

– Most of them have very little education and cannot read or write. They have been sold a dream in Pakistan and spent a fortune to get here. They don't fully understand where 'here' is, and they certainly don't understand the complexities of their situation. Until a few weeks ago, if they registered, they got a paper saying they could stay in Greece for a month. Now, the paper says they will be deported, but they have not fully understood that.

Sofia is completely frustrated at the official agencies' attitude to informal volunteers like herself, even when they are desperately short of translators. Recently, she had persuaded some unaccompanied minors to go and register with UNHCR, promising to stick with them every step of the way, only to have the door to the office slammed in her face when she brought them up there. Unsurprisingly, some of them ran off without registering.

There was a silent protest this afternoon: Moroccans, Pakistanis, Iranians, Afghans and other 'secondary' groups—the ones who have a 'B' on the wrist band issued at registration—sat holding placards on the cricket pitch while the volunteers joined in a protective circle. Wrist bands: the system of categorisation that defines your rights to assistance, not according to what you have suffered or experienced, but simply on the basis of where you were born.

I don't have an answer to the migration crisis, but looking for solutions surely has to begin with certain fundamental principles. One is that people have always moved to try to improve their lives. My Jewish grandfather did, and that is the reason I am alive today. One's chances of life, liberty, and the pursuit of happiness cannot simply depend on geographical lotto. *Bad luck—you are born in a dangerous, corrupt state rife with terrorist bombings or war. No, you may not leave.* If capital can move freely, causing havoc, why not people? *Because everyone will want to come here!* The cry goes up. So how do we make 'there' decent? A global tax on wealth might be a start.[10] *Dream on,* I hear my readers scoffing.

Better Days for Moria, Wednesday 9 March
It's official. The Macedonian border is now completely closed to all migrants, no matter how they are categorised—as are the Serb, Slovene and Croatian borders. Viktor Orban's fences are now *de rigueur.* There is no way to Germany through the Balkans. And, while Balkan governments shout, *He started it!* At one another, the EU plans yet another crisis meeting, and the Greek government says there is a humanitarian emergency—which is true. It's not just the 12,000-15,000 sitting in the mud and rain on the Macedonian border. We stopped in Victoria Park in Athens on the way here. It is packed with families who have been sleeping on blankets for days because the official camps are full, as are the squats in the neighbourhood run by our Greek anarchist friends. One apartment block had 150 families staying there. The ports in Athens are apparently in chaos, and Moria now has 3000 when it is only supposed to house 1500.
– *That was my first demonstration. It was the first time I put up my hand. I am usually a spectator*—Jim tells me at breakfast this morning. He had joined the protest yesterday afternoon.
– *Why did you come?*
– *You sit at home. You watch John Wayne shoot Indians on the telly, then you watch Homs being blasted to smithereens on the same screen, then you walk the dogs in the park, up to the pond, round the church, and you think about those two sets of images on the same screen and it's like it's not happening. It's not enough. I needed to come… If I am brutally honest, we did not give a monkey's when we invaded their countries; we paid no attention to their borders. We chose the boundaries of the Middle East and Africa to suit ourselves. If you believe what goes around comes*

around… the sins of the Fathers… So I'm left with: what responsibility do we bear because of what we have allowed our governments to do? It's a complex and longstanding problem but we have inflamed and aggravated it, if nothing else. So surely we have to hold out our hands and hearts. The Greeks have been incredible, and they are economically destitute.

I am sorry Jim's leaving. He has been friendly and welcoming, helping Asmamaw and I find our feet. He's both sad and glad to be going. Partly because he's exhausted, having done a shift every day for two weeks.

— *You have to remember that people's physical ills occur in the context of extreme danger, after extreme physical hardship. They have been herded onto trucks, walked across mountains, suffered cold and heat. Then there is the physical stress of crossing a sea which many are seeing for the first time. They make it to Greece and let go, and that is when the symptoms appear, just like when you go on holiday and have time to be sick. There are many elderly people who have lived all their lives in one place, then they up sticks for the first time with their diabetes and their high blood pressure and obesity, subjecting themselves to terrible hardship. They say things like 'My baby has died, I have to get to Germany.' Think about that: a fifty-year-old man rolling up his bed heading here, leaving everyone behind…*

Jim bursts into tears. I think about this in the evening clinic. The elderly Afghan lawyer talking to me lost three friends in that boat accident three days ago, and he cannot stop seeing them in his mind's eye. Actually, I was not expecting to do clinics. Asmamaw is doing daily shifts, but I thought I would provide some training for volunteer staff and be available if there was a case where they needed advice, as in Calais. But I have had three referrals in an hour, so I have pinned up an appointment sheet on the wall, where people can book into time slots.

There is a Pakistani man who broke down crying while trying to put up his tent. He had just heard that his father had died in Pakistan. Mehwish, the Urdu translator sitting with him tells me she just brought him here for quiet space. He does not want to talk to me, or anyone else apart from her. She will look after him. I am delighted. The volunteer translators are the frontline staff and are completely amazing. Mehwish is normally the manager of a cosmetic supply chain in the US. She told me she had never realised knowing two languages would be so useful. She sits quietly with the man while he weeps and agonises over whether he should immediately go back to Pakistan. She makes sure he has enough credit to call home, sharing, at his request, pictures of her own family on her phone, and then helping him get settled for the night and making sure others are around to take care of him.

Meanwhile, John, one of the best Farsi translators and a refugee himself, brings in another young man, Samir, a 20-year-old Afghan who had arrived from the boat that morning. He registered in Moria and was given the appropriate 'B' wristband but had ended up in Better Days. John had tried to help and had become increasingly concerned at his odd behaviour and strange way of speaking. His answers were off point and made no sense. He seemed confused, looked terrified and was quite unable to erect a tent, so John brought him to me.

– *Believe me, I have seen a lot of upset people, but this guy is completely different and really strange.*

In the warmth and light of the clinic, Samir is less confused and able to explain that he has been seeing and hearing things for years, since his twin brother died. In particular, he sees three men following and trying to kill him. It has gotten worse since fleeing Afghanistan. He saw them on the boat and started shouting because he was terrified. The other passengers thought he was crazy. I cannot decide in just one assessment if this is an exacerbation of a psychotic disorder or some kind of dissociative experience related to panic attacks. As warmth, light, reassurance, dry clothes and tea have calmed him down, I don't think it's a psychiatric emergency, but the young man needs a safe place to sleep and someone to keep an eye on him, as he's completely alone and unable to organise his own care. Then, he can be reassessed in the morning.

I get on the phone, starting with MSF inside Moria, who, in theory at least, will manage the more serious cases if they are registered refugees. The doctor on duty tells me they cannot take psychiatric cases. MDM is closed. I ring Caritas. They have a camp for vulnerable

A young protestor at Better Days for Moria Camp
March 2016

people, but mental illness is not the right kind of vulnerable case for their facility. In between, I repeatedly try the on-call coordinator for UNHCR but only get through to voicemail. I try a friend in the mental health coordination group. No answer. With the help of a Greek volunteer doctor, I ring the emergency department at the hospital. The duty doctor is extremely reluctant to disturb the on-call psychiatrist, but Giorgiou persuades her. Finally, a very nice psychiatrist and I discuss the case. They are happy to assess him immediately and possibly give him a bed for the night, but, of course, require us to send a translator.

John is the only Farsi translator on site, and we have a queue of patients waiting. On call, UNHCR are still not answering. I text a friend at UNHCR who immediately texts back, and I explain we need a bed for the night. Finally, after three hours of phone calls, someone from Moria rings me. She speaks Farsi, has arranged a bed in a single room for the night and a volunteer to check up on him. The young man is completely calm now. It looks as though it was panic. John and I walk him up to the gate of Moria, where their staff are waiting. We promise to see him the next day.

There is a wary relationship between the professional humanitarian organisations, both UN and NGO, and the independent volunteers. According to Tracy, a volunteer at the Hope Centre, it started out badly. The volunteers handled the crisis alone for all of last summer—greeting boats, saving lives and trying to help refugees on foot across the island. Then, in autumn, UNHCR and a number of big agencies turned up.

— *They basically said thanks, you can go home now, you are doing more harm than good, leave it to the professionals.*

This, understandably, did not go down well with people, both local and international, who had spent all summer saving lives.

— *We were late*—my UNHCR friend said. *I have friends in Geneva who still think we should not be here at all when they lack funds for people who are dying in the Central African Republic.*

— *All the more reason to make use of the volunteers then*—*they fund themselves. You could provide the leadership.*

Admittedly, it is difficult to provide coordination and guidance to large populations of individuals whose average time on the island is two weeks. Moreover, many of them, especially the Greek volunteers, come from solidarity groups whose whole ethos is a resistance to top-down leadership. Last Saturday, Asmamaw and I sat through a fireside meeting on the north coast, in which some fifty supporters of Platanos debated for two hours whether Platanos, as an organisation, should send volunteers to Idomeni, or should go as independent individuals. I don't know the outcome, as no consensus had been reached by the time we went to bed.

By now, just like in Calais, many of the volunteers have recognised the need for some structure and created it for themselves. They communicate on social media pages, like 'Information Point for Lesvos Volunteers,' started by a volunteer who worked here last year and decided this was the most useful thing she could do from home. They join task-focussed messaging groups, which are far more responsive to changing needs than any UN emergency cluster meeting I have attended. Many join established networks like Better Days, turning up for the daily orientation at the information hut. Then, signing up wherever needed, they cook or do clothes distribution or help set up tents.

In between seeing patients, I do the same myself. I particularly enjoy helping keep the lunch queue orderly. Standing there with half a dozen other women—it works best with women—and stopping some 600 men from queue jumping, brings out some kind of inner policewoman in me. We are firm but kind, gently shaking our heads at any place saving. Having clowns wander around in full gear doing card tricks helps even more.

Volunteers also join newly formed NGOs like Drop in the Ocean, Lighthouse or Health Point. All of these organisations sprung up out of nowhere to address the specific needs on Lesvos. They all have long-term coordinators but will happily take short-termers and provide a structure in which the volunteers can fit. Fiona, another British GP, would have loved to work for MSF, but could only spare her two weeks annual leave because she has children at home. Health Point was happy to use her, and she has worked flat out, doing daily shifts for two weeks—all at her own expense. One of my favourites is Dirty Girls, begun by women who realised that the discarded wet clothing refugees were throwing away was creating an environmental problem. They started gathering it up, getting what was salvageable professionally laundered, and recycling it. You see their cheerful purple logo-bedecked bins everywhere.

– *But they don't follow SOPS (standard operating procedures) or protocols*—a colleague in one of the big NGOs complained to me. She had just stomped out of the Health Point Clinic after discovering that they kept baby bottles in the supply room. The baby bottles are an issue. Many of the Syrian mothers arrive already using them. They are not breastfeeding and want new bottles, even though they are a health hazard because they are so difficult to keep clean.

– *Well, why not take the time to share and discuss the protocols with them?* I asked.

– *Just gap year students on holiday*—another said—*completely inexperienced!* I have actually not met anyone having a holiday. On the contrary, the biggest problem is burnout, because many have not learned to pace themselves and feel they must respond to every need. This actually matters less for people going home after two weeks but is harder with those staying longer. I have learned to offer 30-minute daily training sessions in the small carpeted rest room at Health Point because everyone is 'too busy' to sit down for any longer. I am flattered that once they do sit down to discuss subjects like acute stress or grief and loss in refugees, they always stay longer and see the relevance of these topics to themselves. As for psychological first aid, that is what Better Days is all about, and just like in Calais, it is what every single volunteer is doing all the time: providing food, shelter, and vital information, while comforting people, giving them dignity, and helping them connect with relatives and friends. I ask Mehwish to explain to her colleagues how she helped the man who lost his father as a perfect example. More importantly, there are enough of them to take the time to talk, hang out, problem solve, find the diapers or baby clothes or shoes, stand alongside the lunch queue to prevent a riot, sit drinking chai or join in the cricket.

Mytilene, Thursday 10 March

More people are now coming onto the island than leaving: approximately 800 a day, more than 7000 so far in this month alone and 132,000 this year… and that's just those who are registered. I learned this at this morning's coordination meeting chaired by UNHCR and the Prefecture. Along with a briefing on figures and the new relocation programme (more of that later), we hear from the representative for International Relations and Communication:

– *That is me, a phone and a laptop*—he jokes. *Seriously, we expect an eighty percent drop in tourism this year. So, we are asking you—pick your favourite spot on the island, take a selfie, show that Lesvos is a safe and beautiful place to visit. We need your help! If you know any celebrities, we need them. The local community has given everything to support refugees, now it's time to give something back.*

– *Does anyone know how many unregistered migrants and refugees there are?* I ask at the health coordination meeting that follows.

No one has any idea.

– *But if they go to the hospital, the police must be informed, and they should be registered!*

– *That means those undocumented migrants who fear deportation will also avoid the healthcare system completely because they fear police involvement, which will create a public health problem*—says a visitor from WHO.

In fact, it is even more complicated because there are no detention facilities on the island, apart from Moria prison, currently being used to house registered refugees. Pakistanis who do go to register are now being told to wait in Better Days and register on a Tuesday or Friday, when they can be bussed directly to the ferry to Kavala and the Turkish border. Moreover, all of them are entitled to an interview to assess their claim for asylum, and that is not happening. The whole asylum system is overwhelmed.

I meet up with Samir back at camp. He insists on queueing for my tea and then sits drinking with John and I in the children's play area. He is transformed by a good night's sleep and much calmer, although he tells me he had another attack of voices and visions this morning.

We agree to meet tomorrow to do some relaxation training.

Maryam asks me to see Usman, a young Pakistani who is self-harming. He cut himself in a fall and has been refusing to eat since then, and he has been scratching open the wound. He sits reluctantly with us in the clinic. He is obviously not suicidal. On the contrary, he has plans to get to relatives in Germany as soon as possible by going to the border. He has no interest in eating with us, listening to the impossibility of this plan, or hearing what his other options are. Maryam and I decide that eating a meal in front of him might encourage his appetite. We all sit in the carpeted back room with a volunteer he has befriended. I pop out to see a patient, and when I return, I see that good food smells work. He finishes his dinner and then picks up a guitar someone has left. Over the course of the evening, left to play with the guitar and chat with the volunteer, he has completely changed. What a difference social space and company make.

Better Days for Moria, Friday 11 March

In the mobile phone shop this morning, when I was topping up my SIM, the young Greek assistant asked me how to volunteer.

– *I want to work with refugees.*

I tell her that yesterday, UNHCR said they were recruiting national staff, so she should look on their website. She is really excited. I listened to the Mayor of Athens on the radio the other day saying that they had learnt from their own difficulties in the last years and were giving a lesson in solidarity to the rest of Europe. He is absolutely right. The Greeks are extraordinary. Athens appears to be covered in graffiti and full of empty buildings. You have a sense of a city, indeed a country crumbling at the edges. But quite unlike Calais, everywhere I go, whether it is sitting for hours in a café with free WIFI, or staying at a super cheap rate in the beautiful villa Daphnis and Chloe, or simply getting diesel for the car, I am greeted warmly. This afternoon, John brings Samir for relaxation training. I get him to lie down on the couch and explain that these are techniques to reduce stress that we could all use in our daily lives, and then we go through switching from chest to abdominal breathing, using the alternate nostril technique, which both slows breathing rate and requires such intense concentration to get right that it acts as a distraction and thought-blocking technique. Afterwards, I do applied muscular relaxation, and he almost falls asleep, which is very satisfying given the levels of peripheral noise coming through the chipboard walls of the clinic. Later, John spots Samir using the alternate nostril rebreathing technique in the jostle of the lunch queue, so it must help a little.

I am doing these stress management sessions for individual patients three or four times a day here. I like the techniques—they are solid and tangible, address the physical stress symptoms, like shaking and palpitations, that people bring to the clinic, and can be quickly taught. I explain each time that this is not a cure but just some first aid techniques that can be used on a stressful journey, sitting on buses, in the port, or on the ground in Victoria Square, if that is where they are going. It's better than medication because there are no side effects and it won't make them dopey or confused, and I am reluctant to give drugs to anyone I might not see the next day.

Later, there is a rather noisy and disorganised meeting with the Pakistani unaccompanied minors to discuss their options in Greece and ask why so many don't want to register. Usman is there, smiling at us. Because they don't trust the system and are scared of being locked up, is one answer. They just want to travel on to relatives in other parts of Europe, but that option is closed. One of the problems that authorities have not grasped, both here and in Calais, is that unaccompanied minors are rarely completely unaccompanied. They have often joined up with extended family members or made friends with protectors on the journey. Of course, some of these people might be unsavoury, but most are not and have genuine relationships with young people for whom they are a substitute family. Simply ignoring this is damaging for the child. Another problem is that families have sent them to work and send money home. If they go into the protection system, they cannot work or send money back, which defeats the purpose of the journey. And, there is no guarantee of what will happen at 18 years old.

Better Days for Moria, Saturday 12 March

I wasn't planning to see patients this morning because we are driving up north to do workshops, but when I come in to collect Asmamaw at the end of his shift, I am asked to see a Kurdish child. The story is heart-breaking as always. Their town was bombed a year ago, and everyone in the house next door was killed. Their own house also collapsed. Mother, father and 7-year-old daughter survived, but she has not spoken for a year. Indeed, she has gone backwards in many ways, crying, clinging, thumb sucking and bedwetting, and always afraid.

I sit with the parents for over an hour, and a more complicated story emerges. In fact, the girl has never talked, and she has always been a bit different. She was not a cuddly baby and has never played with other children. She is happy with her parents if they stick to her routines but gets very stressed if they are broken. Even before the bombing, she hated loud sounds.

– *Listening to what you tell me, I am wondering if your daughter is autistic?*

The father bursts into tears.

– *My sister is in Canada and she visited and asked the same question three years ago. I did not want to believe this.*

I ask them their plans.

– *Go to Germany*—the same answer every time.

– *But how?*

– *We want to go to the Macedonian border.*

I explain, as I do a dozen times a day, that the border is not open, that conditions are awful, and while it is their choice, I would not recommend it for a highly vulnerable child who cannot communicate, craves familiarity and routine, and whose regressive behaviour will only get worse in a flooded tent in Idomeni. The parents look distraught.

– *There are legal options. There is a relocation plan, and as a vulnerable family, you may have more of a chance. First, you have to apply for asylum in Greece.*

This is not the place to go through the minutiae of what this involves or its chances of success. Everyone I meet has lost trust in all bureaucratic options and believes their only hope is to go where their feet will carry them. In any case, that choice is unavailable at present, as there are no more slots for refugees on any ferries off the island for at least a week. The coordinator at Health Point says she will make sure that they are referred to the camp for vulnerable children. What they cannot do is stay in Moria. It's raining and as usual everyone is sitting wrapped in blankets outside their locked rooms. There is nothing to do and people look utterly worn and miserable.

Skala Sykamineas, Sunday 13 March

The phone rings around 7am.

– Boat coming in.

Asmamaw and I pull on warm clothes and join people hurrying to the small beach beside the harbour. The water is smooth as glass, and when the boat comes in, everyone claps. It is an extraordinary moment. I had been told welcoming operations were often a chaotic scrum with no one knowing what they were doing and competing to help. I see no evidence of that.

There are some twenty volunteers on the shore, some of the Greeks from the village (who have been doing this for years), the Greek Red Cross with their ambulance for any severely affected, Spanish life-guards, and the volunteers from Lighthouse, Platanos and Drop in the Ocean. The lifeguards get in the water to hold the boat and help people off. I am astonished at the number of women and children. The volunteers move forward with emergency blankets, everyone is trained to put them under wet clothes not over, and the refugees are walked to the nearby warming stations. A friend and I end up changing, drying and warming an exhausted mother with two quite flat and very cold infants, and a third screaming child who cannot bear to let her mother go, so that she can remove her own soaking clothes. I hold and cuddle the 4-year-old girl in my arms, but nothing will diminish the screaming. She is Syrian, which means that in her short life she has only known bombing, collapse, flight and the terror of an ocean crossing. Screaming seems an appropriate response.

The idea that there are 'too many' volunteers is completely ridiculous. This is the kind of individual support and attention I wish was available in every crisis. It means that, for a short period at least, people get the personal, human attention they need without queuing in line. They are not a number or a group, but a person from a place, with family, who had a job, or studied, or played, and wants a future. Every contact and connection, every handshake, is a reaffirmation of human individuality and dignity. The more, the better.

Within two hours, all the babies are warm with dry diapers, previously wet and bedraggled children are now playing in the play area among the trees, the men are sitting around the fire smoking, the women chatting. There are no boats off the island until Saturday, so there's no rush to get them to Moria. Lighthouse and Hope are thinking about how they can turn their facilities into longer-term accommodation if numbers on the island are going to grow. Everyone is waiting for the EU meetings next week to see what is going to happen. Opening the borders seems unlikely.

– Aren't we sugar-coating a guillotine? Stefan asks.

He is a German theatre director who has been volunteering on the coast for a while and, along with thirty others, he is attending a workshop I have been asked to run at the Hope Centre. I did the same thing for Lighthouse yesterday afternoon and the same issue got raised. Given what people have to face, isn't the warm welcome they get from the volunteers deceptive and misleading? One of the Arabic translators at one of my sessions in Moria went further.

– I wonder if we shouldn't be telling them the whole thing is a lie—that the best they can hope for, even if they are lawyers and professors at home, is jobs as taxi drivers or care workers in Britain or Germany. My parents have been refugees in Britain for thirty years. So I know what they face.

– Would it be better to be harsh and brusque? Like the Turkish coast guards beating refugees on boats? (Jason from Platanos has circulated a video on social media showing this.)

My own view is that even a brief period of being treated well can increase your courage and resilience to deal with whatever comes next.

– If I am asked questions, I answer them honestly and try to give as much information as I can. I don't think we can do more right here—I say.

I have completely changed the way I train. To start, I go to where the volunteers are based. No slide presentation or flip charts, just an interactive discussion drawing on the volunteers' own experiences to cover my usual topics. We start with a brainstorm on how their experiences resemble those of the people they are trying to help. Small similarities are obvious—confusion and disorientation, uncertainty over where to sleep or eat, not understanding the language, being a long way from home and friends, not sleeping, feeling stressed, running out of money. The big difference is that most of the volunteers have not lived through the horrendous experiences of those they are trying to help, and they have that magical thing: a passport and the right to travel. If they cannot cope, they have the option of leaving. Even so, they get the point that much of what we are discussing does not only apply to refugees. I am impressed with their common sense. What almost all refugees want on arrival is information about how to leave immediately. No one thinks it appropriate to 'make people talk' about what they have been through, but they want advice about to how to listen when people do share their experiences.

One of the participants, Maria, is a Norwegian nurse who married a Greek and has lived here for thirty years. She tells me that half the small villas in the village, including the one where we sleep, were built to house a previous wave of refugees—the Greeks displaced from Turkey in 1922. Nothing changes. Maria saw her first boat arrive in 1991, after the first Gulf War. They were Kurds. As they came close to shore, they were punching holes in their boat to make it unusable after landing. The Greek coast guard arrested them, kept them in cuffs on the beach all day, and then put them back on the mended boat and towed them out of Greek waters to the middle of the channel and left them.

We pack up our things. Asmamaw is working an early shift at Better Days, and we have to drive back over the mountains to Moria. Pink and white blossoming trees punctuate the endless grey-green olive groves, carpeted with white and yellow star-like flowers. The loveliness of the island continues to entrance me.

Better Days for Moria, Monday 14 March

Melanie wants some advice about two tiny North African children who are causing mayhem in the children's tent. She and her husband, Jerome, manage the tent. They are a Dutch couple who moved to Greece sometime ago because they loved it and worked hard in various tourist jobs. Unfortunately, they had become homeless themselves eighteen months previously.

– We spent the summer living in tents—actually, it was very beautiful. Then a Greek neighbour offered us a place, and we have paid it back through work, but it's difficult. Then, we started helping refugees last summer. At that point, they were still walking 70km to Mytiline, so we were meeting the boats and driving them. Then the buses started, so we helped people out of the water at Skala. My son was five and my daughter was three and a half years old. Then a friend said help was needed in Moria. We all started this together in a tiny tent. The friend had to leave so we continued.

What they have created is a light, airy, warm marquee with a carpeted floor and walls covered with children's paintings. A papier-mâché globe hangs down. Healthy snacks are available. Any volunteer who wants to can help.

– We saw that we could make a big difference. We realised that if we are here all the time, we can control it and make sure there are rules.

They have strict policies on NO photos and media.

– Sometimes, people just take pictures through the walls. Celebrities visit who want to be shown with children, but we will not let the children be used or exploited in any way. We had no experience in this area, except as parents, but we are learning fast. UNHCR, MSF and Save the Children have all supported us and given advice.

They still work for nothing. They don't crowdfund, and they only accept direct donations for the tent, or money for fuel for the car and generators. The two children that worry them are running wild through the camp, affectionate with anyone who will allow it at one moment and breaking all the toys in the tent at another or fighting and punching each other. Melanie initially had a policy of excluding them when they were naughty, but while that protected the other

Migrant children arrive off the boats from Turkey
Lesvos, March 2016

children, she realised it did nothing for them, so she wanted to do something more. Mum comes in and we sit with her, encouraging her to spend more time in the tent every day, playing with her own children, explaining the simple idea that if they get lots of affection and praise from her when they are good, they will slowly begin to be less demanding and naughty. Mum smiles and nods, she is delighted with the advice. She has never been to school and says—*no one has ever told me what to do with children. I did not even know how to brush their teeth.* She herself loves coming in just to colour with crayons. While she is doing that, her son sits quietly beside her doing the same.

I have to leave to pack. Tracy, Asmamaw, and I are catching the ferry and driving north to Idomeni with a carload of goods, plastic emergency shelters, hygiene kits, etc. from the Hope Centre. Before that, the volunteers at Gate E2 in Piraeus got in touch on social media. There are four thousand people sleeping in the terminal in the Port. They have heard about my workshops and asked me to come and do some for them.

Ferry Boat to Athens, Monday Night, 14 March

The ferry boat isn't moving because of stormy weather, but we are told to embark anyway. I bump into Usman at the gangway with two Spanish volunteers. He greets me enthusiastically. He is clutching an out of date ticket and unusable papers, lacking a photo and with one clearly photocopied last page. I wonder what he paid for them. There is no Urdu translator anywhere, and once Usman grasps that his papers are unusable, he runs off into the night. I text Maryam to let her know. I hope he will have the sense to return to BD.

On board, every chair, every bit of floor space, is occupied by Syrian, Iraqi and Afghan families. The smaller children are laid out on blankets on suitcases or across chairs. Fathers and mothers make blanket beds on the floor. On one television screen in the corner, Brad Pitt is storming Troy, while on another, they are reporting on migrants trying to get into Macedonia by wading up the river. The migrants have been stopped and thrown back. Three Afghans, including a pregnant woman and a child, have drowned.

Tracy has printed off small leaflets with useful websites where migrants can get accurate news and information about their ever-changing rights. We go around the boat, handing these out, and then I sit, chatting and listening to those who want to talk. There is an Afghan mother with four girls under ten. She was a shopkeeper, but she has lost every single possession, including her valuables, because the captain on their boat told them to throw all their bags overboard. Mohammed lived in a city controlled by Assad and besieged by Daesh. His parents made him escape to avoid conscription, but then he was kidnapped by Daesh, held and beaten for three weeks. He does not know why they let him go, but they did, and he walked to Turkey. Beside him sits Nur, with two daughters sleeping on either side of her, under down blankets, their feet poking out over the seat edge. Her husband is in jail in Damascus but she smiles and smiles and smiles. In the early morning, as the boat chugs past snow-capped mountains, I chat with Adib and his wife, with their three-month-old baby. He is an agricultural engineer. He wants to know what I think he should do. *Not go to the border with the baby*—I advise—*there is so much sickness there at the moment.* Anyway, there are now continual announcements over the tannoy as we near Piraeus:

– *We will arrive in thirty minutes. Please be ready for disembarkation. The border to Macedonia is closed. There will be free buses that will take you to safe accommodations. Please trust the Greek government, and do not spend your money.*

As we get off the boat, I see the buses and interpreters standing shouting instructions to the disembarking refugees. People are exhausted and compliant. Meanwhile, we head across to the E terminal building, easily identifiable because of the crowd of tents outside and the mass of families camped out on blankets on the floor inside. There is no space left at all. A young man called Sam with short hair, spectacles, and an American accent greets me:

– *Have you come to do the training? We really need it. It's total chaos.*

In fact, as soon as some fifteen volunteers have sat down on crates and boxes in what appears to be the storeroom next to a makeshift kitchen (there is no other quiet space), it becomes obvious they don't need me at all. They all agree that their biggest source of stress is the lack of coordination between volunteers, and that is because they all feel overwhelmed and have no time to sit down and meet each other and organise. So, I simply suggest that instead of me saying anything at all, they take the time to address this problem now—and they do.

I sit listening as Kat, who lives with her family in Athens, suggests having small groups form around each need: for food and cooks, for people distributing clothes, for people doing health care. Then a coordinator from each group should turn up for a daily overall coordination meeting. It's the humanitarian cluster system invented on the run, from the ground up, again. Everyone agrees, even the Greek anarchists and the vice Mayor of Piraeus, who happens to be sitting next to me and introduces himself as 'a volunteer.' He tells me it was he who broke the lock on these office doors so that they could build a kitchen. Apparently, he has squared it with the owners. Sam says he is off to buy a gazebo tent from IKEA to build an information booth, both for incoming refugees and for new volunteers—brilliant.

Idomeni

Northern Greece, March 2016

Eko Camp and Idomeni, Thursday 17 March

If you have to put a migrant camp beside a closed border, choose your site carefully. A gas/service station is ideal, but not just any old gas station. It needs large empty parking areas where astonishingly tolerant owners will allow refugees to pitch tents and other agencies to set up tented clinics, distribution centres and porta-loos; a café where they will let you hang out and project movies for children in the evening; and a shop where almost the entire stock has been adapted to the needs of refugees. I have never been in a service station that sells waterproof boots, small tents, sleeping bags, down jackets alongside baby food, non-prescription medicines, dustpans and brushes, and camping stoves. This is the Eko service station on the main road from Athens to Skopje—some thirty minutes south of the Macedonian border.

I listen to a woman behind the counter teaching an Afghan man the Greek word for gloves. She is friendly and delightful. The man is laughing.

– *You must live with us and learn more*—she says.

Outside on the empty forecourt, small boys play with toy cars and girls play hopscotch.

At the volunteers' orientation session last night, Phoebe said she thought one thousand people were camped there. At a glance, it looks more like three thousand to me, living in a combination of UNHCR marquees and small camping tents.

Phoebe is impressive. We met her at the Park Hotel in Polykastro yesterday, where yet more extraordinary Greeks have allowed their hotel to become a volunteer hub. Caravans and tents fill their yard. Volunteers, talking earnestly and staring at laptops, cluster around every table. The warehouse for donations is across the road, and as we learn on the social media page, 'Information Point for Volunteers in Idomeni,' an orientation meeting is held every night at 8pm.

— I just decided to start coordinating volunteers a couple of weeks ago. There's no central committee or organisation. I don't tell people what to do, just let them know what's happening and how to connect with already existing teams on the ground. One hundred and fifty have come in the last two weeks. The truth is, you are not going to know what is going on most of the time. We are all just trying to make a bloody mess better.

— We have good relations with the police. They see how messed up it is. I saw one of them taking baby food to a tent yesterday. Please don't alienate them.

— And we have a warehouse. Aslam rented it. He's a Syrian refugee who came in September and has not left. He is the centre of everything here. He raises money and spends it on what's needed.

— We could use more help with distribution. Some volunteers haven't quite grasped that you cannot save Syrian babies if they don't have socks. And there are still lovely people throwing stuff from cars. I saw an elderly couple bring a cake up a few days ago. They had baked it themselves, but I was really afraid for them.

We have joined two messaging groups: the medical one and the general coordination. As a consequence, both of our phones constantly beep with messages—direct requests for help, mixed in with personal jokes and hellos and goodbyes. I am learning to filter. Lighthouse is here, putting up a baby tent, which will have a washing and breast-feeding area. Asmamaw and I have already been asked to help with protecting breastfeeding and promoting infant stimulation, but as the tent is not ready yet, we are learning the geography of the camps.

Eko Camp is a five-star hotel compared to Idomeni. There, large canvas marquees and a cluster of Portakabin huts stand beside the railway line that crosses the border. They are surrounded by a sprawl of small camping tents. Some are in waterlogged, muddy fields, which are also open sewers, because there is rubbish and human faeces everywhere. Some are pitched along the curved farm road and some are on the railway tracks themselves, perilously close to the one train I watched come through this afternoon. It is like a miserable rock festival with no performers. The medics report skin and respiratory infections, gastroenteritis, even some cases of hepatitis A. Impossible

Housam Jackaly,
protesting on the
railway line at
Idomeni
March 2016

to estimate the numbers, it could be anything between 8,000 and 12,000. Until a few days ago, there were 500 to 1,000 arriving every day. Phoebe told us some people are leaving. But the volunteer tent crews still go out every evening looking for the most vulnerable to add plastic to existing tents or set up more.

On the way back to our car, I notice a man standing stock still in the middle of the railway tracks. He holds a roughly penned sign on a piece of cardboard: "We survived War, but you make me wish I didn't." Something about his stillness draws my eye. I go over to chat. Housam tells me he is a law student from Damascus. He lived in the Yamouk area and barely escaped with his life, as DAESH had named him as a target for his secular beliefs. He escaped to Lebanon where he worked for local NGOs and as a photographer for a couple of years, before being targeted and threatened again. He decided he really wanted to continue his studies. So, he sold everything, including his beloved camera. After captaining a boat to Greece, he reached the Frontier just in time to be told by the Macedonian border guards that Damascus was a safe city, so he should go back.

– I don't have any plan—he says quietly. *I will stand here every day.*

Idomeni, Friday 18 March

So, it is agreed. Large new snakes have suddenly appeared on the snakes and ladders boardgame that all refugees must play if they ever want to get to Northern Europe. This particular snake has its head in Greece and its tail in Turkey, and you slide down it if you had the temerity to make it here by 'illegal means' (i.e. a sinking boat that cost your life savings). Apparently, if you are Syrian, you will be swapped for someone less audacious than yourself. If you are Afghan or Iraqi, you are not worth swapping for anyone, you will just be sent back. If you are none of the above, you are probably on an even longer snake back to your home country.

Recognising the complete illegality of group expulsions, a caveat has been inserted—all claims must be individually assessed. Where? When? By whom? We heard at a meeting yesterday that the Greek Asylum Application Service is now getting 200-300 applications a day, but it can only handle twenty. And, you can only apply for an interview via a dedicated Skype address, which certainly excludes most of the people sitting here in the mud on the border, and for those lucky enough to have internet on their phones, even an hour online does not get through. Housam told me he had spent hours trying. So how is the government going to sort out the one thousand a day who are still coming in by boat?

Many things remain completely unclear, so the rumour mills grind away. Are all the Syrians currently here with their papers allowing six months in Greece, going to be sent back to Turkey? The belief that this is the case has made people even more reluctant to move into the government camps that are being created. We were told about those yesterday as well as the awful conditions inside. People would rather stay with the misery they know, and the illusion that the border will open.

I had an argument with Ai Weiwei this morning. He is staying in our hotel, making a documentary. Yesterday, Tracy, Asmamaw and I all smiled, shook his hand, and said how much we liked his work. But a friend working on one of the mobile teams came back very upset in the evening after they had been doing a medical consultation with a mother and child outside the ambulance because there are no indoor spaces in Idomeni. Ai Weiwei had started filming with his phone. Both patients and medics asked him to stop, but he kept standing there filming and smiling, stating that this was a public space, and, if they wanted privacy, they should go inside a clinic. Apparently, it escalated, and one woman even tried to damage his camera.

I approached him and his team at breakfast, asking politely if I could just explain about the lack of private spaces here and the need to create confidential spaces for medical consultation, and respect dignity, even in these circumstances. He told me I had my facts wrong; he would not film a child, but he was filming the whole scene, as it was in a public space. Moreover, I should fire the aggressive woman who kept telling him it was a private consultation.

– *I am not in a position to fire anyone, these are my friends and colleagues, not employees.* Ai Weiwei obviously does not get independent volunteers.

– Hmmph. I don't believe you are a doctor!

– Well, whether I am or not, I would just like to understand. Are you saying that, if, as unfortunately happens here, some medical consultations have to be done in public because there is no private space, and if I, for example, am seeing someone and ask you not to film, you still feel you have the right to do so?

– Of course! It's public! It's a human tragedy, it's necessary to show people! We are all exhibits now.

Housam is on the tracks again today. This time his sign simply has the number of days he has been here marked out.

Walking back through the camp in the evening, sunlight catches the plastic of the tents and the pools of water that surround them. In the distance are snow-capped mountains, in between there are woods with the lovely mixture of soft greens that appear in early spring. Blackthorn blooms in the hedges. It is this toxic combination of beauty and pain that is both compelling and addictive.

Idomeni, Saturday 19 March

The sign at Harar Hotel says, "Welcome to Greece." Next to it is a larger than life figure of a man in Greek national dress with arms stretched out. This is a roadside motel, down a slip road off the main highway. Once again, the hotel owners have been welcoming, allowing refugees into the shop and café, renting them rooms and allowing tents to fill their yard. It is still a disorganised and miserable place. Some families are camped out under blankets attached to balconies. Across the road, there are some even more miserable encampments in and around ruined, graffiti-covered buildings, set in scrubby forest beside another gas station. In this one, the owners have made it clear that we should all keep out.

The Baby tent at Eko is still not complete, so Asmamaw and I have started doing tent-to-tent outreach, sitting and chatting with any mother with an infant under two about how they are feeding and coping. The problem is, not surprisingly, many of them have given up breastfeeding. As in Moria, they are using poorly mixed formula in bottles which are impossible to keep clean in these conditions.

UNICEF has produced good guidelines in multiple languages about what to do in transit. Asmamaw discusses these and hands out cups that are safer to use for those who no longer breastfeed.

The mothers are both welcoming and interested. We also give out baby clothes and nappies, and I discuss the importance of continuing to play. What's impressive is how clean and cared for the babies are, despite these conditions. I watch a mum give her baby a complete and thorough wash with water heated in cans on an open fire, the baby crowing happily. Both our translators are mothers living in the camp themselves and say they will carry on giving out the same messages. Muna had an important job at a government ministry in Kabul but fled when her own life was threatened, and there was a bombing close to her home.

– *I had to for my children's sake.*

While we are eating lunch, we get an online message that all refugees currently on Lesvos are being shipped to the mainland, to empty Moria in preparation for interning those designated 'illegal' arriving after Monday. Where is everyone going to go? UNHCR has already said the new camps are either full or simply not ready.

Amnesty has completely condemned the new deal: "Guarantees to scrupulously respect international law are incompatible with the touted return to Turkey of all irregular migrants arriving on the Greek islands as of Sunday. Turkey is not a safe country for refugees and migrants, and any return process predicated on its being so will be flawed, illegal and immoral, whatever phantom guarantees precede this pre-declared outcome." I wonder if one day our treatment of migrants will be seen in the same light with which we regard the slave trade today.

Back at the border, Housam has changed his sign to a completely blank piece of cardboard. Three other refugees stand silently beside him.

Thessaloniki and Idomeni, Monday 21 March

Today I stood where Paul preached to the Thessalonians in 52 AD. Mark Cousins is here, showing his films at the Thessaloniki film festival, so we went together. We were the only people in the tiny chapel. I could look down the hill over the city to port, sea and mountains, or turn and look at what once must have been stunning wall paintings. Almost all had the small faces chipped out by incoming Muslims who saw the paintings as a desecration. The strange thing is that the blizzard of white holes in the plaster had its own peculiar beauty, tinged by the sadness that nothing much has changed regarding our tolerance for other people's icons. But if you follow the city walls down, there is another tiny ancient chapel in a garden, where the paintings of extraordinary loveliness are still intact, and I could contemplate the sad face of the lion having its thorn removed by St. Jerome and a tranquil sleeping Madonna.

I had to get back to the border, as Save the Children had asked me to train their infant and young child-feeding counsellors on enhancing mother-baby interactions. The relationships between the professional agencies and the independent, informal volunteers are exemplary here. They get on really well. MSF has appointed a staff member to liaise with volunteers. So now, there are regular appeals on messaging groups, asking for volunteers to come and put up four hundred beds in a new tent, for example. I chat with Konstantin, who runs the Park Hotel.

– *Greece is amazing. I have never seen anything like this hotel.*

– *The Gods speak to me.* He grins. *Solving the problems of one person can give happiness to another. We are all brothers and sisters. Did you know the Greeks are descended from one of the Sons of Noah?* I confess I did not.

– *And what about Heraclitus?*

– *What about him?*

I am deeply embarrassed by my lack of classical and philosophical knowledge.

– *Everything flows*—he moves his hand in a waving motion—*and everything changes.* He brandishes the kettle at me. *Look! Water! Then steam...*

He pours my herb tea. He taps the counter.

– *At one point in the future, this piece of wood could be a man.*

I am temporarily lost trying to connect this to the twelve thousand refugees up the road.

– If people have love, they can see we are all the same, all connected, all one. Everything flows.

Eivar texts and asks if I will come with her tomorrow to talk to a man who is threatening to set himself on fire at the railway tracks in the morning. She is a psychosocial worker who has taken unpaid leave from her work with unaccompanied minors in Norway and lives at the Park Hotel in a shared caravan. She saw him making the threat this evening. I promise to be there.

Idomeni, Tuesday 22 March

Up at the border, the mood on the tracks has changed completely. It is no longer a quiet, dignified handful of people supporting Housam, but a large, restless crowd completely covering the lines—some sitting on blankets, some standing. A tannoy is being handed around. A young man in a red sweatshirt is winding up the crowd. They are chanting, *No food, no drink, until the borders open!* Eivar recognises the man who was saying last night that he would set himself alight. Aashif is a slight, middle-aged man in a brown padded jacket, standing to the side. He agrees to come and talk to us with our translator. He tells us he did not mean what he said last night; it was just a moment of anger.

– I know such an act is against Allah, but what should I do?

I tell him I admire his courage.

– You are clearly a very brave man with great moral strength. But that is the reason all these people need you alive, not dead, if you want to change this situation.

Eivar makes similar points and we chat for some time longer. Aashif is completely without family here, which concerns me. He smiles at us, he looks relieved. He shakes both our hands and says he will not do this.

– Please do promise us that—I ask. *People need you alive. We will come and visit you every day to see how things are going.*

Then he plunges back into the middle of the demonstration. The trouble is the man in the red sweatshirt is now making 'lighter' gestures with his hand, both at us, and at Aashif, who squats down,

115

Eivar is beside him. Then she comes to join me at the side.

— *He assures me he is not going to do it, but he says there is another young man who might do this. He does not know who he is.*

— *I just worry that Mr. Red Sweatshirt is going to wind him up.*

Another man has taken the tannoy now. He is asking Germany to take everyone sitting here and asking the crowd not to disperse but also not to cause trouble as—*they can control us if we get upset.* There is a slightly calmer feeling as he speaks. How easy it is to shift a mood in a crowd. I am slightly anxious that Housam might be the other young man, and we go off to look for him. When we come back past the tracks an hour later, the demonstration is much larger and a number of buses of police have arrived. I cannot see Housam, Aashif, or Red Sweatshirt. Fortunately, no burnings have taken place.

We are sitting eating lunch, when we get a message online: two men have set themselves on fire. The pictures are vivid and horrific. A young man I don't recognise is running ablaze. Aashif stands with the lower part of his jacket in flames. People put blankets around them and they are rushed to the hospital. So much for our intervention. I should have stuck by his side.

Minutes later, another message: bombs have gone off in Brussels (at least three) and more than thirty people have been killed, hundreds wounded. Almost immediately, another picture follows. A child is holding up a sign on the railroad tracks in front of a much quieter, mostly seated crowd. It says simply: "Sorry for Brussels."

In the early evening, I counsel a mother and baby group in the newly created baby tent at Eko. It is bright and cosy. There is a bathing station and a breastfeeding corner. A small circle of mums and infants sit while we share ways of playing in these circumstances and why it is important to do so. They are lovely, intelligent mothers, and the infants are all lively and happy.

It's a pleasure to do something so life-affirming on a day like this. They share some lullabies, and as they sing, I go out to play with older children. I have been doing this every evening because there is so little going on for them here, so now four or five children at the southern end of the camp rush up to me shouting *Hokey Cokey.*

116

I can think of worse names. We gather about twenty children and go onto a grassy space at the end of the camp. I think I get as much out of the singing game as they do. I particularly like the shouting bit at the end.

Idomeni, Wednesday 23 March

Refugees are demonstrating on the Polykastro road. Eivar and I get past and up to Idomeni before they block it completely. We want to talk with people around the railway racks and try to discourage any more burnings. This morning, there is just a quiet group with placards. Aashif and the boy are still in the hospital. No one has news, but we find Housam walking along the road with a group of friends. It is pouring rain—the drenching kind that penetrates every corner. The only dry place to sit is Eivar's car.

Housam tells us he hated yesterday's demonstration and wanted no part in it. He never had any intention of setting fire to himself and felt those who did had been pressured by the crowd.

– *It's not good to be so provocative.*

But he does feel very confused as to what he should do about his own situation.

– *I need you to imagine my life for the last five years. First two years in hell in Yarmouk, trying to help every day, people eating dogs and cats, finally getting out to Lebanon. Another two years, helping small NGOs translating, helping people every day, refugees all the time. I just imagine a small room, somewhere, anywhere where I can be alone and quiet and listen to music and continue to study law.*

The UNHCR legal advice team has told him he has good grounds for asylum because he has documentary evidence of Daesh threatening his life. But if he applies for relocation, he could end up in Sofia. You don't get to choose the country to which you are located.

– *What will I do in Sofia? Should I just apply to stay in Greece, where there is no work and thousands of refugees?*

Eivar and I explain that Bulgaria might not be so bad. Sofia is beautiful, and it has to be better than this. We take him to meet Abdi, a Somali friend working as a translator for an NGO whose father got asylum in Russia, then moved to Slovakia where he grew up as the only Somali. He laughs and jokes with Housam in Arabic—*Everyone will help you. Everyone helped me.*

Boats are still arriving in Lesvos, undeterred by the awaiting snakes on the board game. When they arrive, they get a leaflet on their legal rights from UNHCR. UNHCR has refused to cooperate with the transformation of Moria into a detention centre and no longer provides the transport from the beach. The Greek government gives the refugees a quite different leaflet. This tells them that they have been arrested and should behave quietly, and that among other things, they have a right to a lawyer, consular assistance and for their family to be informed. They also have the right to know what their offence is (but this is not spelled out on the document) and that they should be brought before a magistrate within 24 hours. So far, none of these rights have been granted to the families interned in Moria. It would be funny, if it was not so serious.

I do my workshop for the mobile medics in the late afternoon. Among other things, we discuss what to do about self-immolation. It is new for all of us. Everyone agrees that we need to look out for the single men and for those doing the winding up and talk to them. One of our Arabic translators points out that we should remind people of the teaching in the Koran, to kill one person is to kill humanity.

One of the team members asks advice on what to do about a woman who is due to have her fourth baby imminently. The previous three were born by arranged Caesarean. A C-section has been arranged for her in the hospital tomorrow. But she has been saying she won't go. She won't bring her baby into this situation. She has finally agreed to go in early tomorrow on the understanding that the hospital will keep her for two or three days, but no one wants her discharged to the camp, and all hotel rooms for vulnerable refugees are full. I promise to talk to UNHCR protection.

Idomeni, Thursday 24 March
The road is still blocked by demonstrators, so we take a back road

up to the border. We drop Asmamaw off to continue his tent visits, and I go to tell UNHCR about the mother. She has just delivered a baby girl. A very sympathetic man says he might be able to find a foster family to take in the whole family. This is a program started by another Greek solidarity group, where they support Greek families prepared to take in vulnerable refugees.

Then Eivar and I head over to the old railway station. I am not sure which is better: drenching rain or howling wind. Today it is the latter. Grey and white clouds pour over mountain tops like breaking waves, tent sides and doors loosen and flap in the wind. Some smaller ones are down completely. Bits of cardboard and rubbish blow across the mud. This is not a good time to walk through the encampment carrying rolled up tarpaulin under one's arm. Everyone wants a bit of it, and I have to repeatedly explain we are using it for at least fifteen mothers and babies to sit on.

At the Old Railway Station, more than one thousand people are camped in small tents on two platforms in a disused siding that still has a roof. We lay the tarp down on the tracks between the platforms. This is the first time in my life I have organised a mother and baby group on a railway line, but it's a covered space and out of the wind. As more and more mothers see us, they jump down to join in. A young man carrying another young man in his arms like a baby comes up and asks if he can join the group too—much hilarity all around. Then, two actual fathers with 6-month-old babies strapped to their chests join us. The session goes well, largely because we have a brilliant enthusiastic translator. She is a nurse from Aleppo who has spent the last few months watching people die in her hands. She has a 15-month-old daughter who will not allow her mother to separate from her for a second, which is not a problem as she joins in the group. At the end, everyone asks us to come back. Any structure, any activity is a respite from the boredom of life in tiny tents.

When we leave, we bump into a group of young men brandishing long poles, running towards one of the trucks distributing hot meals. Yesterday, a similar group had insisted on the tea tent closing, and then went to the new circus tent where children were playing outside

A woman cleans out her tent, Idomeni, March 2016

on a trampoline. They demanded the games stopped—they did not want media pictures of people looking happy. But back at the main railway tracks, it is still quiet and calm and Aashif is there, standing holding a card. When he sees Eivar and me, he looks very sheepish and embraces us both. Apparently, he was not badly burned at all, nor was the young man. Red Sweatshirt is standing beside him but in a completely different mood. There is none of yesterday's hysteria. Both tell us they realise that, in the context of Brussels, dignified non-violence will be far more powerful. People know this is the way. I tell Aashif that it broke my heart when I saw the pictures yesterday. He takes my hand and promises not to do it again.

The food trucks have stayed open in spite of stick-wielding young men, and I get other good news: UNHCR has identified a foster family for the woman with the new baby. Dad and other children are already there waiting for mum to come out of hospital. Amazing Greeks!

This evening, I learn that Radovan Karadzic has been given forty years for genocide and ethnic cleansing. By some strange coincidence, this is the 17th anniversary of the NATO bombing campaign of Serbia. That was the military intervention that precipitated the mass expulsion of some millions of Kosovars out of their province and into neighbouring Albania and Macedonia. I went with them and stood in a muddy field where the Macedonian police had penned some thirty thousand without water and shelter, refusing to allow them into the country. On that occasion, NATO came and built camps that housed the Kosovars decently until they could go home. This time, it is Europe doing the expulsions back to a country sliding into dictatorship. MSF and Save the Children have both issued statements condemning the detentions in Moria, expressing their concerns about the dubious legality of the whole EU-Turkey Deal, and they, too, have withdrawn services from the centre.

Idomeni, Friday 25 March
I wake up to find an intense debate going on through messages. Groups of Spanish and Italian activists are coming for the week-

end to demonstrate 'solidarity' with the refugees by protesting with them. The longer-term volunteers, especially those who witnessed the burnings and what happened in the river two weeks ago, are completely against this.

– *Independent volunteers! Sunday at 5pm, we call you to meet at the train tracks at Idomeni for a gathering to unite the refugees fighting to open the border. We are not here just to give food and clothes but also to help facilitate the return of dignity to these people. Nobody is illegal! We fight against the fortification of Europe because it is not representative of what we believe. Welcome refugees! We invite you to join us!!!*

– *Active political demonstrations by volunteers are discouraged within Idomeni camp. Tensions are extremely high, and incitement of protests has the very real potential to cause violence, riots, and harm to the many vulnerable individuals and children in Idomeni. Police are looking for any excuse to evacuate the camp. Furthermore, actions by a few volunteers affect us all. Retaining the trust of police and authorities is the only thing which allows us to continue our work and provide access and aid to Idomeni. As humanitarian workers, we must prioritize the refugees, not our own politics.*

– *Refugees who want to protest should be allowed to protest. Refugees who want to have the calmest life possible should be allowed to be calm. It's not our job to start protests. It's our job to help. It's not our decision, it's theirs…*

And much more of the same. Yesterday evening, Housam was back on the tracks with another card. Some twenty buses had appeared, along with extra police. It was not a forced evacuation but free transport for voluntary transfer to a new camp. One of the buses had a logo: 'Crazy Holidays.' But not many seemed to be moving. Housam said he thought it was a bad idea to move.

– *Because the media are not there, and they protect us.*

The buses are still there today, and there are empty spaces across the fields where some people have packed up and left. But many don't want to move. *We don't like big tents*—one of my friends explains— even though they are stronger, waterproof and warmer. The tents offer no privacy or safety, and families are often separated. In one case, a man with a disabled son was given a bed at one end of such a tent and his son was given a bed at the other. They also fear it will be more difficult to register for relocation, although UNHCR assures them this is not true.

Housam is sitting with his 'family.' Four small tents make a square around a fireplace over which they have rigged a tarpaulin on metal poles. There is an elderly couple, and a younger couple with one of the happiest infants I have seen, always smiling and laughing, and seemingly indifferent to mud and cold, perhaps because her mother and father are always playing with her. There are a handful of small children running around and two Yazidi brothers. As in Calais, I am astonished at people's ability to create community in the middle of nowhere, out of almost nothing. It is not surprising that they are reluctant to move and have this community broken up.

– *I love this place*—Housam tells me, laughing. *I know it's weird, but we have made a home here. If I go off somewhere else in the camp, I have to hurry back, because I love it—it's where I feel comfortable.*

Housam has completely changed in the last week. He is no longer the sad young man I met on the railway track; he's engaged in trying to make things happen constructively. He wants to get musicians together to make music in the circus tent, and perhaps do peace education with smaller children. Twice, when walking across the fields, we have come across small children fighting physically, and he has pulled them apart, then brought them together, and reconciled them.

– *Is it true that the Red Cross and journalists are coming to open up the border tomorrow and everyone will be able to walk across?*

– *Absolutely not, Housam! It's just a rumour, you have got to tell people. If they come and that is not happening, they will get more frustrated and angrier.*

– *I already am. I was sure it was not true.*

I tell him about the 'activists' and the worries that, when things are so volatile, their presence could be provocative—*The last thing needed after Brussels is a riot here.*

– *Tell them if they want to do something, just to join us in standing in silent protest. No marches, nothing else.*

There is a big meeting in the Park Hotel in the evening, continuing the messaging discussion. An Argentinian man from Italy makes a speech. He has been here for a few days and he has heard from 'the Refugees.'

— *They all say, 'thank you for the clothes and food but what we want is for you to help us open the borders.' Assemble with us at nine o'clock so we can really go forward to the border. They believe, if we are with them, things will go well.*

There are many similar speeches. The main thrust being that: it is not enough to hand out bananas. The Argentinian asks a refugee from Eko Camp to speak:

— *This is not the proposal of the refugees. Right now, the police and military are putting pressure on the camps, so people won't join any demonstrations. What they are thinking about is food and blankets. We need a kitchen so we can eat.*

The Argentinian man had clearly expected something different.

— *Well, that's your view, but there are just 1000 at Eko and there are 12,000 on the border.*

— *And you have spoken to all of them in a couple of days?* Someone asks.

— *Two weeks ago, we had volunteers willing to assist something similar with completely disastrous results, NOT for the volunteers, but for the refugees*—another volunteer chips in. *So, I am begging you, if you want to help, you can be very helpful. The refugees need you, but not in this way.*

— *The crowd can change its mood in a minute, we have had burnings and drownings.*

Phoebe is even clearer:

— *The border will NOT open, no matter how much you shout, it will not, and your presence on a demonstration gives people hope and prolongs this situation.*

I decide to join in:

— *A friend of mine in the camp has explained to me that simply insisting on living here is his demonstration. He does not want a march; he wants to continue to camp here in protest. Perhaps the best way to show solidarity is to provide the humanitarian assistance that allows him to do so if he wishes and provide clear information for those that want to leave.* I turn to the Argentinian. *Why not demonstrate in Austria, where the problem begins, or on the Macedonian side of the border?* I ask him. *Don't forget, You get to go home. You have passports. It's the refugees that will suffer from any clampdown. At the moment, no one is forced to move. We don't want a forced eviction. I have already seen that in Calais.*

Idomeni, Saturday 26 March

I didn't stay for the end of the debate. In the morning, there's a message from the Spanish on WhatsApp, saying they have cancelled their afternoon action, and another from the coordinators, saying they don't support the demonstration and will remove anyone from the messaging group who calls for it.

We drive up to the border. When we get to the turn-off from the Skopje Highway to Idomeni, we come across large groups of people carrying packed bags. Each group tells us the same story: The Red Cross is going to open the border today. The disappointment on their faces when we explain that this is a false rumour is unbearable. In the last group, a large elderly woman is pushing a pram with two toddlers in it. She must have walked at least five kilometres from the nearest camp.

Up at the tracks, there is an enormous crowd, but it appears completely peaceful. They all hold large posters and leave a clear walking space between themselves and the double line of police—this time, in riot gear with white helmets, obviously prepared for disorder. Two hundred metres beyond the police line, the barbed wire topped gates across the railway track remain firmly closed. No one from the Red Cross is visible.

Then, we meet a couple from my mother and baby group at the old railway station. The mother has the baby on her chest. The man is carrying their tent and bags. They thought the rumour was true. When I explain that it is not, the man says:

– *I cannot stand it here any longer, we cannot live in this place.*

Stijn, a Dutch volunteer friend, joins in the conversation. Other volunteers have gone to inspect a new government camp at Katerini. It really is not so bad—basic but improving every day. He recommends they consider going there.

— I am thinking of going back to Syria. I am tired of promises.
— Of course you are, but there really is no illegal way to cross, and beyond Macedonia is Serbia, where the border is also closed, and the same across the Balkans. And if you do get through, you will be pushed back. That will be so hard with the baby.

Push backs are actually illegal. If anyone makes it across, the Macedonians should consider their application, even if they have crossed irregularly. If it's decided they are from a safe country, they can be 'handed over,' but it must be formally done to the authorities of the country from whence they came. The Macedonian police are taking any irregulars to a hole in the fence and literally pushing them back through with the help of a punitive beating. But who is bothered?

As the morning goes on, the crowd grows in size and tension. At one point, we find two mothers and six children sitting inside the fence on the railway tracks, between demonstrators and police. They are Kurds, all packed up as if waiting for a train, except none is coming. I manage to find a translator:

— We are NOT moving until the border opens—says one mother while breastfeeding. I beg her to consider the risk to the baby if the crowd surges forward or the police hit back.
— You will be trampled—I repeat. She shakes her head, crying.
— I have no other option.
— You do, I promise you.

In talking, I have discovered she has a husband in Germany, so family reunification is a real possibility. Another woman comes up and sits beside her to comfort her. Suddenly, the crowd does push forward. For a terrifying moment, I think we will all be crushed, but as I grab one child and the translator another, the women are on their feet clutching the other four, and somehow we have swung around to the safe side of the fence, where they sit on the ground again. It takes another hour of slow discussion. Someone from UNHCR brings pictures of the new camp and reiterates that it will be as easy to register for asylum claims from there as here, possibly easier, as there will be fewer people in the camp.

— But if I give up my tent here and I don't like it there, how can I come back?

Border protest, Idomeni, March 2016

— The trouble is they just don't trust us. They think their chances of leaving are greater if they just sit here—says the man from UNHCR.

I have to leave her with the officials, as I have a final mother and baby group to run at the old railway station. As I leave the tracks, I can see Housam standing in the centre of the crowd saying—*Go back! Go back!* To those pushing forward against the police line and they seem to be listening. Another man makes a speech that makes me uncomfortable: *Do not allow Afghans and Pakistanis to provoke us into stupid actions.* But we set up the discriminatory system in the first place; they have learned the categories from us.

In fact, I notice there are more people in the lunch queue than on the demonstration. And some people are in a good mood. On the road to the Old Railway Station, we bump into Red Sweatshirt and a crowd of young men, all singing loudly. They surround me—*Britani we love you, Britani we love you*—they sing, circling, arms linked, before rushing off to encircle other volunteers.

We spend our last couple of hours sitting at Housam's fire. I do some face painting on the children, and we discuss his hoped-for musical event. Finally, it's time to leave, which I find extremely hard to do. This has become my home as well. At the tracks, the demonstration is just the usual quiet handful under an awning, sitting on blankets. The two women and their children have gone, but a new family has taken their place.

— These people have just arrived here from Athens—a volunteer tells me. *We are finding them a tent and food. They say people in Athens think the borders will open soon, so they are still coming.*

Lagkadikia

Northern Greece, Summer 2016

Lagkadikia, Sunday 12 June

I feel like I'm travelling in a flying creche. I had not expected the plane to be so full of children. Northern Greece is now the holiday destination of choice for young British couples with infants and babies—quiet beaches, lovely people, good food and no terrorism. The woman queuing next to me at the car rental counter tells me no one wants to go to the southern side of the Mediterranean anymore. Her angelic, blonde, blue-eyed infant waves his arms to some internal music as he sits atop the large family suitcase.

– *Where are you going?* The mum asks.

– *To work in a refugee camp*—I reply.

It's an immediate downer, and I feel guilty for intruding on the holiday mood. It is not her fault that 57,000 refugees are now scattered across deserted industrial wastelands and old military barracks all over Greece. These are the unfortunates who got here early enough to avoid the EU's illegal deportation return scheme, but too late to make it across the border into Macedonia. That route is completely closed, and they are stuck in Greece with the choice of seeking asylum here, or, if Syrian or Iraqi, requesting relocation in another European country. In the last two weeks, the Greek government has closed almost all the informal camps around Idomeni and moved people to new 'accommodation' run by the army and Ministry of Migration.

I have a GPS guidance system for the first time in my life. Much as I love paper maps, I decided it might actually be helpful for locating these places. The square box is stuck mid-screen and it successfully guides me over Chortiatis Mountain and down to the two lakes to the northeast of Thessaloniki. Lagkadikia lies between the two. It is a sleepy village off the Thessaloniki Kavala highway. Just outside the village is an abandoned army base, where some two hundred UN-HCR tents house one thousand refugees.

This is what you see when you walk in. DRC
are here, the police are here, the UN is here.
The boy is carrying a peach and he is looking
back. This is like a first glimpse of the camp.
There are taps and dumpsters. This is the
main road and people are out doing their
errands and you can see what it is like living
here. We are not used to living in tents.
Picture by Ayatt, age 12

Housam and some of his friends moved here in mid-April. He had started helping children in Idomeni and UNHCR had told him of this small camp where they thought he could help.

— People were just sitting there, saying 'the border is going to open, it's going to open.' I knew it wouldn't, and I knew they would evict us soon. We came to have a look here and found just a few families. We knew we could do something good.

Four sleepy policemen sit at the open gate. When I say I am a doctor working with the Jafra team (the name Housam and his friends have given to their group), they smile and wave me through. Housam and some other men are putting up tarpaulin over the fenced queuing area.

— It gets very hot when people are queuing for food, and people start to fight. He gives me a hug and wants to show me around. We sit in the 'school' he and his friends created in one of the old army buildings. They have scrubbed it out, painted it, built benches, and hope to start soon. Meanwhile, they started daily informal education in two containers provided by UNHCR.

— UNHCR kept saying, 'We are going to build a school,' but they haven't done so yet, so we just got on and did it. We want to show that refugees can help refugees. We don't want a lot of NGOs coming and doing everything. If they do, people will just sit in their tents all day doing nothing, there will be more fights and violence.

Lagkadikia and Eko Camps, Monday 13 June

— I am that dreadful thing: an independent volunteer—I explain to Julia, when Eleni from MDM introduces me. Julia laughs, and I explain that Housam had invited me to come and train the Jafra volunteers before her agency had taken over organising the camp. She heads the protection team and makes me feel very welcome, saying they were looking for someone to do training in psychological first aid and more on psychosocial support. She wants to send her own staff to the sessions. They will arrange a meeting room for training in the village, with the Mayor. I can be an official agency volunteer, which will help with getting in and out of the gate.

I spend the rest of the morning with Jafra, helping them collect rubbish. There is a contracted cleaning firm, but as of yet, they are not doing a very effective job and leave litter scattered everywhere, so the refugee team cleans up three times a week.

Eko service station, the last of the informal camps, was cleared today. I had really hoped to get there before it happened and see all my Hokey Cokey friends. Too late. I knew it must be an eviction when I found they had blocked the main highway to Skopje at the Chalkidonia entrance, and I was diverted in a great queue of transcontinental lorries up the back road to Polycastro. My GPS navigator had a nervous breakdown. It simply could not adjust to the new route and kept repeating—*turn around at the next opportunity*—until I turned it off.

Up at the Park Hotel, a handful of volunteers sat around the tables in the late afternoon sun. I bought some dinner and asked Kostas, the owner, if everything still flowed.

– *Everyone is going*—he said gloomily.

A handful of new volunteers had turned up for the orientation meeting, but messaging groups and social media are full of discussions as to how difficult it is to get into any of the new camps unless you belong to a Ministry approved organisation. The fact that all the official organisations are slow to address the acute needs of water, food, and shelter in these grim places, makes no difference. Many of the volunteers are moving on or adapting to new circumstances. Tracy, who spent the last three months working with Phoebe as a volunteer coordinator, is starting a new organisation to look for housing for refugees in Thessaloniki. At least four thousand refugees from Idomeni avoided being bussed to the new camps and have gone missing or are visibly sleeping on the streets.

I head back to Lagkadikia. The Skopje highway is now open, and I stop at Eko. It's a strange sight: thousands of shelters and tents still standing—many of them half full of blankets, cooking utensils, gas stoves, half eaten meals, cast off clothes and shoes, as if everyone left abruptly. There is an old woman and a teenage boy wandering and poking through the remains. There is a car refuelling at the gas pumps, and the owners are sitting outside in the last of the evening sun. I wonder if they will miss the community they welcomed for so many months. I drive on.

In the evening, I watch the news for the first time in two days. Orlando: at least 49 dead, probably more, the deadliest attack in the US since 9/11. All the horror and details fill the airwaves—tearful survivors, silent vigils, angry protests, questions as to whether the killer is a terrorist? It is heart-breaking. Every violent death is heart-breaking, but in Lagkadikia, every single person has been through years of such attacks, so their losses are neither visible nor of interest. Terror that takes place every day, against large numbers of civilians, goes unremarked and unhindered. It's called war.

Lagkadikia, Wednesday 15 June

I like Lagkadikia Village. It has one main street with shops and cafés. Refugees walk the half mile up from the camp to shop in the local store, where the owner, his wife and staff are always very friendly and patient. Just like in the Eko gas station, they have adapted their stock to refugees camping out, with torches and calor gas stoves prominently on display, next to the fresh vegetables. In the evening, we sometimes sit on one of the café terraces watching the family of storks nesting on a telephone pole across the road. We are made welcome and served without complaint. But not everyone is so friendly. At the end of my teaching session on 'Grief in Children in Emergencies' yesterday afternoon, two men came into the meeting room to tell us it was time for the children's karate session. They were very friendly, assuring us we could use the hall the next two days, and that it was completely free on Wednesday, with no karate. Then a middle-aged woman with dyed black hair came in, upset by the sight of women in headscarves.

– *You are kidding me*—she kept repeating as the men explained the schedule and the available hours to us. *You are joking! Refugees in here?*

Dan received a message from the Mayor. They are extremely sorry, but the hall is not free. No matter, this afternoon we will squash into a container on site. Meanwhile, I help Jafra with rubbish collection again. We are ill-equipped—the plastic gloves are too fragile and we need more brooms and spades, but everyone pitches in, including a 3-year-old who loves pushing the wheely bins and takes the task extremely seriously.

Lagkadikia Camp, Thursday 16 June

In the afternoon, I train on 'Taking Care of Ourselves' and 'Psychological First Aid.' The Mayor has allocated a new room in the village. At least people enjoy the breathing and relaxation, but I am suddenly aware that I am utterly exhausted myself. When we get back to the camp, I flop down on the bed outside the Jafra office. Someone passes over the blue plastic bag that contains supper—airplane style, every item is sealed in cardboard plastic or tin packaging. Potatoes again tonight. Apparently, this caused a near riot. Food is an issue. People throw at least a quarter of every meal away, along with the quantities of packaging, so, in between the clean ups, there are piles of waste and flies everywhere. What everyone wants is to cook for themselves, so Jafra planned to build a communal kitchen. Indeed, communal kitchens are in the UNHCR plans pinned to the walls of their offices, but unfortunately, the Greek government has vetoed this.

– No single camp can have a kitchen until everyone has a kitchen, because, they argue, refugees will try to move to the camps with kitchens and cause chaos.

So, people vote with their feet and walk into the village to buy camping stoves and cook for themselves in their tents. There has already been one serious fire. How long before a death?

It is not just the kitchen. The agency received a message from UN-HCR that the school had to wait another two months to open until a properly designed school could be built. So much for Jafra's efforts.

Here is the problem: this need for uniformity and control flies in the face of what every handbook, every guideline that you read on working with refugees talks about—the need for empowerment, consultation, and the need to allow refugees to control their own lives, to avoid passivity and dependency. Any psychologist will tell you that psychological health starts with self-help and a feeling of control and engagement in the environment. In many of the long-term camps in which I have worked, I have been asked to come in and 'activate' people who have become depressed. After months of fending for themselves on the Macedonian border, these are the most resilient and activated groups of refugees with whom I have ever worked. Do those in charge really want to kill that spirit?

It is obvious to everyone that sitting in tents in the growing heat, waiting for the next meal, queuing to use the showers, taking care of bored children who long to go to school, leads to stress and violence. Housam tells me of growing numbers of fights, men beating women in their tents, divorces. On one occasion, a man beat up his wife in front of both the police and a Greek social worker. I am glad to say they intervened. The woman is pressing charges, but the man escaped with his child to Turkey and is blackmailing the wife.

Last night, Housam was called to help with another incident where a woman complained that a man from the neighbouring tent was harassing her 15-year-old daughter and insisting she be given to him in marriage. Again, when confronted with police, pointing out this is illegal, he backed down and promised to refrain.

The tensions and frustrations play out in other ways too. When I walk around the camp with Eleni or sit with her in her clinic, people approach her constantly for reports that will show they are too stressed to live here and need hotel accommodation. In fact, the small stock of such accommodation is almost full.

Housam's solution is to accept the reality that, at least for now, people are stuck. So he wants to give people the chance to use whatever skills they have to create a functioning community, whether through building and/or teaching in a school, giving informal classes to adults or children, or building a kitchen where people can cook together the food that they like.

Luckily, the agency agrees. They cannot do much about the kitchen, but they recognised that children in the camp cannot wait another two months and asked Jafra what they needed for a 'temporary' school. They have found benches for the rooms Jafra cleaned up and are already advertising for teachers. Interviews are next week.

Helping to clean up the rubbish
Lagkadikia Camp, June 2016

In the evening, we all walk out to the river—just beyond the camp fence. It's actually a small stream flowing through water meadows, where horses graze and wooded cliffs rise on either side. We sit at a small concrete dam where water pours over into a pool below, and loud frogs sing to one another. It is a lovely contrast to the aridity of the camp, with its gravelled ground and wire tents. Other families are out walking or cooking over small open fires, breaking their fast as dusk falls. Later, we gather around the small fire pit the Jafra group have made near the office. Housam plays his drum, others sing.

Lagkadikia Camp, Friday 17 June

I'm sick all day with some bug, but I manage to get in for meetings with Julia and Dan. They are happy with the trainings and like the idea of the children's storytelling project, so I am welcome to come back. But the meeting is repeatedly interrupted. The container area, where the offices are, has a locked gate, but it is easy to get in through various holes in the fences, and two boys are shouting and arguing outside the locked container that stores clothes. One boy with dark brown hair and a flushed face says, if he is not allowed in, he will come at night and burn down the container. Julia patiently explains when distribution times are and that personal distributions from the container are just not possible.

– *I have an appointment at the German Embassy. I must have clothes.*
This seems unlikely; he has no paperwork, but she relents and allows him to look. He looks around for ten minutes and then comes out.
– *There is nothing I want*—he says in disgust and stomps off.
Understandably, people don't want to look shabby when they are meeting officials, but the whole registration process is still a confusing mystery to most people, including me. Housam gives me a demonstration of the difficulty of getting onto the Skype number to make an appointment for an interview to be considered for relocation. He takes his own and a borrowed mobile phone, gets an internet connection, and starts calling the dedicated Skype number on both phones. It rings, and rings, and rings, and after twenty minutes of trying, he stops. Yesterday, two of the Jafra women took the

bus into Thessaloniki to use the free internet connection provided by a supportive Greek legal firm. They too failed to make an appointment. If you do finally get through, they will give you an appointment to come to Athens, interview you, ask your preferences out of the eight countries offering relocation...

– So, I would like to go to Spain, but I can still end up in Bulgaria or Lithuania, or I can be told no country wants me and I must apply to take asylum in Greece.

In fact, the Skype calls may become redundant because a 'pre-registration' process is starting in which all refugees living in camps who arrived before that magical date, 20th March (those arriving after remain liable to deportation under the infamous EU Turkey Deal), can be 'pre-registered' in order to start the process of seeking asylum, relocation, or family reunification. Apparently, a bus will turn up at the camp on some unknown date and take people to a pre-registration centre. Unfortunately, this information has not been widely disseminated. No one knows why not, but rumours spread, and people fear that, as the bus has not got to their camp yet, they will be at the back of the queue.

Housam does not think about it. The young man I met in Idomeni who just wanted to find a quiet room where he could study and listen to music has, at least for now, disappeared. All he wants to do is help his fellow refugees make this small community into something bearable.

– UNHCR keeps telling us the camp will be 'heaven' in the future, and we should do nothing but wait. We cannot wait, we need to make it liveable right now.

Lagkadikia Camp, Saturday 18 June

Housam, Hannah, and I, with a few others from the Jafra group, ran a trial storytelling workshop today. We gathered together six girls and two boys (between seven and eleven years old) in the schoolroom and explained that we wanted them to help us try out the equipment for a project we hoped to do in the summer. We wanted children to be able to tell stories about any aspect of their lives, in any way they wanted—drawing, writing, talking and taking pictures or videos. To-day, we were going to give them some cameras to see if these were any good to use.

The children were so excited. Initially, we just gave them cameras, translated the three buttons on the side, and told them to play with them in pairs and work it out—they did. Then Housam went over the camera in detail and gave them simple tips on taking pictures. I talked about asking permission, not taking pictures of people who asked not to be photographed and encouraged them to take pictures of anything that interested them in the camp. We sent them off in pairs for an hour, telling them to take turns for thirty minutes each, and then to meet back. Together we would download and look at what they had done.

In that moment, a major fight erupted in the camp. Apparently, there were two rival Kurdish gangs, Syrian and Iraqi, constantly fighting in Idomeni. The Iraqis are here in Lagkadikia. A Syrian Kurd arrived at the camp and wanted to marry a young woman here. The Iraqis were having none of it. In a flash the northern part of the camp had gone from sunny tranquility, with women washing clothes at the water points and children playing on swings, to a great crowd of shouting angry men—some waving tent poles—surging through the children's play area.

The volunteers grabbed all the children and pulled them into a safer place. I found one of the boys trying to follow and film the action and stopped him—too young for war reporting. Later, when we met up, we discussed the importance of keeping safe and that filming fights needed special training. In fact, they had taken some lovely photos. Interesting to see the children had a preference for still pic-tures: all the details of a market stall, women washing, and lots of pictures of the garbage. One of them had done the most delightful interview with her friend, but unfortunately, had a thumb over the lens for most of it! Nothing like learning from experience. None of them got hassled by anyone for having a camera. No one tried to grab or steal it off them, they did not have any technical problems, and they all loved doing it, so I think from a practical point of view, the project can work. The technical failures were all on my part.

– *What do you mean you have no external drive or extra memory?* Housam asked me in amazement as we were downloading.

At the end of the workshop, we discussed other storytelling methods and gave each child a notebook, so they can write stories and/or keep a diary. They all want to do this, except two who cannot write. Cyra, the 7-year-old (and quite the brightest), said it was the first time she has ever used a camera, and she was so happy.

Lagkadikia Village, Thursday 21 July

I am sitting in the Church dining room waiting for a code of conduct training session. No one has turned up, but some Greek ladies, who have just finished cleaning the Church, insist I join them for cake and coffee. When they discover I work at the camp, an agitated conversation follows in which they mime grapes being pulled off vines, while one gets her daughter on her mobile phone to explain in English.

– *My mother wants you to understand that the refugees are stealing grapes off the vines and people are very upset.*

– *I am so sorry, I already heard about this yesterday, and I know the refugees themselves are meeting today to discuss what to do about it, because it is just a few who are causing problems.*

– *Well, it is not good.*

– *You are absolutely right, I am just a visitor, but I know the camp managers and the refugees are discussing it.*

Apparently, it is not just grapes. One group stole a sheep and then took the animal to the local butcher!

I head off to look for the training and find it taking place in the Spanish volunteers' living room.

Julia, from protection, is explaining:

– *As humanitarian workers, we hold power over resources. We have been given that power in order to support refugees, IDPs and other affected populations—we must not abuse it. Refugees must participate in all matters that affect them.*

I am back after a month, and there is definitely a much more tense relationship between refugees and camp management than there was in June. Unfortunately, no one really discussed bringing in Spanish volunteers to help with children's activities with Jafra. The Spanish seem competent and friendly, but Housam is gloomy and fed up. I sit with him in the corner of the camp where some of them are trying to plant small trees and shrubs transplanted from the wilderness beyond the fence. Housam feels the camp managers still don't understand that refugees can organise and take care of themselves if given resources and support. He now has thirty seven refugee volunteers for Jafra who feel excluded and pushed out. On the other hand, the staff working in the containers behind the (now much more impenetrable) fence say that Jafra often fail to deliver, don't turn up when they say they will, and not everyone likes them. Although, they acknowledge that not everyone likes the camp managers either. Never mind, I am given permission to start the camera workshops with Jafra.

Lagkadikia Camp, Sunday 24 July
I drove into Thessaloniki last night to pick up my translator—Dalia, a lovely Palestinian woman studying law in Sussex. When I parked my car by the port, the man in the parking ticket booth simply said:
– *English? Brexit? Are you crazy?*
– *Please don't blame me*—I replied. *I completely agree.*
Never mind politics. This afternoon, we started working with an excited group of ten children who we then sent off into the camp to take pictures. We immediately discover that there is a situation: some angry young men have thrown the hated lunches in blue plastic bags, into the rubbish bins and stopped the food trucks from coming in. The trucks then drove off taking the food with them, so now there is growing tension in the camp. On one side, the angry young men who want a full-blown food strike. On the other, a number of older men who simply want food for their families. I meet them down at the gate, talking to one of the staff on duty, asking why he let the trucks leave. Later, some of them come to see Housam, who I find standing in the Jafra area, trying to mediate between both groups

144

who are yelling at one another.

– You cannot have a strike if you have not prepared an alternative supply— says one of the older men angrily.

– The food is inedible, and everyone should support us—the young men shout back.

Housam tells them that he is not part of the argument. However, given that the prepared food is not going to be delivered today, he does not want people to go hungry. His solution is to call on independent volunteers that he knows, to bring both food and cooking equipment, so that Jafra can at least feed people tonight and stop them from getting angrier and hungrier. I leave them to the discussion and run around the camp, warning children not to film any arguments. As they are mostly having fun filming each other, it's not a problem.

Lagkadikia Camp, Monday 25 July

I came to camp this morning; no signs of a riot, but there is a food delivery going on. Some families tell me this is the first time they have had breakfast given to them since before Ramadan. Meanwhile, Mustafa, one of the older men, tells us the cooking was only complete at two or three in the morning, and, even then, the rice was not ready. Jafra announced it with a loudspeaker, but he and his family had gone to bed. What he wants is for those who don't want the packaged food not to prevent the trucks coming in, so that those who want prepared food can get it. Housam goes to talk to the protestors and gets them to agree they won't stop deliveries anymore.

Lagkadikia Camp, Tuesday 26 July

Sunday it was the food strike, today it's a thunderstorm. Much needed to break the horrible heat of the last few days, but then again, not the moment to release children into the camp with their cameras. I look for children trying to film in the rain but find none. Although, I wonder about the lightning strike risk posed by the new metal poles that have gone up in the last two days outside every tent. Their purpose is unclear.

145

I am on the swing with my friend's sister on
my lap and I took this myself. The trees and
sky look so nice.
Lamees, age 10

The camera training workshops are going well. We spend some time with the children asking what they want to show others about their lives. As before, it's the food, the rubbish, the toilets, their family. Then we discuss and recite the rules: always ask the subject for permission to take their picture; don't film arguments or any distributions, including food (this is a new request from camp management after yesterday); wear the camera wristband and treat the camera gently; don't let anyone else borrow your camera.

Four Jafra volunteers, as well as Dalia and myself, each work with two children to make sure they are completely comfortable with their cameras and hopefully will not delete all their pictures as two children did on Sunday.

I think I now have almost every child of the right age on my list. We had to limit the workshop to 8–12-year-olds, as we did not have enough cameras to include every child in the camp. Consequently, as Dalia and I walk around the camp, there is a constant crowd of small children running up to us saying when can we use the cameras? The age restriction is now common knowledge and small children who are obviously only five insist they are eight, while solemn pubertal older girls and boys insist they are only twelve.

We use the evening time to visit families, asking their consent for their children to join tomorrow's group. Almost everyone seems very happy. Indeed, parents keep coming up to ask for their child to be involved, but some are more cautious. One father asks what his responsibility would be if pictures of a woman without her hair covered or feeding a baby ended up on the internet? A mother asks what to do if her child films her sleeping or breastfeeding? We assure them that all pictures come back to us and that we won't use pictures where the children have not been given consent by those being filmed or photographed, but that so far, we have had no pictures like this. Most children are taking pictures of nature, puppies, infants, dancing, toilets and rubbish, or doing delightful interviews with each other and their families.

Two fathers have come and politely withdrawn permission for their respective children. One explains they are leaving soon and he wants

I took this picture because the sheds in the distance look like a train, and it is my dream to go on a train. I want to go round and come back here. I have only been on a train once, and it was such a short distance.
Abdullah, age 9

no trouble, so it's best that there are no photos. Not surprising after all the batterings and legal changes of status in the last few months. People are tired. Perhaps a faction-ridden, war-weary camp where half are in conflict with the camp organisation (who themselves have their issues with the Greek government, Ministry of Migration, army and police) is not the ideal place to do a project like this. But then, I watch a small girl filming another washing her hands at the taps, while interviewing her, and holding the bright red camera with an intense seriousness worthy of Lanzmann. We sit with each child as they review their work on the computer and choose the pictures and films they want to keep. Their pleasure at doing this is so great, it is all worth it.

We plan a show with selected photos and videos for the whole camp before I leave. Jafra will keep all their work on the computer so that they can come and look at it any time. We will also print off their favourite ten pictures for them to keep. Beyond that, we plan to put their favourite picture and video online (migrantchildstorytelling.org).

The food situation appears to have settled. Jafra have used one of the shelters in their area to create a 'kitchen.' Families come themselves to choose the food they want from the donated supplies and cook their own meals with the equipment and stove provided. This is surely a safer option than the calor gas stoves in tents or open fires nearby. I think the camp managers are adopting a three monkeys position, because they have not come near and have not discussed it with Jafra at all.

There are other issues. As I go around the camp, I am repeatedly asked if I am the 'Canadian Woman.'

— *I am afraid not. Why?*

— *Because she is taking families to a better place*—a woman explains.

This sounds both biblical and disturbing. But after multiple fragmented conversations, I get the story. An Iraqi woman with Canadian citizenship and apparently limitless funds, turned up a month ago and went around the camp interviewing families. The managers asked for her credentials and, initially, did not prevent her from coming in the camp, until they realised she was selecting families to move to a housing settlement that she was funding herself, without any discussion as to where the settlement was, who and how it would be run, who were the most vulnerable in the camp, or who had the greatest needs. The managers asked her not to do this, and she disappeared. But yesterday, a bus came and took thirty families away, and more will follow. Apparently, she went directly to the Greek government and got their permission and has just taken her elected group. Whether more will follow remains unclear, both to the managers and the camp community. Hence, as I go around tents with my interpreter, people hope I might be a selecting angel and they will be among the chosen.

I feel sorry for the camp managers, and for the unselected. But I am astounded at how tidy, clean, organised, and home-like most families have made the insides of their tents, with carpeted floors and beds and shady shelters outside. They have created deep shade between the tents, where they have covered the lanes with tarpaulin, and deep shade along the fences, where they have built small day shelters with reeds and the now-discarded first-generation beds. These are single-metal bedsteads whose springs are so soft they are unbearable to sleep on, but when they are turned on their ends and woven with rushes from the field, they make good shady walls.

I am faced with other problems. Yesterday, we spent time with Adem. He is eleven and had been one of the keenest filmmakers in our first group. He had come across as bright, sparky and talkative, but he has bad nightmares since the crossing to Turkey with fifty people on a boat designed for four. The crowd was so great that his younger brother was in danger of suffocating, so he and others had to get in the water with rings around them. They had a rope and he held onto an older man, but he was terrified.

— *The waves came over us, but we were OK because another big boat came and saved us.*

He tells me he has bad dreams every single night, and in the dreams, a devil comes and tells him to kill his sister or even his mother, both of whom he adores, and he is afraid. I ask him what he does when he wakes up.

– I read the Koran to try and feel better.

He also dreams about Daesh and the things he has seen on television: the throat-cutting and heads on poles. So I will take him to Eleni the MDM psychologist tomorrow, as I will not be here long term, but in the meantime, we do some dream scripting. I explain that this is a game he can play just before he falls asleep. I want him to make up a new movie to play in his mind when he is lying in bed. He thinks for a bit then tells me Shatan will still appear, but this time he, Adem, will have a superpower:

– What will that be? I ask.

Adem chooses the power to summon up water. He shows us how he is going to make a great wave and drown Shatan. In fact, it would be boiling water, and Shatan would explode into steam.

– And then I will have cold water to wash my face and awake refreshed.

– Great dream—I say—*now you are going to play THAT dream in your head before you fall asleep tonight and every night. It won't work at once but after about three nights, I promise you, you will dream that dream instead.*

Adem listens and looks at me with great seriousness, and I am hoping my suggestive powers hold true. I have found dream scripting does work with some small children, so it is worth a try.

Lagkadikia Camp, Wednesday 27 July

Today the camp is full of kite-flying children rushing around with kites made out of the blue plastic food bags. The Spanish volunteers have done a great rubbish recycling class.

I am getting used to the rhythms of the camp—the hot silence in the morning, except for the odd child careening down the main drag in a cart made from a container, or a few children on the swings. Just before noon, no one is up. Dalia and I start running around getting the consents we missed and reminding children the workshop is at 2pm. They all turn up as planned, and we let them loose with the cameras. No more incidents. Today is remarkably trouble free.

As I am now three cameras down because of breakages, the children are working in pairs and have to share the cameras—it's working out.

Just one boy came back to see us and tell us his partner would not hand over the camera. The boy handed it over at once, as soon as he saw Dalia coming. The other problem is children deleting all their pictures by mistake, despite us going over the delete buttons repeatedly in the workshop.

While one group is out with the cameras, we are doing feedback with the previous group. The children choose the one picture they want to exhibit and to tell us why they like that picture. They also choose the ten they want to keep. One small boy spent a considerable amount time thinking about his exhibit picture and finally chose a rather blurry tree. Then, half an hour later, he came back with his sister, and she told us he actually wanted to choose a selfie but was too shy to say so. In fact, it's a lovely picture of him. A number of other children have chosen selfies. The children's pictures of each other are some of the best, because they capture an intimacy normal pictures don't get. The children look straight at the camera, unabashed. Most of them have chosen pictures of family or friends or volunteers, and when you ask why, the response is always—*because I love her, because I love him*, or *I love them*... It is all about love. One girl says her friends are what make life at the camp bearable.

Then around 8pm, the camera group returns the cameras, and we start downloading.

I have found out the reason for the new metal poles; they're not for winterisation, apparently. They are belatedly to protect the tents from the heat of the sun. Ad hoc shade created by stretching tarpaulins between tents is unsafe, apparently, as it may fall into all those illegal cooking fires. A tarpaulin will be stretched over the whole area. Blue signs are appearing on buildings indicating EU funding for this and that, and new roofed water points are being built. It should be a perfect camp... in a few months' time.

Lagkadikia Camp, Saturday 30 July

There is a cold wind from the north over the lake this morning, then dead calm, and a great crowd of birds come flying from the east: cormorants, heron, storks, pelicans, grebes all mixed together. They circle, swoop, spread in long dark tendrils, then beat up the water by the reed bed beside the hotel. The utter peacefulness of this place contrasts with a sort of continuous quiet roaring in my ears. The sound of distant thunder, or waves that crash on other shores. The almost daily death toll—today Texas, last week Germany and France. The sources are multiple, not just ISIS but aggrieved and angry teenagers, angry husbands, angry second-class citizens of any description, black, white, refugee, migrant, right, left. It is not ideas that are infectious, it is action itself. All anger, all dispute, is now played out on a public stage with the whole world watching. If nothing else, one can go down in a blaze of Twitter fame.

In Lagkadikia, the storks are in their nests again. I thought they had left, but they are stretching their wings, going for long looping sorties over the rubbish-filled fields beside the camp, practising for their longer migration. Dalia and I are in town all afternoon interviewing Maria who continues to tell her horrifying story with extraordinary grace. In her short, eleven years her school has been bombed while she was walking towards it. Two teachers were killed. Then her neighbour's house was bombed as they turned and ran back. Then they got in a boat and travelled to Lesvos, ending up at Eko with a closed border. She loved it at Eko Camp and remembers me playing Hokey Cokey. She dreams of being a teacher and an artist, but having only managed first grade, she still cannot read and write.

Adem tells us some more of his story. Like Maria, his home and school were bombed. The good news is that, last night, his superpower worked in his dream. When I ask him how he is sleeping, he mimes pulling up the water, expelling Shatan and washing his face. He then flops back in his seat with a smile. But he has another problem—he is being badly bullied. Other children beat him up and break his toys. We find some of these others in the village playground and Dalia talks to them. She makes a passionate speech about how she knows their lives have been terrible so far—nothing but shit—and she cannot change that, but they are all Arabs who stand together, and they should not behave like Bashir Assad. They should remember how they felt when they were afraid—that is how they are

154

making Adem feel. I watch the boys' astonished faces as she talks. It works. The five boys embrace and say they will be brothers now, then they all get to ride in my toffee coloured car back to the camp. Then Maria asks me to teach the Spanish volunteers Hokey Cokey like we did in Eko, so I do, with Maria dancing into the middle of the circle and taking the lead.

Lagkadikia Camp, Sunday 31 July

I wake early to walk along the lake shore. The birds are there but fly off as I approach. I wish I could walk into a natural landscape without changing it and engendering fear.

In the evening, we visit Majd's father and his family. I admire all the plants they have put outside their tent, and they beg me to visit two ruined barracks rooms, which they have bedecked with homemade sofas and hangings. They have hung fairy lights and coloured mats on one wall and placed small artificial trees in pots. They found all the things among the donations left at the Church. Then, Dad berates me for an hour about how terrible life is here and how the UN and camp managers are liars because they promise everything and do nothing, and how if he could, he would return to Syria because there is no respect, no dignity in Europe.

— My son is a master chef, just give us a job and we will make money. We don't want to take it. We don't want to take anyone else's work, we just want to work. Maybe they will make this a perfect place one day, but we want to leave.
His hand is damaged because he was caught in crossfire in Damascus. He has had eight operations and needs more to get it working. He tells me his wife has had a nervous breakdown but no one will help. As always, I feel overwhelmed and useless, but they seem happy with me writing it all down.

When we go outside, Adib, a teenage boy with learning difficulties, is in the centre of another fight. A mob of smaller boys is attacking him as he lashes out. Two of them are from yesterday afternoon's group. Dalia and I grab them to ask why they are yet again bullying another weaker boy. They don't know, they don't have an answer. *It's fun*—they say as they run off.

155

It's a beautiful memory. Look at his face, he
is an old man now. It is a good face. He is a
good-looking man. I love my dad, he has had
a lot of experience. He is sitting next to the
tent where he always sits with his friends.
Majd, age 11

Vasiliki Camp, Tuesday 2 August

– We are farm animals—one of the men in my parents' group said to me this afternoon. *In the morning, they give us food. In the evening, they give us food, then they close the doors. Isn't that a farm?*

Everyone in Vasiliki Camp knows they took the chickens out of the hangers to stuff over a thousand people in, and this fills them with fury. It is the lack of respect and dignity that this symbolises as much as the physical conditions themselves. The camp consists of seven large hangers with concrete floors, filled with rows of army-style canvas tents—one for each family. Outside there is a large, hot, treeless space, with rows of hated chemical toilets that stink, and showers that are too hot. The ground has been covered quickly with loose gravel that is hard to walk on. There is one tiny shaded area for children's play, a kind of cardboard box room that functions as a school, and one empty hanger used for sports and meetings. Grim is an understatement. Conditions are even worse this week because the camp is being 'improved,' which seems to mean bringing in more gravel, piling it in heaps, and then flattening it, along with digging deep trenches to improve drainage. So the air is full of heat and dust and the roars of the diggers and levellers, and there is no respite.

Nor is there anywhere to go—no walk beside cornfields to a village with shops and cafés as in Lagkadikia. Vasiliki is in the industrial suburbs that stretch to the east of Thessaloniki, an area of empty shoebox-style office buildings, factories and half-built mansions. Many appear to have been abandoned as Greece went bust. Outside the hangers, there is a major highway on one side, where any small child might run to their death, and a scrap metal yard on the other. Refugees as just one more waste product, with added benefits in terms of employment opportunities for Greek construction and catering companies. The refugees are angry about that as well.

– Please tell the Europeans you cannot take one million Syrians and use us as a commercial product!

I am doing a consultancy this week and have the impossible task of asking groups of parents and children how things can be made more bearable. But they don't want to discuss this.

— *The biggest problem is that we are completely lost. We saw a lot of people since we crossed the Syrian border, but we have not seen any humanity. Everyone has used the children for different political and economic agendas. We are used as a playing card, first by Turkey, then Europe.*

— *I am a human being, you are a human being. I ask you how many hours you could endure it here? Everyone is using us to get money.*

— *I never thought the problems could be worse than in Syria, but living here, they are.*

Vasiliki Camp, Thursday 4 August

In the girls group yesterday, one little girl with a boyish haircut and a dirty white shirt just could not sit still—she left to get water, she left to join a game. When she came back, the other girls were discussing how their parents taught them to be good. All of them had already told me that *talking* and *discussing* in Syria had changed to *getting a beating* here in the camp. They knew it was because their parents were tense. One girl tearfully told us that her mum and dad argued every day and her dad kept saying if her mum went on about things, he would just leave them all and go back to Syria. She was terrified he might actually go. The white shirt girl came back. One of the girls turned on her.

— *She is always in trouble, she gets into fights and runs around, and then other mothers complain to her mother and her mother beats her.*

White shirt burst into tears, pulled an angry face at the girl speaking and ran off. This evening, I visited her family and got a clear picture of a very overactive little girl. The parents tell me their usual benign methods of discipline have broken down and the children run wild, pick up bad habits, and do what they like.

— *Just now my boy took a shower then ran in the dirt and came back filthy. I was so annoyed, I said, 'How many times have I told you, if you take a shower stay clean!' Because it's impossible here, you suffer so much to take a shower. At home, he could be clean again in minutes, so I beat him.*

The miseries of camp life pile on top of the horrors of the past. In the last two days, I have listened to a 9-year-old girl who cannot get the image of a boy with a burst stomach out of her head. She spent three months living in a garage in Turkey without any furniture or running water and worries all the time about her mother's health. There's an Iraqi Kurdish boy who spent days crossing mountains in the snow and wading across a river, and a 10-year-old who worked (for weeks or months—he cannot remember) as a cutter in a Turkish tailor shop. He and his brother cut pieces of cloth ten hours a day. They were not allowed to sit down and only got a one-hour break. They were never paid.

The children's stories fill my head as I drive over the mountains back to Lagkadikia in the evenings. The winding route is familiar now, and I have abandoned the horrible GPS. I buy fresh vegetables and watermelon in Panorama, and always stop at the viewpoint where I can stand in the hot sunset, watch cumulus piling up over Mount Choriatis, and look down on both lakes filling the long flat valley stretching east to the sea. I try to clear my head. I haven't helped myself by buying a Herald Tribune and reading about the amazing courage of doctors working under siege in Aleppo.

Vasiliki Camp, Friday 5 August

– First thing, change the toilets! Second, the NGOs who come and write our names and lie to us, don't ever come back because you are giving us false hope. A lot of organisations come and ask us what we need, and, in the end, they do nothing, so I am fed up with their lying.

This is from a 12-year-old in my girl's group this morning. Although, curiously, by my second day here, when word had got around that a woman was holding discussion groups with children, more and more kept coming up asking if they could join the session going on, or when I would do a group with them. And the girls sitting with me all said they wanted to be there—their answers pouring out without restraint. I think it is because people rarely come and sit with children for a couple of hours and ask them in depth what they think about things.

What they have to say is worth hearing. Every single one of them has either witnessed or been directly bombed. Most have seen woundings and injuries directly and then travelled over mountains and

159

oceans to get here. All are clear that they want to leave as soon as possible. At this point, I apologise that it is not in my power to achieve this, but I would like to know what they would like to happen right now to make life in the camp more bearable. The two things they say they most need are toilets with water, so that they don't feel sick when they go inside, and a proper school—a large clean one, with much more space, regular classes, discipline and proper subjects— not informal playing and teaching all mixed up in a squashed hot box where you can come and go as you please. At least half of the children I have talked to cannot read or write because, like Maria, they missed the chance to learn. They are desperate to do so. Many of the 11 and 12-year-olds have had no schooling for at least three years. They tell me their lives have *stopped* and they are *losing their future.*

I learn some other interesting things. Eko gas station was better because the owners put on free movies every night and let people watch TV in their café. Independent volunteers did a better job in distribution than UNHCR. The children told me that, if they needed something—clothes, toys, milk—it usually arrived from somewhere pretty fast. Here, however, they ask constantly and it does not come. The medical care was better there, with some presence on the site at most times. A woman burst into tears in my group yesterday, saying her daughter has a hole in her heart, and she has all the papers, but the medical providers here are not interested and do nothing. I took her to meet the site manager from UNHCR today, who promised to get his health coordinator to look into the case. On the other hand, here in Vasiliki, the factory roof provides shade and protects them from the rain, the tents don't blow down, and there are fewer fights.

But even so, the children don't feel safe. They told me about a knife fight between Arabs and Kurds the other night, which got quite vicious. Meanwhile, the police apparently stood and watched. There are other things that frighten them as well.

– *There is a guy here who is trying to use food and sweets to tempt young girls and boys and take them to another camp and sell them—*one girl says. Her comment opens a floodgate and the other girls all raise their hands to tell me more. It is hard for Mahmoud and me to keep up.

— I always see a guy outside the camp. He is a refugee. He is a drunk and beats older children.

— We see that drunk guy every night, he comes to this section. We are sitting on plastic chairs in the area where they play basketball. And he gets boys to stay with him.

— There is a guy here, he is taking children to do nasty things with him by the sea.

— He was also in Eko. He is not a refugee.

— One day I was taking my little brother outside the camp. A man came to me and said, 'Come with me, I have a lot of toys for you and your brother, come and play with me.' He spoke Arabic.

— There was a foreign woman. She was like a friend for me here, and she told me she wanted to buy me a necklace but she said we have to go outside to get it. I said no, I must ask my parents or the police first.

— Very good—I said. *And you are quite right. If anything like this happens, go and find your parents and go with them to report what is happening to the police.*

But apparently the police are not a solution.

— We are so afraid of the police because the police sometimes ask me to go out with them and my sister and my friend—says one of the 12-years-old girls. Two other girls jump in, saying that they know police ask girls out.

You might hope that putting refugees in a fenced camp with police and army guards who rigorously inspect my documents and check me off on a list every morning, would offer some protection. But apparently not. Indeed, it strikes me yet again that encamped refugees are a sort of honey pot that pulls all the dirty buzzing flies towards it. Yet another argument for using all the EU money to allow refugees to live independently in the city. If they are given vouchers or funds to spend on necessary food and accommodation, or even better, allowed to work, they will be much less trouble, much less depressed, probably just as safe, and contribute to the economy.

The geography of this honey pot is particularly bad. All the tents are in the hanger sections facing one another, and it's not possible to see out to either the yard or road to watch over the children. The

161

police office at the gate is next to a thick wall, next to a drive, which leads to the main road, and has no visibility onto either, so no one is watching who is hanging around the camp. At Lagkadikia, everyone has a line of sight onto the road to the village. 'Hangers around' are noticed in an instant.

I promise the children I will write a report without mentioning their names and give it to some people who I hope will do something. I have, and I did. Let's see.

When I get back to Lagkadikia Camp in the evening, Jafra have organised a chess club, and there is a line of children intensely engaged around tables. Jafra have created a large new psychosocial space—a tented structure open on one side to the fields and carpeted and decorated. They have also created a clean, tidy office, and put up laminated signs around the camp saying: "Self-organised group engaged in cleaning and children's activities, etc. Come and visit us." The one beside the gate to the management offices, hung on the impenetrable fence, was taken down immediately.

I am sorry the camp management people are not here at night to watch Jafra at work. They might understand why they are not always consistently efficient during the day. They are not paid staff who go home in the evening or volunteers like me who can retreat to rest in a room by a lake. They never stop being available—night and day. Between 6pm and midnight is when the camp is most awake and busy. As well as children's activities, there is a constant stream of people coming to ask for help, advice, or just to hang out and be social. Housam wants to create social spaces around the camp where people can mix and cook and eat each other's foods. I am glad to say I found some funds to give all the Jafra volunteers one evening off by the lake. Not enough.

Lagkadikia Camp, Saturday 6 August

The Greek authorities and the site managers want Housam to sign an MOU on working cooperatively in the camp. I point out the extraordinary fact that the Greek government is making an MOU with a self-organised bunch of refugees who are not officially registered as an NGO and have no legal standing. That is an achievement in itself. The MOU talks about cooperation and shared decision-making and training, and also asks for structure, timetables and consistency. I note that it says food cannot be cooked or distributed, but Jafra has already closed its kitchen. Housam wants to add some points and asks me to help him with the English.

Dalia has been running around the camp making sure everyone photographed by the children agrees to their pictures being used on social media. Tonight we get it finished. Only a couple of people say no. I am sitting, typing in the Jafra area when there is a sudden burst of elation. News has come through that the Siege of Aleppo has been lifted. Even so, it is not an end. Once again, I am struck by the paradoxical tranquillity of this tiny corner of Northern Greece, compared to the roaring noises coming from other places. The children play on the central street in the evening sunlight. Women and men sit in groups in shady areas, gossiping. At least there is peace. This place is a holiday camp compared to the hot aridity of Vasiliki. But there is no point in saying that to anyone here. They are not in Vasiliki; they are here, and as far as most are concerned it is a *hot boring trap* as one father told me. Telling them they are better off than others in other camps or telling people in Vasiliki that they are more comfortable than people in Aleppo, or refugees in Kenya, or on the Somali border, achieves nothing.

I have long ago learned that one person's suffering is never lessened by pointing out that they are better off than someone else who is suffering more. On the contrary, they simply feel worse because you have added to the feelings of guilt, worthlessness and shame that so often accompany feeling low. I once made this mistake as an inexperienced trainee psychiatrist. I had come back from a terrible crisis, somewhere in the Balkans, and was seeing a young university student who was obviously miserable. But she seemed unable to put her finger on anything but the most trivial reasons—a quarrel with girlfriends, feeling she was on the wrong course, hating her bedsit. She had no serious biological symptoms of depression and I thought, naively, that a reality check in the form of, *well at least you are not being shot at*

163

by snipers in Sarajevo, might do the trick. On the contrary, it caused a catastrophic reaction. The girl burst into tears and wailed that she knew that already, thank you, and even thinking of what other people were suffering made her feel suicidal with guilt that she had nothing to complain about, so why was she miserable? Was I there to help her or lecture her on how boring and trivial her life was?

I was mortified and ashamed of myself. Misery and discomfort will fill the space allowed. It cannot be lessened by measuring it against another person's suffering.

Lagkadikia Camp, Sunday August 7th

I do believe I know the names of almost every 8 to 12-year-old in the camp. When I walk in, they call out my name as I pass, or rush up to hug or high five me. I also now know who plays with who, and who is different and gets left out. Hanan, for example, is a grown up in an 8-year-old's body. Her father is already in Germany and her mother is sick, so she is always getting the lunch or fixing things up. In distributions, she fights with older women to get to the front of the queue. The Cinderella girls, as I call them, the ones who were working on the play in June and are always on the swings together, don't play with her.

The camp is changing; there are now covered, shiny, new water points with tiled backgrounds. There are water fountains with drinking water, and the beginnings of a shaded distribution area. Although, the promised extended tarpaulin has still not been added to the protruding poles.

I sit with some fathers in their small shady area next to one of the ruined barracks. I ask them what they think about Aleppo. Interestingly, they are not happy. One tells me:

– *All sides want to sell the country.* The speaker is no friend of Bashir Assad. *The West needs to kill him. Even when he kills us with chemical weapons, no one stops him. Bashir is a dictator.*

– *Yasser Arafat was one of the best presidents in the Arab region, he was a smart man, a real man*—another man, sprawled lengthwise on the couch behind the first speaker, says. (This is for Dalia, my Palestinian

164

translator, who is talking simultaneously in my ear at remarkable speed.)

– But Bashir's dad was good! And so was Saddam Hussein—says another. *He fought for Syria and Iraq!* says an older man opposite. He is making coffee and gestures to see if I want any.

– And his treatment of the Kurds? I ask tentatively.

– The Kurds were trying to take land that was not theirs! Says the sprawling man.

– After Saddam Hussein left, the Arab region just collapsed—Egypt, Libya, Syria—a young man joins in.

There is a mother sitting opposite me, and I ask what she thinks.

– The men in our region do all the talking—she says, smiling.

– But I would still love to hear what you think.

– I liked Bashir's father. He was a successful politician, and our country was completely secure. We could go out on the street at 3-4am. Now, you have to be in by 5pm.

– Was it democratic?

– No, it wasn't a democracy. It was good there was no democracy, because we were safe.

– Were there any people in prison?

– Security is much more important than freedom.

Everyone around the table is nodding agreement as the older man carefully pours out the coffee.

– Look what democracy and freedom have done for us!

– Before all these events in Syria, you could not tell Muslim and Christian apart, it didn't matter, Arab and Kurd, we all lived together.

– I like everyone—said sprawling man. He paused—*except some Alawis.*

Mostly I have avoided discussing politics unless the children bring it up. It is clear there are families with very different viewpoints in both camps, and parents have taught their children to be careful of what they say. However, I did discuss my own time in Kurdistan with an Iraqi Kurd. I told him how everyone I visited in Erbil had Blair and Bush photos in their houses in 2003. I wondered what they thought about our intervention now.

– People did not have a clue! They had no idea what was coming. America

and Britain put Iraq in the hands of the Mafia, the whole of Iraq in the wrong hands, and now people are not OK. Look at the price we have paid. And at the end of one group in Vasiliki, I asked some of the boys how the war in Syria could end?

– *We should become one hand*—he said holding up his with fingers spread. *We should organise a huge demonstration and go to Syria and stop the war*—said an 8-year-old. The others all agreed.

It has grown dark. Majd arrives with his cart adorned with a metal pole and flag. This has suddenly become the fashion in Lagkadikia in the last two days—I wonder if they are digging up those unused metal poles—so many of the children's carts are sprouting them. Some include a totemic stuffed toy atop the pole, and they charge around the camp like pirates with their banners blowing out behind them. Then it suddenly starts raining, and all the children run from under cover to spin in the downpour and turn up their faces to catch the heavy drops of water.

Lagkadikia, Monday 8 August

I spend my last afternoon writing by the lake. It is incredibly hot, and in the span of three hours, the water has gone from glassy calm to whipped up waves as thunder sounds over the hills and a hot wind blows. Undaunted, a proud pair of swans lead six large grey cygnets behind them. A baby grebe scuttles among the rocks while larger ones drift far out, and a large white heron pokes in the rushes beneath me. As usual, the restaurant terrace is half empty. The owner of Dalia's guest house told me that thousands used to come for the thermal waters every summer, but it all changed with the financial crisis. In the evening, we have the picture show. At first, I think no one is coming, but then, most of the camera workshop children turn up with mums and dads, along with the Spanish volunteers, and the Jafra tent is packed. Giorgos, a filmmaker friend in Thessaloniki has made a rough edit, including a tiny bit of film from every child. Unfortunately, the LCD cable is bad and the projection is poor, but everyone loves it, clapping and cheering and laughing as well-known family members appear, and children do interviews. I promise we are going to make a better film.

Then we show each child's best picture, and Dalia reads out their description of it in English and Arabic. The best moment of the evening for me is Abdo's tree. Abdo is nine and often in trouble: never where he is supposed to be, often where he is not. When he discovered he was in the second, not the first, camera group, he sat down and refused to leave the workshop, arms folded and heels dug in, face set—a tactic I have seen him use on many occasions. At the end of the evening, we share his favourite picture and read out what he said about it.

I love trees so much, but I couldn't get the full picture of this one. I like this tree the most though. It's the most beautiful, it looks like a painting. It's pointy at the top, a perfect tree. And I also asked the tree permission to take her picture, and she said yes. It reminds me of the greenery in Ladkia, there was a tree there that looks like this one, and I loved it. So when I saw this, I loved it, too. It looks like one of those ancient trees; they've been through everything and have seen it all. They've seen refugees from all over the world. They witness our lives. Allah loves trees and created them to be good for us. Nature is good to us and cares for us, I feel safe when I am around it. And trees never die until somebody harms them—that's why God punishes those who cut trees down. However long they live, the tree sees everything and never forgets. Every leaf on it protects you, so every time you pick a leaf, you'll be punished. Each leaf was born for a purpose and has a past and a story. For every refugee it sees, a new leaf grows. It protects us from the sun. The prophet Mohammed loved trees too. This tree is a source of strength in the camp.

After listening to this, the room erupts in cheers, and Abdo, squashed on the floor at the front with the other children, squirms with pleasure and smiles and smiles and smiles.

'Tree' by Abdo, age 9

Maria's Story

Maria comes from Syria. At the time that she told this story (August 2016), she was eleven years old and living in a refugee camp in Northern Greece.

Life at home was amazing. I went to kindergarten, and it was nice. All the children played. My mum was always very good with us. No matter what I asked, my parents would be there for me and I for them. I dreamed of registering in school and studying, and I wanted to grow up in Syria. I still want to grow up in Syria, and I want to see my siblings get married. I was seven years old when I went to school. I loved it. All the teachers loved me and I loved them. I loved English and when I grow up, I want to learn English so I can pretend to be Western, so I can go on TV. I would like to be a translator and I want to teach children English.

We had a nice house with a pool. I would come back from school and swim after I finished studying. My brothers loved swimming. My dad made the pool so they could practice. My dad was a truck driver. He travelled all around Syria and came home at night. On Friday mornings, he would always swim with us. My brothers taught me to swim, and I can swim in the middle of the sea.

I love sports a lot. I used to want to train to play football. I liked football and I wanted muscles. Half of the boys called me a tomboy, the others let me play. When I did all the sports training, they taught me some self-defence moves and I used them. I used to dream of seeing my cousins. We played in a football field near our house and they decorated it all over. My mum could see me when I played. I used to love to draw. I wanted to do it professionally. One of my cousins taught me how to draw. Now, looking at you, I can sit down and draw you.

We would go on road trips in the truck. We would go to my grandfather's house. He lived in an Alawi area, and there were no bombs there. They protected the Alawis. We used to go there to get a change of atmosphere. My gran was staying with us, and she had a heart attack so they took her to another place. I dream of my life returning to the way it was.

The war started when I was six years old. I remember everything. It came to my town when I was seven. On TV, I used to see bodies falling in the news constantly, and I asked my dad—*Why are these people dying?* And he said—*Bashir wants to annihilate the people.* And I was afraid, because I would watch TV, and I worried the same thing would happen to us. Then I saw Damascus on TV and Homs. For a year, they were burning. Then it was our turn. When I saw Homs burning, I immediately knew all of Syria was going to burn. Whenever I saw a plane fly by and drop bombs, I would ask my dad—*Why are they doing these things?* And he would say—*They want to burn all of Syria.*

I really wanted to see my cousins, and I had nightmares that I would die before I met them. In my dreams, I would see an F-16 come above us and drop a bomb, and my heart would start beating fast. I don't dream that anymore. When they started bombing my city, I still went to school, they put us in the basement. For a little while, the war stopped and that is when I went to school. Then it started again. The teachers would tell us—*If we hear an F-16, go inside the building, so it does not hurt you.*

The first bomb I saw was on a neighbour's house. I saw the F-16 go low and then I saw them drop the bomb and I was really scared. I thought it would hit me. Because when you see a bomb falling it looks like it is going to hit you. So I ran and hid in the bathroom. They had told me before to go there because it was a safe place. When it hit, two of our bedrooms were destroyed and the kitchen. The bathroom stayed standing. My grandparents and friends were in there, about fourteen people. It is a big bathroom, but we were all huddled. I was on a chair right in the middle. I lost my hearing because it was so loud. I was deaf for four days, then I started hearing again.

Two of my neighbour's children were killed. They were eight years old, a boy and a girl. I used to play with them at school. I felt it was unfair. I used to cry a lot. My friends and I went to the funeral. That is what happens if a child dies. We went and buried them.

I stopped going to school when a bomb dropped on the school. It was the same day. My father took me to school. We were walking toward the building when we saw the same F-16. The bomb dropped on the school, so we sprinted back home. Then we saw the other bomb falling, so we ran inside the bathroom. I saw my friends running out of the school. Only teachers died, because all the children ran into their parent's arms. I pissed myself when I saw the first bomb. That's when I lost my hearing.

After that, there was no more school to go to, and that is why I cannot read or write. Two days later, we left the city and went to another. It was in an area of Syria where Daesh were in control, but we did not know that. For the first year it was OK. I played, and I went to Koran classes in the Mosque, where you had to memorise the Koran. There was no war there.

Then my dad, my mother, my brothers and I went to Turkey. Crossing the border was easy. The police let us through—we crossed legally. We went to a very nice town, and we stayed one month. Then we left Turkey on the boat with smugglers. We wanted to join my brother in Europe. My father had to pay; I don't know how much. It was two hours on the boat. The waves were big and it was crowded—fifty people. We had life jackets. My cousins' boat flipped when they were on it, but they were saved by a big boat and taken to Greece.

I wasn't scared. I was scared at the beginning, but when we were on it, it was very nice. The captain was another Syrian. It was night time and, in the middle of the sea, we saw a light flashing and we thought we will go there. The boat stopped working a couple of times. People got in the water to help. Then we got to an island. People gave us clothes and a room to dry ourselves and there was a little park. Then we went to Mytilene for four days. We slept in a room, and a Syrian cooked really good food, and they gave us cards to get a boat to Athens. When we got to Athens, some Westerners gave us a caravan. It was near the water, and I would wake in the morning and hear the

'My cart' by Maria, age 11

sea, but there was a fence, so we couldn't go to the sea. But we played a lot and went to the beach. We stayed there two or three days. Then people told us there is a camp in Thessaloniki that is better than Athens. So, we got on buses. It was nine hours because the police stopped us for three hours on the way.

The borders were open and we wanted to go to Idomeni, but the police stopped us again and would not let us pass. I am glad because it was raining and the tents were awful and anyway there were not enough. The Police made us go back to Eko. We were the first in Eko. There were white tents like here.

The people in the Eko garage were amazing. They gave us food: fried potatoes and cake. Eko was better than here. We had TV in the café and they sometimes projected movies at night. And there were not too many people. This camp is crowded and dirty. That one was clean. There were a lot of fights, but I am just remembering how I liked it there.

Then people came and told us we had to move. The doctors stopped working. They stopped the food, so we had to cross the highway to get food. But there was no place to put a tent on the other side. We came here in June. It was so nice when we first came here, but now it has been a long time. There was a field to play in, and they used to give the children toys, and there were no fights around the camp. Now, there are many fights. But now, all the troublemakers are travelling, so maybe it will be better.

I will tell you about my day: I wake up and brush my hair. I brush my teeth. If I have laundry, I do it at the taps. It is not hard. I really like washing clothes. Then we play with the Spanish volunteers, and afterwards, I have the breakfast they bring us: zatta, eggs and rice. We wash it and make it better. After I eat, we go with the Spanish and draw or play with plasticine or sing. After that, I go and shower because I am very sweaty. Then I sit in the tent for an hour, and then I go around and play. Girls and boys play separately, unless they are playing with a ball, because if we play with boys, they make fun of us. We say every person is free to do what they like. All the girls are friends and love each other. Then I go to school, and then I go and get food for the family. I use the little cart; I made it before you came here. I stole the wheels from a big garbage can. I broke them off with a rock and took them. The man in the supermarket gave me the box. Sometimes, Dad comes and takes me into town, and we walk around until night. Then I go back to the camp. I don't like this life. I want to live in a house, and I am getting too tanned and I want to rest. I do sleep OK and my dreams are nice. In my dreams, I see my brother in Germany coming and hugging me.

I am imagining myself in the future, being able to read and write. I want to go somewhere, anywhere. But, if I end up in a bad country, I will be sad because I have already had some bad experiences. I don't want to go to France, because people have told me they are mean to Syrians and don't treat them well.

I want to be a teacher very much. I would like to teach English and Arabic, and I want to teach everything to 7 and 8-year-olds.

Calais

France, October 2016

The Jungle, Thursday 21 October

It's my crow and cat I mind about most. I picture them discarded somewhere, lying bedraggled in the mud. They have been everywhere with me for the last ten years and know everything: how to run from a tsunami, what to do if there is an earthquake, how not to tread on a landmine…but not how to avoid being stolen from the back of a car outside a migrant camp. I can imagine the disappointment on the thief's face when he opened my small rucksack and found nothing but puppets. I see him checking every pocket, going through the purple plastic bag, picking up a small bird, spider, woolly caterpillar, mole, fingering each in increasing disbelief and disgust, hurling the lot (including cat and crow) into some wayside ditch, then trudging away, hood up against the driving rain. Perhaps he kept the water bottle. I hope so. It was a good one.

Rowan did warn me about the increase in petty crime in the Jungle. He suggested parking by St. Michaels. But no one was around, and the church looked desolate in the grassy wastelands that have grown up around it since the last eviction. So, I left it with a row of other cars on the south side, hoping my rented grey Fiat would be unnoticeable next to a large Sedan and a Range Rover.

It's not just the grassy wilderness that is different. The first street of restaurants leading into the northern zone is deserted and closed down. The abandoned feeling is somehow accentuated by the brightly coloured posters plastered everywhere. Primary school children have made welcoming pictures with slogans, such as "All refugees are welcome in our school" or short, hopeful, personal letters to particular refugees in coloured crayons, wishing them well and saying they will like England.

When I get to the junction that leads out of the camp under the motorway, or onto the congested northern area, I become completely disoriented. There are more tracks and more houses than I remember, but, in spite of cobbling, there are large pools and muddy verges to navigate, just like last year. A young Sudanese boy says he will take me to the Youth Centre, but it's closed, so he invites me to his 'home.' This is in a small dome tent under an awning stretched between wooden box dwellings belonging to his friends. Inside, there is nothing but a heap of wet blankets.

He tells me he is fourteen and his name is Ali. His father is dead, and he has not seen his mother since he was three, because she sent him to live with an uncle to have a better life. But the uncle died when he was thirteen.

– *So I went to Egypt.*

– *What did you do there?*

– *Worked in a coffee shop, from early morning to late at night. It was hard work, and if you are black, people are not kind. But then a friend said, 'Let's go to Italy.' I said OK, but I only have 5,000 Egyptian pounds. Then my friend called the guy who had the boat and said, 'We have a small brother, can he come?' And he said OK.*

– *So how was the trip?*

– *There were 300 people in the boat—lots of women and children—but a big boat came and took us to a 'hotspot.' We stayed there in a camp, but then my friend said Italy is not good. So, we ran away and took a bus to Milan, and then we got a train, but they took my friend off the train. I don't know where he is even now.*

Ali looks extremely sad, rolling and unrolling the blankets in his hands.

– *What do you want to do now?*

– *Go to England.*

– *Do you have family there?*

– *No family.*

– *So why?*

– *I love it. I love One Direction, and Top Gear. I try every night.*

– *What happens?*

– *They find you. Dogs, they smell you. Last night they found four of us.*

It is dark and drizzling when I get back to my car to find the smashed driver's window, glass everywhere and a note from a policeman on the front seat saying the crime had been 'interrupted,' and I should make a report. In the police station at Place de Lorraine, I sit in the glass-partitioned lobby alongside a woman waiting to complain about her sister, staring at a poster full of missing children: innocent looking family snap type pictures of girls and boys, all white. "Help us find them"—the poster calls. Through the partition, a young man in handcuffs is grinning and pulling faces at us. He has just been arrested for possessing a gun. Then I am summoned, and a policeman called Oliver takes my statement in broken English and adds it to his file on X.

— It was a migrant. There were two. We caught one and we have him here, but he won't speak. No name, nothing, so I call him X.

The policeman smiles and shrugs. He somehow manages to combine irony and sympathy as he eyes my ID badge saying "Volunteer, L'Auberge de Migrant." "Volunteer doctor with migrants," he writes on the form, "just arrived…"

Luckily, I have roadside assistance and comprehensive insurance. The kind woman on the helpline asks me:

— What's going on in Calais? You are the second this week. Don't tell me, I know the answer.

The car is taken away, and I am promised a new one in the morning. Back in the hotel after making my report, I am still grieving for my crow. How much we invest in inanimate objects, particularly those that accompany us everywhere. They are signposts for memory, allowing us to navigate our way back through the mists of the stories that make up our lives. I think about Ali sitting on his sodden blankets with no possessions at all, no family, no old friends, just a dream.

The Jungle, Friday 21 October

The eviction—the definitive attempt to get rid of the whole Jungle— will go ahead next week. Migrants and volunteers have a meeting this afternoon at the Khyber Restaurant, and Annie goes through the facts.

The eviction will start on Monday at 8am. People will be asked to go to a warehouse and queue in one of four lines: vulnerables, children, families, or single men. They will then be asked to choose from one of two regions in France, registered, given a colour-coded wristband and sent to a room to wait. Once there are fifty people corresponding to one destination, they will be put on a bus and dispatched to the accommodation centre at that destination. Those who are 'vulnerable,' as certified by MSF, will go to an accommodation centre in a city where they can access the medical help they need.

Once there, they will be asked for name, nationality and age and be given a month to think about their options, which appear to boil down to: apply for asylum in France or risk deportation.

– *There should be fifty buses coming on Monday to take at least three thousand people away from here, and this process will continue all week.*

– *What about children?* Someone calls.

– *The first place to be cleared is the containers, and all unaccompanied children will be brought back there and looked after by the French authorities. All unaccompanied minors will be interviewed by French and British officials there.*

– *So when do they start knocking down the shelters?*

– *They will start clearing manually on Tuesday—no bulldozers. And if you want to take down Mosques and churches and send them abroad to other refugee groups that will be allowed.*

– *What happens to people who arrive after the eviction?*

– *No one will be allowed to stay in the camp after the eviction has finished. If they do, or if they stay in the city or in small camps around, they risk arrest and deportation.*

– *So what if we have Dublin fingerprints?* (Meaning they have already been registered in another country.)

– *The French Government says, but this is a verbal promise, that those with Dublin fingerprints can still go to the accommodation centres and claim asylum here in France, but we cannot guarantee this will be followed through.*

The questions go on. Apparently, French government officials are coming in large numbers on Sunday with ten thousand leaflets. They will hand them out and answer questions. There is a quiet, depressed, resigned feeling to the crowd, quite different from last February.

Then the government was refusing to acknowledge the numbers in the camp and providing no alternative accommodation. The nightly meetings were all about fighting the eviction through the courts, and how to prepare oneself to remain unprovoked in the face of possible police brutality. On this occasion, the 'No Borders' crowd don't appear to be visible, and no one talks about resistance, although, many say they will just take off.

– I am going to Belgium tomorrow—the man sitting next to me says.

– Please be aware that, after the eviction, the authorities are likely to be very tough with anyone found in Calais or the surrounding area—Annie emphasises again.

I have to leave. Tom, one of the volunteers asks me to come and see a man who is really unwell. He has already seen the MSF psychiatrist who gave him medication but has remained distressed and agitated since. They are worried about him, but MSF are not here over the weekend. Tom takes me to one of the deserted shops and we tap on the door. Inside, a middle-aged Afghan man with grey hair is sitting on a wooden bench with two volunteers. He is hunched over, head in his hands, but looks up to see me and gives a sort of smile.

– Hello, Wasim, I am a volunteer doctor in the camp, I hear you are feeling unwell—I explain, sitting on a plastic stool in front of him.

He leans forward to look at me intently with fixed, staring eyes and grabs my hand.

– Thank you doctor, thank you, thank you! He speaks perfect English.

– Can you tell me what the problem is? I can see how upset you are.

– Yes, yes, yes… because of the smells. I can smell blood doctor, I smell it on people, and I see it. I see terrible things…and the smell.… He looks up across the room to middle distance. *It's terrible… dead bodies.*

As we talk more, he gives me fragments about his symptoms and how they affect him: visions, nightmares and pictures in front of him, particularly staring eyes and the smell of blood and how, when these things happen, he gets a choking feeling and a pain in his chest. He is afraid all the time. *I remember being in the woods and it is like I am there now. I feel people touching me.* He clutches at my sleeve and stares across the room again. Tom tells me this has all got worse in the last few days with the pending eviction. And, Wasim was mugged a few days ago.

– I asked them, why are you doing this? I am not hurting you; I have nothing…I don't want to go to the hospital, Doctor!

He has already been hospitalised in two other European countries, and he would rather kill himself than have it happen again.

– They beat me doctor, they beat me and tied me, and I felt so sick.

He talks of running away. It is obvious to us all that if he does so in his current state, he will end up restrained and drugged in a hospital again. He pulls a wad of papers from his pocket, formulations from previous doctors that, unsurprisingly, say chronic PTSD. The MSF psychiatrist has put him on a strong prescription that makes sense to me given his extreme agitation, and the instability and uncertainty of the next few days. He has not taken any of the prescribed tablets yet, so I suggest he does take the prescribed Risperidone—a major tranquilliser—to help him calm down.

– Am I crazy doctor?

– Definitely not. You are not crazy, but I do think in your past, you have had some very bad experiences, and the stress has affected you so that sometimes it feels as if you are back in the past, and that's very frightening. And the stress of the camp at the moment is not helping. So, we have to help remind you that you are here with us and quite safe. We are looking after you, and a good night's sleep will help you and then we will talk again tomorrow morning.

We arrange between us to check on him every hour, although volunteers cannot stay overnight, so I hope he will soon be asleep.

I spend the early evening giving out information leaflets. Sarah and Rowan now run 'The Refugee Information Bus' from a converted horse trailer and have been printing them off in multiple languages. Ali tells me he is going to register on Monday and move into the containers. I tell him I think this is a safer option than trying the lorries, and if nothing else, he gets a dry bed, food and a chance to discuss what his options are. I am relieved to find my car intact by the highway when I head for home.

The Jungle, Saturday 22 October

Wasim is transformed by a good night's sleep. He is sitting up, dressed, hair combed, refreshed looking and smiling. The staring looks have completely disappeared. Eloise, another volunteer who has been helping, asks if he will come and join the cricket game in the afternoon.

– *Definitely.*

– *Did you play cricket in Afghanistan?* I ask.

– *Cricket? I love cricket, I played in my village.* Wasim smiles. *Those were good years. But it all changed.*

Eloise and I remain silent, and without any prompting, Wasim starts to tell us about his life—his job as a mechanic, looking after his parents, his wife and children. But when the Taliban came, the whole village refused to join them and they attacked the community, and so many people were killed. He describes finding a friend's body and twists and contorts his body in his chair as he does so. I see the fear and agitation return. He is back there.

– *Wasim,* I say quietly, *you are here with us now. It is over. You are safe here now.* He looks at me, bewildered and distraught.

– *I am going to show you some tricks to do when you feel like this.* Sitting there in the dusty empty shop on uncomfortable chairs, we do breathing and relaxation until the agitation has subsided. Wasim promises to practice, and we promise to come back for cricket.

Eloise is on 'the vulnerabilities team' and wants me to check on other people she is worried about. One is a man with severe sciatica and stress. Another is depressed and on a toxic mixture of medications, because, like so many, he has been seeing lots of doctors but not telling them what he has been previously prescribed—an unfinished course of antibiotics, two different sleeping tablets that should not be taken together, a strong antidepressant which he takes *now and then*, and four different kinds of painkillers. I try to sort this out by confiscating most of them and leaving him with the simple, logical prescription from MSF. Then, another volunteer asks me to see a man who is also depressed and anxious, suffering frequent panic attacks and who is slightly suspicious and paranoid. He has not been assessed by any doctor and therefore has no kind of vulnerability certificate. This means he will just end up in the general scrum of young men on Monday, which is likely to exacerbate all of his symptoms, unless someone takes him to MSF first. I will need to find someone to do that, as neither Eloise nor I have access to the camp on Monday.

In the evening, I sit with other volunteers on the bank below the fenced off motorway, watching migrants and volunteers play cricket. The sun lights up the match, the top of St. Michaels Church, and the roofs of all the shelters in the camp beyond the embankment.

Then I take Solomon to buy petrol for the Church generator, and beer for his friends.

– What will you do with the Church? Will you keep the paintings? They are so beautiful.

– It will all be burnt. Give it back to God.

As for himself, he has no idea what he is going to do. He has a wife in the UK but does not know where she is. After Sunday, it feels as if he is stepping into a void.

– What have I been doing for the last year?

– Holding a community together, keeping it safe and peaceful, helping people stay sane, helping people express their faith. There are so many people who would not have survived here without you Solomon. You were needed here.

– And now?

I don't know what to say. Telling him I would welcome such an extraordinary man in my own home is not enough when I have no means to help him get there.

Calais is overflowing with policemen, journalists, government officials and volunteers (new, old and returning). I bump into Mary outside the packed family pub in the old town. She says she's going to a party at the Kids Café back in camp, so we head back along with Miguel, a photographer from Colombia, who got all the children to photograph their lives last year.

The Kids Café is packed as well. It is an offshoot of Jungle Books and provides free food, a pool table, and plenty of space to hang out. Some of the boys want to discuss their options. I explain what I have learned already: the process is straightforward for young people because after they have registered at the warehouse place and gotten their wristbands, they will all be brought back to live in the containers. They won't be dispersed across France.

– *But then what?* They all ask, and the trouble is, it's not clear. The British government is supposedly finally getting its act together over those who have family in the UK, albeit too late and too slow, and I have already walked a couple of boys around to the containers where UNHCR has been registering them. But what happens to young people like 14-year-old orphan Ali, who have no family there or anywhere else? Or Afzar who is twelve and almost blind and who stands beside me in the café in a too big white jacket, smiling and smiling? The Dubs Amendment,[11] which has been stuck in a bureaucratic swamp these last months, remains opaque as to exactly which children are vulnerable enough to be considered eligible to come to Britain.

The matter is not helped by different charities in the camp having different approaches to assessing the children's needs and vulnerabilities. I spent part of one morning with a group of social workers doing assessments for a firm of lawyers who are campaigning to make the Home Office accept its responsibilities under the Dub's amendment. The social workers make it very clear to the children that the assessment in no way guarantees that they will be going to the UK, but it could help in advocacy. The children understand this, but even so, other agencies and groups of volunteers insist that these assessments are raising false hopes and should not be carried out. Some volunteers complain that there are too many groups making lists, and it is confusing. Personally, it seems to me that duplicate lists and registrations are better than not being registered at all, given how easily children get lost. But I have stayed out of the argument. The vulnerable adults take up enough time, and as usual, no one is batting for them.

I do tell the young people talking to me in the café that I think going through the formal camp eviction and registration process and then staying in the containers is a good idea—much better than running away, or risking their lives jumping on trains and lorries. If they are living there all together, then they are getting food, clothes and a dry bed, while those advocating on their behalf know where they are, which makes it much easier to act.

While we are talking, a row erupts. One young man is playing a guitar. Another comes over, grabs it from him and hurls it to the floor. He is angry because he thinks the music disturbs another young man who is kneeling to pray in the corner. Although, the praying young man appears unbothered. I pick up the instrument and place it against a wall, then carry on talking to a Somali boy. Jamal tells me he has tried lorries and trains nearly one hundred times in the last year but had to stop because he injured his leg. So, he has no choice; he is definitely registering and staying in the containers. He actually has an aunt in the UK, she lives in Tottenham but does not answer the number he calls, so he does not know what to do.

Another crashing sound, another boy has taken the guitar and jumped on the back, smashing it. *A pity*—Miguel the photographer says stroking it gently. *It was a good guitar.*

We have to leave, as it's getting late. Walking under the graffiti-covered motorway bridge we come across a woman, four children, and a man, all pulling heavy cases along the highway towards the camp. They have just arrived here from Damascus in Syria, via Morocco, Spain, and France. The man says he is a Palestinian. He met the family on the way and has helped them, because the husband is dead. The youngest little girl is six. She's wearing a pink jacket, has neatly brushed hair, and has a rucksack with a picture of Winnie the Pooh.

Mary starts making phone calls, and we turn around and head back to the camp, helping with the luggage. Three policemen get out of their vehicle and come to meet us. Luckily, the Syrians speak French, but even so, a helmeted policeman in riot gear wants to make a full inspection. His colleagues look awkward and embarrassed as the officer insists on raking through every item of clothing in the stuffed cases. At one point, the mother awkwardly holds a bundle of brassieres. He insists that she shake them out and checks each cup with his hand. Meanwhile, one of the embarrassed policemen points at the Winnie the Pooh bag, which I am holding. I pull out a Barbie doll, a kangaroo, a book and an obviously empty smaller bag. *Open that!* says helmeted policeman. I do. Meanwhile, I have been taking surreptitious photos of the search process on my phone.

– *Are you filming?* Helmet guy yells at me.

– *Absolutely not*—I say—*just finding a number.* I slap the phone to my ear and pretend to be listening. To my surprise he does not check. Mary has found them a caravan. Simon is going to give them his and share with a friend. We walk them in, carrying their bags, and promise to take them to the Women and Children's Centre in the morning. I want to ask why they came here now? What do they hope for? As French speakers, they might want asylum in France, and at this moment, this might be the fastest, simplest way. The pending eviction, combined with the promise of accommodation, is possibly acting as a draw. Some people are coming to the Jungle in order to be given accommodation…

The Jungle, Sunday 23 October

The ratio of journalists to Jungle residents appears to be one to one. It's a cold, clear, sunny morning. I have come in early to help the Syrians move to La Vie Actif, which still houses women and children. There are small clusters of press with tripods and cameras on every corner.

Then I sit in the sun outside the Kids Café and my phone is stolen, pulled directly out of my hand as I am making a call. The thief bolts into the Café, out the other side, and up the embankment across the wasteland, with me yelling in pursuit. I have a large crowd with me but cannot keep up. I am distraught, as it has all the numbers from the people I saw yesterday and want to keep track of, not to mention my last pictures of the camp.

– *Don't worry*—a man says to me making a soothing gesture—*we will solve it for you.*

I spend most of the rest of the day trying to connect volunteers who have the magic passes to come on the site with the vulnerable men I met yesterday. I know Tariq, the paranoid man, will never make it into the registration point if someone does not go with him, nor will Wasim. Johannes, a local Catholic priest, arranges for a volunteer to meet Tariq at 10am tomorrow.

Jamal bumps into me on his way to collect his supper and insists on sharing it with me. While we are eating, he tells me how all his friends were being forced into Al Shabab in Somalia, and if you did not want that, you had to leave.

— *One of my friends was forced into a black car and I have never seen him since. They call you on the phone and tell you to fight for your religion and if you say 'no, that is bad Islam,' they say 'we will kill you.' So I left. In 2014, I went to Dolo Ado* (a refugee camp in Ethiopia).

He spent nine months in the camp. But there was nothing there for him, and when some people offered him the chance to leave, he took it. Jamal then described a nightmare journey involving being crushed with fifty others on a truck. At one point, the truck drove so fast to avoid an ambush, his friend could not hold on and fell off and died. There was another crowded car, which broke down, then a five-day trek across the desert, during which they drank water mixed with petrol. Then he was imprisoned by an Egyptian boss man, who made them work on his farm until they had earned the money to pay for the boat ride.

— *Sometimes he made us work, sometimes he beat you like an animal. It was a game for him.*

Friends helped him get out by collecting money and he crossed to Italy. He made his way north, hiding in the toilet on the train from Italy to France because he had no money for a ticket. For the last six months, he has been trying to cross the channel every night.

— *You find a method to slow the truck, and you have three minutes to get on. But the last time, the police used tear gas and I got confused and fell over that wall between the highways. My friends took me to the hospital.*

He promises to let me know how things go the next day. I check on Wasim, sitting at the Khyber restaurant, which is packed and noisy. Not the most calming place, but he says he is alright. The incoherence of the first day has completely disappeared.

Out along the street of restaurants, groups of people are sitting around braziers fuelled by deconstructed shelters. These provide nice towers of black smoke for journalists to film, and thus, convey the completely misleading impression of the whole Jungle being on fire.

In fact, most people are just keeping warm and using the material at hand, given that it will no longer have a purpose after tomorrow. And yes, some are burning down shelters that have no use anymore.

The good news is that both my SIM card and my memory card have been found. I had sent out a message saying—*Please do keep the phone but just let me have those back*—and it worked. There is some kind of narrative symmetry to losing a phone on both my first and last days inside the Jungle.

Funny thing, I have not seen one single French government official handing out leaflets at any point today.

The Jungle, Monday 24 October

A bunch of nurses asked me to join their first aid crew just outside the perimeter, so I spent the first couple hours of the morning sitting in my car, following various sources of live news. Then, we got a message that the French were providing ambulances and fully equipped paramedic teams, so Emma, Eloise and I decided to go into town to hand out more information leaflets, water and snacks to any lost or bewildered migrants.

– *There are quite a few people around the railway station*—a volunteer tells me. *But they have cancelled all Calais-Dunkirk trains, and they have removed the bus timetable for Dunkirk from bus stops.*

I am not sure how this rather Orwellian attempt to stop migrants moving to the Dunkirk camp can be sustained for long. I am curious to see how far it extends and am just investigating a bus stop near my bed and breakfast when we bump into an Afghan man and two small boys. They just got here, he explains, he is taking them to the camp. It turns out they are two of a family of five children who arrived last night with their mother. The man had found them all at the train station and put them in a cheap hotel room last night. Now, he wants to help all of them get to the Jungle.

So, Eloise and Emma look after the boys while I run a shuttle—first driving the smallest children and their mum out to the camp and then the boys. I make friends with a French policeman called Frank who, seeing a wailing little girl in a mother's arms and two small children clutching my hands, takes pity and allows me to walk, passless, up the road to La Vie Actif where, undoubtedly, they will meet the Syrian family we took in the other night.

Hamza comes out to meet me and the children and translate. He runs one of the restaurants and is friends with many of the French government officials, and he cannot believe how unprepared they have been:

— *They did not bring enough buses!* He expostulated. *Everyone lined up and went quietly this morning, queued and everything, and then they did not have enough buses to take those they had registered to the accommodation centres! Can you believe it?*

— *They told me they did not expect so many to agree to the process on the first day. They were not prepared for people to be so cooperative! So they were not equipped. So people are registered and waiting in the warehouse to be sent somewhere and of course they are fed up and angry.*

— *Looks like everyone did a good job informing people. All those leaflets and meetings helped*—I say.

Hamza nods, but Tariq has disappeared. Hamza went to look for him first thing to remind him of his appointment with the volunteer, but he had already gone. Where?

— *What about you, how are you? What will you do?*

— *Go of course, but not yet.* He smiles.

— *Good, you are needed at the moment!*

There is a small restive crowd of young people outside the entrance to the containers. Jake, one of the youth workers, is having an argument with the man behind the glass screen. He sees me and comes over.

— *Crazy! Young people who have wristbands and have registered for the containers are coming back from the warehouse, but because they are not coming in buses, he is not letting them in. They are supposed to stay in the containers after registration.*

— *There are not enough buses. I'll find a journalist*—I say. *They are all lined up on the southern edge, bored because there are no riots and they are looking for stories.*

And I do. A nice man with red hair from a French TV station listens to the story I tell and says he will go at once and ask the man at the container gate why he won't let the young people in—good. Nothing like the power of the press for confronting obstinate bureaucrats. – *It's deliberate*—a volunteer tells me, listening in. *They deliberately brought in too few buses and lots and lots of CRS, because they want to provoke people so that they have the justification to get heavy.*

Personally, I tend to favour cock-up over conspiracy, but I cannot wait to see what happens, as I have to catch my train home to go back to work.

– *You will be back*—Benoit says when I bid him goodbye. *Remember Sangatte?*

Cornwall, Tuesday 1 November

In the end, they cleared the site in three days. Wasim rang me on Sunday, he is in Rouen. They tried to hospitalise him, but he persuaded them not to, and Eloise is going to visit today. Another of our patients is comfortable in Dunkirk. But Tariq still has not been found.

Nothing has been solved. Migrant tents have increased in Paris, in spite of regular clearances by police. The containers housing 1500 young people and children are totally inadequate. Apparently, there is no running water, inadequate food, no activities, no structure or care of any kind. Meanwhile the French and British governments argue over who is responsible, and they refuse access to volunteers who want to help. Other children still sleep in the ruins of the Jungle in far more danger than they were before, when some kind of community existed.

One of the volunteer kitchens put out a statement on social media: "The idea that these children are being adequately provided for, simply because they (or at least most of them) have received accommodation, is false. They have, once again, lost their communities and homes and social spaces and schools. They have been given misinformation, and are currently without adequate care, many without any idea what will happen to them next. They are now without the accountability and guidance provided by older community members and are perhaps more vulnerable than ever. There is so much frustration and uncertainty and boredom. This leads to tension and fighting. The only consistent adult presences provided by the state are the CRS (the French riot police) and the CAP security. This cannot be."

I am completely furious with myself for trying to convince young people that the containers would be a good place for them to go. It is clearly not. Finally, I get Jamal on the phone. He is just queuing for lunch. *Not enough food and not enough water*—he says. *But don't worry, I am fine.* He sounds really upbeat. Apparently, he is getting a bus to another accommodation centre in France tomorrow:

– *Do you know where you are going?*

– *I have no idea.*

Sadiq's Story

Sadiq comes from Somalia. At the time he told this story (November 2016) he was sixteen years old and lived in Syracuse, Sicily, Italy.

I come from a small village in Somalia, near the Somali border. I lived with my mother and father and my brothers and sisters. I am in the middle. We all lived together in a typical Somali house, like those in your pictures. I went to school when I was very little, five years old. Before the fighting came and I left, Father worked collecting food from a warehouse and selling it at the market. My mother was at home.

The fighting started when I was seven years old, with two groups fighting in the street with guns. Two villages were fighting with one another. There was fighting all over Father's workplace because there was a lot of food there. Our house was bombed, so we had to leave the house and go to another place. When the fighting started, two of my brothers ran away, and no one has seen them since. We don't know where they are. My father, mother, sisters and I went to another village. But every day there was fighting, and my father was killed—I think he was in his workplace. And because there was fighting, I had to run. I was very small, I was running but I did not know where to go, so I followed some people and I got to Jijiga in Ethiopia.

But when I reach there I don't know where to eat or sleep, so I just find somewhere on the street. People give me food. And after a month some people say they want shoe cleaning. So I see one man with a car and I say I want to help, and the man says OK and gives me some water and I clean his car, and he gives me some money and I go to a shop and buy some stuff to clean shoes.

When people have seen what I have seen, it makes you older than your age. Because I was small and I did not have a mother or a father, I had to be my own mother and father. There were people who helped me and gave me food, and I did find things by myself.

I worked things out. I woke up at six. People gave me breakfast—Somali people—whatever there was. I went to the market and found people who could help me. So, every day, I was in the market cleaning shoes and cleaning cars all day. I slept on the street for almost one year; every day I found a new place to sleep.

Then when I was eight, I got sick. I found a way to call my mother. In the New Year at that time, I found a place to sleep with four other Somali people and paid money to sleep there. And I found a woman who made coffee, and I helped her. I cleaned everything and that woman gave me money for that; and I cleaned shoes, and I cleaned cars, and I kept all the money from cleaning. I saved as much as I could and only used a little for the food and the house. I did this for another year until I was nine years old.

After that, I took that money. I could buy clothes and I took a house alone. I don't have a father or a mother, so I have to think about life. I worked in this same work for another year. When I was ten years old, my aunty came. She came to greet me and asked me what I was doing. I told her I had a house and work, and she came to my house that night. I asked about my mother and she told me she was good.

— But your two brothers, no one knows what happened to them. Your house and everything in the village has gone. There is nothing left. Your mother and sister are living in another village and staying with other people.

At that time, I could not do anything for them. I am thinking, what to do? Then three boys came from Somalia to Jijiga. They wanted to go to Europe. I told them—*Wait here, do like me, find work here.*

I help them. I show them how to work like me and I let them live in my house. I don't ask them for money because I know what it's like for them. If I had more, I would give it to them. At that time, I have three jobs, so I share the work with them so they can see how to do it. I am happy to help them. One was sixteen, one fifteen and the other ten years old. My aunty cooks for us and lives with us in the house. She cleans it and we help her. I don't play. I am not thinking about play, I am just thinking about how to work and find food. I forget how to play.

That woman I worked for, she trusted me, and so I was given another job in the market. I packed tea, coffee, and spices into plastic bags and hung them up for sale in the market. It was the same with chilis and peppers. You pack it up and hang it, and people buy it. So, I helped the woman with her market stall. Then she put me in another market and opened a restaurant, and I worked there cutting vegetables and cleaning up after people left. I got up early to clean and get it ready. I worked there for a long time—two years.

When I was twelve years old, she took me to the big supermarket, and I arranged things for her. Those boys did my other jobs. But, in my last five months in Jijiga, my mother called me. There were many problems with Al Shabab people. Everyone knew what was going on, everyone told one another. For example, one of my cousins killed another man, so another came and said—*I saw you kill this man in my family.* So, then people are killing each other, and there is more and more fighting, and my mother calls me and says—*They want to kill you. They are trying to find you.* Because we all know each other. Because I am in that family which killed a man. And the people looking for me are from one of these groups killing each other. So, I stopped work. I thought, what shall I do? I didn't go outside. I stayed at home. I went out sometimes, but only for a very short time because I was afraid they would find me. And if Al Shabab found me, they would also kill me. They say—*If you don't work with us, we will kill you.*

It's not just Al Shabab, there are many groups. So, I stayed like that at home, thinking what to do. I told my friends what was happening and that I didn't know what to do. So they said—*OK, we are going to Europe together.* They helped me because I helped them in the past. I had some money because I had given my aunty what I earned and she kept it for me. And my friends were working, so they paid for me, no problem. We went to Harar and slept there one night, and then we got a car to Addis Ababa.

I had been seven years without my mother and sisters. I called my mother and told her I was in Addis. She prayed for me and she told me—*God help you, I am not happy that you go from me, but it's better for you.* I told her—*Don't worry, just pray for me.*

I stayed in Addis with friends, and we left at night on a bus to Gondar, where we stayed one day. We found some people to help us because we did not want the police to see us and catch us. We slept there, woke early, and asked where the bus was to Metema, on the Sudan-Ethiopia border. When we got there, we got out of the bus and walked into Sudan, because if we went in a car, the police would catch us. We slept there one night and found a car to some place before Khartoum. We walked for four days and then we asked how far it was to Khartoum and they told us eighty kilometres, too far to walk. So, we found some good people who took us. They asked us—*Where are you from?* We told them we are Somali.

We got to Khartoum and stayed there three nights, in some empty house where no one lived. Then we found a Sudanese man and told him—*We are going to Libya.* He asked—*Are you Somali?* When we said yes, he said—*I will help you, but there is fighting in Libya. I am going in a car close to Libya.* The Sudanese man and a Libyan man worked together. The Sudanese man asked the Libyan man to help us. He said—*They come from a country with fighting and many problems.* The Libyan man said—*OK, I can help you, but in Libya I cannot do anything.* We said—*No problem, just take us*—and like that, we reached Libya. It took one week through the Sahara.

We stayed one month in many empty houses. Arab people helped us, and afterwards, we found where the capital was because we did not know where we were or where we were going. We found a car and asked them to help. He said—*I will take you to Sabratha, not Tripoli.* We said—*fine*—and he took us there and we stayed two nights and then we found another man who asked us—*Where are you going?* We told him—*We want to go to Europe*—and he said—*Fine.* But he kidnapped us. He took us to a house with forty people staying there. That man wanted money from me and my friends. We told him—*We don't have money. We don't have any people to send money.* And he said—*If you don't have money, I will kill you.* So, we told him—*We don't have money, so kill us.* I was there eight months. It was all Somalis—forty people. The Arab man said—*This country is my country. Why did you leave your country? I can do what I like with you, so give me four hundred dollars.* I said again—*I don't have it, so what can I do, so if you want to kill me, kill me.*

They brought us food in the morning. Not food—bread and water. Then they did not come again until evening. We did not have a place to go to the toilet, nowhere to shit, nothing. It was like a prison. This man had one phone. He said—*call your family to send money.* And then they start beating you, so your family knows it is going badly. But I had no one, I did not have a number, so I never called anyone. They beat me for a year, and I never called anyone. They were always putting pressure on me. I did have one number and I called, but they never sent money to me. And after I called, I thought my life was ending and I would escape this room. I told these people—*My life is over.* And then the conditions changed, and we only got bread and water once a day. I kept calling the woman, and she found my mother and I talked to my mother. So, my mother went to the city to beg for money. She begged and she was weeping, saying—*My son is dying in Libya.* She got a small amount and sent it to me.

Then they threw me out, because they were worried I might die in Libya, because I was very sick. They took me to the seaside, to some people with a boat. They said—*We don't want this dead boy in Libya. We don't want this boy dying here.* So, they got me on a boat. The boat man called his boss saying—*One Somali boy is going to die today or tomorrow.* And the boss says—*If he is going to die today or tomorrow, throw him on the boat. He can die at sea.* I stood on the boat for two days. There was no room to sit. There was no food, so I did not want to shit or pee. God is wonderful.

Two of those boys came to Europe. One ran away. He is in Libya. We left him there, because we lost touch.

It is two years since I left Jijiga. I spent one year in Libya and I have been in Italy for eight months. I have seen many bad things since I was little. I would like to be a mechanical engineer or a doctor. Then I can go and help people in Somalia.

Before I arrived here, I didn't think I would stay in Italy. I didn't want to stay. Now I am staying because I was sick. They took me to the hospital, and then I was put here, so now I am going to school and it is OK. I have peace here... but later... I think all the time about how to help my family. Everything is not as it appears to you. I look OK, but I am not. I have a house, food, somewhere to sleep, but my family doesn't have food to eat, and if I go to Switzerland or Germany, I can send money. I can do something if I go to Germany. One of my friends is in Germany. They give him 300 euros, and he goes to school, and he can send money to his family. If someone is a refugee here, they only give a small amount. That is why I think about leaving.

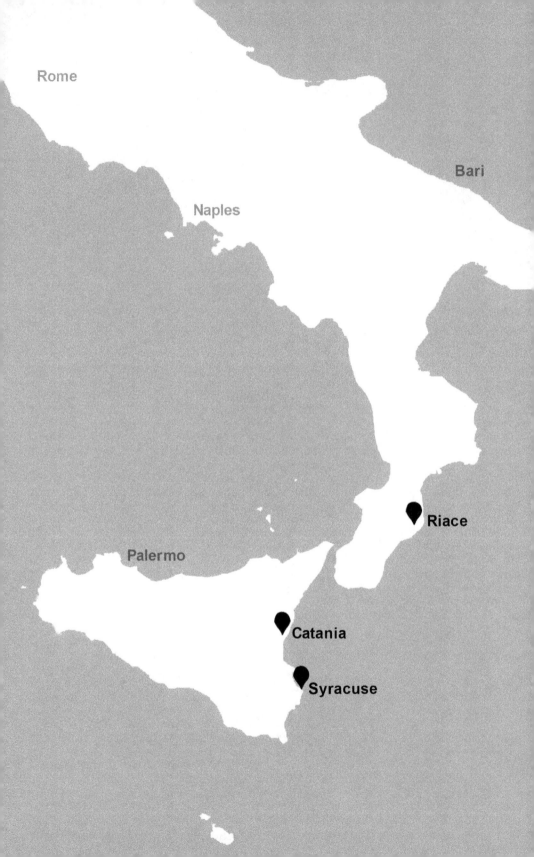

Sicily and Calabria

Italy, November 2016

Syracuse, Sicily, Tuesday 8 November

Sadiq cannot believe I have pictures of Jijiga on my computer. He stares at the photos of the dusty town in Eastern Ethiopia.

– *A tuk tuk*—he cries delightedly at the sight of the small three-wheelers that we used for public transport …*the water!* It seems we both loved the reservoir outside the town… *I think I know this man! Look, this is how we build houses!*

He wants his friends Mohammed from Ghana and Fazil from Egypt to see everything. Sadiq is from a small village in Eastern Somalia. We have worked out that we must have been in Jijiga at the same time, when I was working in the neighbouring refugee camp. Now he is living in this small children's home in Syracuse in Sicily with eleven other migrant children, aged between twelve and eighteen. Sadiq has just finished school for the morning and eaten lunch. We are sitting in the dining room. Mohammed volunteers to translate while Sadiq tells me his story in Arabic. It is both heart-breaking and extraordinary. And when he reaches the part where he tells me about trying to phone his mother from the prison in Libya, Sadiq is crying, and Mohammed is crying, saying he never heard this story before. I tell Sadiq there is no need to continue, but he insists, he wants to tell the whole thing. With tears running down his face, he mimes his mother holding out her apron—a mother he has not seen for eight years. I am crying as well now.

We take a break at the point where he gets to Italy. I promise I will hear more over the next few days, but I want to take the three boys out for pizza. Fazil leads us across the old town of Ortygia. He has a particular destination in mind, and, as we walk through the narrow, medieval streets, past the sculpted mermaids holding babies and riding fish on the fountain in Piazza Archimedes, Mohammed tells me he has never been happier. He left Ghana when he was thirteen.

– *I cannot tell you why because it will make me cry.*

Somali woman constructing
home in refugee camp.
Jijiga, Ethiopia 2008

Mohammed had no plan to come to Europe and had worked and lived happily in Libya for a year. But then, like Sadiq he was imprisoned. He managed to escape after six months and then got picked up in the street by some other men who forced him onto a boat. *They said 'Get in the car' They took me to the sea. There were a lot of black people being beaten and put on boats, and they said to me 'If you don't go, we will kill you.'*

He is now seventeen, has been here a year, and has a place to study. He plays football and is training with a local team. *There are no big problems here. We are all human beings, all minds are different. I came with a lot of friends, but they all went to Germany and France. I call them. They don't have documents. I say I will be patient and sit here. Now I have a document.* He shows me his card showing he has humanitarian permission to stay. *What I really love in Italy is the people. They don't fight with Muslims. They don't insult us. There is a Mosque in Syracuse. They respect us.*

We order pizza, and they want one with lots of meat. When it comes, it is covered with prosciutto, which I have stupidly forgotten is pork! *I can't eat this*—Sadiq looks distressed. *Don't worry*—I say handing the whole thing to a delighted group of passing tourists and buying another.

Then the boys take me to church. This is the reason the boys have walked me across Ortygia. They want me to meet Ramzi Harrabi, a Tunisian artist who has an exhibition there. Ramzi migrated here alone legally fifteen years ago. He and two fellow artists, Elizabeth Atkinson and Salvatore Accola, have created an exhibit called 'Uprooted,' inspired by the migrant crisis. There are also paintings by young migrants, like 16-year-old James Vin Brown from Guinea:

– *I lived this. Four days at sea. I was painting in Guinea. I always wanted to do this.*

Ramzi had started a workshop, encouraging the children to paint. *Ramzi is a father to us*—Mohammed tells me. *He always wants to help us.*

After the boys head home, I go home to bed and read John Julius Norwich's 'History of Sicily.' I am still immersed in Greeks and Carthaginians. It gives me a sense of perspective. Thank goodness we no longer live in an age where democracies willingly hand themselves back into the hands of tyrants, I think to myself, or where neighbouring superpowers, when asked to intervene to save some oppressed city-state from subjugation, never stay on uninvited to massacre and pillage. I fall asleep.

Syracuse, Wednesday 9 November

I wake early and turn on the World Service and turn it off again. Perhaps this is a bad dream, and when I wake up the next time, things will be different. Unfortunately not, Trump has been elected as President of the United States. Nothing to be done. My Italian friends seem remarkably sanguine, but then again, they have lived through Berlusconi.

Not all the migrant youths I meet are as happy as Mohammed. The association that runs Sadiq's home, also runs another in a neighbouring town, and the boys there have been making a protest. Cristina, who is a cultural mediator and works there, takes me with her for her morning shift. It's a similar set up—friendly apartment with shared bedrooms for twelve boys, but when we arrive, most of them are sitting on the sofas around the unwatched TV in the communal living room, looking bored and disconsolate. Cristina is briefed by the night shift staff while I sit and listen to two Gambian boys:

– *These people don't give us food. They don't give us money. We don't have documents here. They say, 'We are trying, we are trying,' but I am here five months and still no documents. No one has documents, this camp is no good.*

– *I think the association is having a problem with getting the money they are owed by the government*—I say.

– *The problem is not the government; it is the people here. They collect money and don't give it to us.*

In fact, the main problem for a migrant child arriving in Italy is trying to understand the system taking care of them. I have had it explained to me in detail four or five times, and I still have not fully grasped the Kafkaesque series of bureaucratic steps through which a

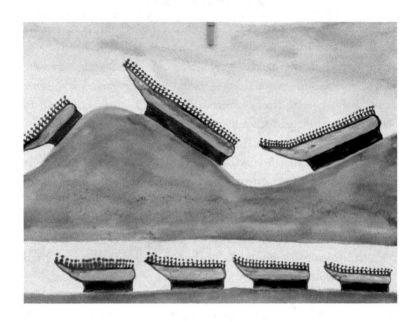

Picture by James Vin Brown
Age 16, from Guinea

migrant child has to pass in order to stay in this country, or the various arrangements that are made to look after you.

It starts when you get off the boat—the one that rescued you from the rubber death-trap in which you just spent two to three terrifying days after reluctantly boarding in Libya. I say reluctantly because Mohammed is not the only boy I have interviewed who told me they were forced at gunpoint; others, who paid large sums of money but had second thoughts when they saw the state of the vessel, were beaten or threatened. So, you arrive in a port like Augusta/Port Salo and you will be put in an emergency camp—a big tent with around 700 people. If you are over fourteen, you get fingerprinted there. It is fenced and policed and crowded, but some children do run away. You are only supposed to stay there for a few days, but it can be as long as a month. Then you get moved to a 'first stage shelter.'

– *And the dispersal process is chaotic*—Roberta, a psychologist with Terre des Hommes, who works with unaccompanied minors in the Ports, tells me. *Two Bangladeshi boys, who were related and among the very few Bangladeshis coming to Sicily at the moment, were sent to quite separate shelters.*

The maximum stay in these shelters is supposed to be three months, but the reality is between six and sixteen months because so many are arriving. You may be living with 175 others. Your basic needs are met but nothing else. There is no education or assistance in planning your life. You should then get moved to a more permanent centre run by SPRA, the Italian government system for the protection of refugees and asylum seekers. If you are lucky, it will be a family-type place like the ones I have visited, with a psychologist and cultural mediator providing support, school for those under sixteen, and Italian and cultural integration classes for the older boys.

At some point in this process, an unaccompanied child gets a legal guardian appointed to them. This used to be a local magistrate, lawyer or social worker, who could sometimes be responsible for around one hundred children without knowing much about them. But various civil society groups realised that the lack of sufficient guardians was keeping children trapped in the emergency and first-stage shelters.

— I was visiting the ports in 2013 and I asked why so many young people were stuck in the big entry camps and was told it was because there were not enough guardians. Or, children were sort of ghosts on lists and no one actually cared about them.

This, from Simona who I met providing legal assistance and information to migrants on her night off in Syracuse. She and others founded Accoglierete, an association to train more guardians and personalise the care for migrant children.

— There are now 150 of us. It's not an easy job because these guys are in a difficult place. There are not enough places for them. They spend too long in the first-stage centres and many of the secondary camps are not so good.

One of the main tasks for the guardian is to understand what the migrant child wants—*their history and life projects*—as Simona puts it—and then to help the minors get their documents. In Italy, all minors are entitled to humanitarian protection until they are eighteen and they get an underage residence permit. But, by eighteen if you were fleeing war, persecution, or discrimination, you should have applied for asylum. To do this, you must go in front of a commission and must have a guardian. Or, if you don't have grounds for asylum, you must show that you are integrated through work or education. Then, you may get humanitarian protection.

My Gambian friend applied for asylum but was turned down. But, because he is under-age, he still has the right to stay as a vulnerable person, so he is appealing. The trouble is, at seventeen, he is running out of time. He has already spent a year doing nothing in a horrible first-stage camp; he does not know what's going to happen, and he is bored. No wonder he is protesting.

— They have free WIFI, they can call home, they have pocket money. There is respect for religion, and they can go to Mosque or cook their own food. They are free to go out but have to be back by midnight. They have school. In the community, they have such good chances. But sometimes, they just cannot see beyond their own perspective—Cristina says.

In theory, the association gets 40 euros per child to cover all running costs for their care. This money is from the EU but should come from the local authority. Each child should be paid 1.50 euros a day for pocket money. Unfortunately, the local authorities have not paid the association for months. Not just here, it is a problem affecting second level communities all over Italy. At first, the association was simply advancing the money, but now, they have run out of funds themselves. Cristina goes over all this again with the Gambian boy, and this time, he appears to accept it. She tells him they are exploring possibilities of paid internships with a stonemason—this gets his interest.

Work, and acquiring the skills to do it, is the major concern. The other night, I sat with three young migrants waiting to see Simona. They have been here legally for five or six years, but none of them have permanent jobs. Two were doing irregular agricultural work around Rome. One showed me a video of himself picking vegetables on his mobile phone. They lived in cramped, shared flats, while the third was sleeping on the streets.

Last year, the association found internships in local restaurants for some of the children. The young people got work experience, and four of the five who did the internships went onto proper jobs. Ramzi thinks the internships are a form of exploitation. *Project coordinators are paid proper salaries of 4000 euros a month, but child migrants only get 400 euros a month for eight hours of work per day. The restaurants get free labour. This is pure slavery. Why not use the funds to start a restaurant run by migrants?*

In the afternoon, I wander through the old town, and in a dark church, I stumble across 'The Burial of Saint Lucy.' Who needs cinema when you have Caravaggio? I am transfixed. Not just by the mastery of the painting. The massive gravediggers, the frail, floodlit, blinded saint with her hand dropping into the grave, the misery of the crowd, the darkness around them, and the light about to be buried, it seems so appropriate to the times.

Catania, Thursday 10 November

At least if you are under eighteen there is something for you. If you are an adult man and not in some way classified as vulnerable, your only choice is to apply for asylum. If your application is refused, you will get an expulsion letter which tells you to leave in seven days, including where from: e.g. Rome Airport, at your own expense. You can imagine how many migrants actually do this. If you are found, you get another paper, or you might get sent to an expulsion centre, but they are currently full, or you can appeal within thirty days, provided you have identified a pro bono lawyer to help you. Did I already mention Kafka?

I learn all this from Andreas, sitting on a bench, looking over railway tracks to the sea, outside Catania Railway Station, where he is running the Open Europe project for Oxfam, reaching out to the most marginalised. A number of the migrants around the station have the backpacks he hands out. They contain underwear, hygiene kits, and shoes. The winter ones will have blankets.

– The biggest need is information. I am meeting more and more migrants who have been arrested for alleged smuggling, because they were 'driving the boats,' so they get sent to jail which makes appeal impossible, unless they can prove they were not smuggling. But lawyers at jail get a reputation for getting people out by plea-bargaining. The migrants don't realise they should never plea-bargain and should always fight the charges because they will NEVER get protection with a criminal charge. Their only option is to go to trial and prove their innocence. But, it's a big risk because, if you lose, you could get a long sentence. Most of these guys were forced to drive the boat. Like this man.

Andreas introduces me to a tall young man from Senegal who was arrested for being a 'captain' and plans to appeal against his expulsion. Oxfam connected him with legal assistance, but they don't provide shelter or material support, and the municipal shelter closed recently. So, like many, he is sleeping in the station. And the whole process is incredibly slow. Andreas took some people to the office in September, and their next appointments are in February.

– It's difficult for West Africans to get international protection. Applying is a way to stay legally because the system is so slow that you have time to learn Italian and try to get integrated—then, you may get humanitarian protection. Some people do ask for voluntary repatriation. But if they have a criminal conviction, IOM cannot help. So we tell them they are

not wanted, but do not help them take the obvious route home. So they have to disappear.

Andreas has to leave, but I wander past the fountain and through the bus station to join the disappeared. Caritas provides dinner and breakfast. This is the route out of Sicily, so it is busy. There was a crowd of young Eritreans, but they do not want to talk beyond telling me they are heading to Germany.

– So many minors want to get out, the Eritreans particularly—Andreas says. *The EU's restrictive policies of closing the borders, with no alternative solutions, is just reinforcing the criminal networks. Those with good links manage to go where they want.*

It is not just migrants in the jostling queue waiting for Caritas to open its dining room. There are elderly Italians, men and women, and a mother and baby. Besides the Eritreans and the Senegalese, there are Gambians and Nigerians. I talk to a Somali man who has slept on the street for the last four years without papers, always being told to leave, never getting permission to stay. Then the door opens and we all queue to enter a big dining room. I too am offered a steaming bowl of pasta.

I don't stay too late. I have to drive back to Syracuse in the dark, and I am filled with gloom. Nothing is going to get easier. The numbers coming in continue to grow. Last week, more than 3000 migrants arrived in Italy, some 500 more than the previous week. The total arriving in Italy by October of this year was already 155,000, matching the total for the entirety of 2015. Almost 25,000 of those were children and 91% of those were unaccompanied. Prime Minister Renzi has repeatedly complained that Italy can no longer cope. The arrival of winter weather does not seem to be slowing things down. On Monday this week, Roberta had to run off and meet another 800 who had just arrived in Port Augusta.

When I am not actually listening to children, I remember that a dangerous buffoon has just been elected to run the world's most powerful democracy—one who has not noticed that the ice caps are melting and deserts are expanding, pushing more and more people into war, starvation, and yes, flight. His answer to people moving in search of a better life is to build more walls and allow more guns, and this is an infectious idea. I wish Trump could meet Lami who I met this morning. He has never been to school, but he learned to be a carpenter and worked his way across four countries at fourteen years old.

– In Gambia, there are no rights because the government is too nasty. I am Madinka. The President is Jola, and Jola and Madinkas don't have a good relationship. So, it's difficult for Madinkas to have a job in Gambia. That is why I say I need peace and a means to feed my family. I wanted to come to Italy to learn at school and have a better life and earn money to feed my sister and grandmother. I like it here, but I want to go back to Gambia—that is my home. But first, I want to learn! I want to learn more, I want to be a carpenter.

Syracuse, Friday 11 November

– It's a business! The whole thing is a corrupt business. Why do you think young people are forced onto boats? Because the Mafia wants them here. Why does the Italian Navy leave rubber boats lying around in the Mediterranean? So they can be used again! And here in Italy, who gets the contracts to look after migrants? The hotel is paid to take the boys, the police are paid to hang around. Very nice work for all of them. But the boys are trapped here doing nothing all day. It's a business!

Ramzi is ranting while driving me out to one of the first-stage centres for migrant youth. He works with the health team and is doing some research on health status for IOM. I am his assistant for the morning. He tells me he rants a lot and not to worry.

Inside, I find the familiar scene: a lot of very bored, sad, young men sitting on sofas watching daytime TV. *Actually, it's not good for us*—a Nigerian boy says. *We don't get to do what we do best. There are some Italian classes but our teacher speaks no English. There is football, and the food is OK.*

They feel suspended and trapped. They are not allowed out. And if they were, where would they go? They are miles from anywhere. He has been told that he must stay there for at least four months. I, at least, provide some variety in their day, and they are happy to answer the health questionnaires and tell me about themselves. More stories of impossible poverty, of broken, dysfunctional families, and courageous journeys. More stories of extortion and torture in Libya, of being captured, taken to the beach, and forced onto boats at gunpoint. I am speechless. I have nothing to offer, except to encourage them to be patient, having come so far.

On the way back, Ramzi wants me to join him in skulking around a moderate sized apartment block in a particular neighbourhood in Syracuse, where there were three migrant shelters. The neighbours did not want them and mounted a petition; two were closed, but this one remains open. *Because it is run by the Mafia. It has been repeatedly denounced, and there are many abuses going on in such places, but it cannot be touched.* After complaining to the press, he is now barred from entry. Our skulking reveals that, although it is supposed to be for women and children, it now has lots of young, single men staying there, along with two remaining families, which breaks all protection rules. Ramzi is plotting further denunciations.

We head to a sports store to buy shirts. Ramzi is forming a Bangla Syracuse cricket team, and the boys need clothes. Then he takes me back to Ortygia. He wants to walk me around the Arab quarter of the old city, and it is lovely. He takes me to a building that combines Muslim and Jewish elements in one graceful façade. The Jewish quarter is just next door. Afterwards, I sit drinking coffee outside the Cathedral—astonishing in its combination of ancient Greek, Norman and Italian Baroque. In every part of this ancient city, you cannot escape from the fact that its beauty arises from everyone having lived here: Greeks, Carthaginians, Normans, Arabs, Jews, French, Spanish. So what does it mean to be Sicilian?

Riace, Calabria, Tuesday 15 November

Cosimo is seven years old. He speaks fluent Italian with the local dialect, as well as some English. *My country is Italy*—he says when I ask him where he comes from. Daniel, his soft-spoken father, laughs. Cosimo was born here a year after Daniel arrived here from Ghana. Daniel spent a year in one of the centre's but now has a job doing garbage collection for the Comune, and his family has a home in the small village of Riace, in the Calabrian mountains, where almost a fifth of the population are migrants.

Riace's story is now well-known and documented: when the first Kurdish migrants arrived on the beach in Riace Marina in 1998, the local Mayor, Domenico Lucano, had the simple idea that, if he helped them, they would help revive the fortunes of his tiny hilltop village which, like so many in the area, was being abandoned by the locals fleeing in search of work. So, the mayor offered migrants accommodation in local empty flats and created projects to teach them work skills while they waited for their documentation. The village blossomed and continues to do so. Domenico Lucano, who is now number 40 in Fortune's listing of the 50 'World's Greatest Leaders,' is off to lecture at Cambridge University at the end of the month and to meet the Pope shortly after.

Domenico told me these last two facts while I bought him coffee in one of the local cafés. Unfortunately, as a consequence, he was too busy to do the promised interview today but promised to meet the following evening. Meanwhile, Daniel wanted to show me around. So, I spend a delightful evening wandering around the art shops that are part of the project, chatting to a mother of six from Somalia, who is making glass jewellery.

– *All of Africa has worked here*—Maria Irena tells me. She started the shop eight years ago. Around the corner, an Afghan woman does embroidery, and across the way, two women have just started learning weaving from Angela, whose striking applique pictures decorate every wall.

– *These pictures come out of my mind*—Angela explains. *I hear the stories, and I want to honour them and their traditional techniques.* Angela was born in Riace and remembers the village as a teenager.

– *People were leaving to look for work in Germany, Australia and Canada. The village was practically deserted; there were no children and the primary school closed. When I came home from high school in another town, there was no one to play with. Everything changed with the first boat. At the beginning, it was difficult. We had no experience with foreigners. We didn't even know where Kurdistan was. Now it's completely normal. We treat everyone as one. You don't look at colour, you see people like brothers and sisters. For me, we are all the same. I don't understand why some people say we are white, they are black, we are European, they are African. We are all the same blood, we are all one, and I think we can live as one.*

Most people in the community appear to share her opinion. There are 175 migrants living in the village at any one time, including families with babies and teenagers in a young people's centre. I spend the next three days hanging around the village and the surrounding area, and, on not one occasion, do I witness any hostility between locals and migrants.

Riace, Wednesday 16 November

– This place is very good. The people are good and nice. They see us like their own—says Betty, a Nigerian woman I meet in Mirela's Café on the main street. She ran away from Nigeria to escape a forced marriage to an elderly man who had made a loan to her family. He said—*make your grave, I am going to kill you*—so I ran away. She made a living hair plaiting in the city, and a woman spotted her and offered her a job in a hairdressing salon in Italy. Except that she discovered in Libya it was not going to be hairdressing but prostitution, and when she said she was not going, she was told she had no choice. She was 30,000 euros in debt and the woman had her beaten up by some Nigerian and Libyan boys. She was forced onto the boat. But then, the procuress got into a fight with an Arab man on the boat and was pushed into the sea and drowned. Betty escaped, spending two months in an emergency camp before coming here. Now she shares a small flat with a mother and child. *It's wonderful! I have a toilet and bathroom.*

Mirela gives us another coffee. She has allowed me to set up my office in her café. She is a migrant herself, coming here from Romania ten years ago. Her home was a village like this, but much poorer. She worked with cows for eighteen months before falling in love and marrying a local. Her children do their homework at one table while a mother from Eritrea feeds her baby at another. The mother

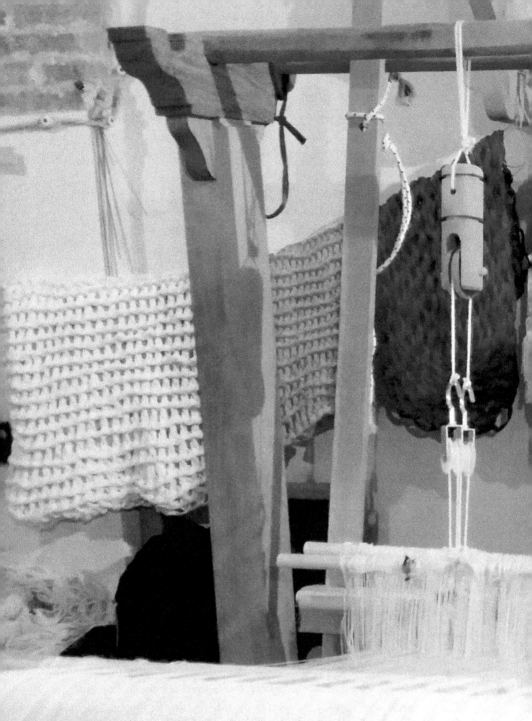

Woman learning weaving
Riace, Italy, November 2016

pays Mirela with the local paper currency that the mayor has issued. The Comune has the same problem as in Syracuse. The government has not passed on the EU funds owed to support migrants for many months. Domenico's solution is to print local money. I particularly like the picture of Nelson Mandela on one of the notes.

I sit in the main square with my new friend Stella from Ghana, who is helping me as a translator, and her landlord. We look down on the reopened school as children come out at lunch break, and down the main street with three cafés and small shops. There is striking artwork on every corner, and it is easy to see that it is not just the migrants who benefit. Her landlord, Nazarene, says he has rented to migrants for ten years and loves doing so. There have never been any problems. I watch a young Nigerian woman walk up the street, her small infant following, going home from nursery. There is a warmth and energy in the community.

— *In my daughter's class, there are thirty children, and fifteen of them are migrants*—Rosemarie tells me. Rosemarie was born in a neighbouring village, studied languages at university, came back to work as an interpreter, and now works in another project in Riace Marina. She gave me a lift up the winding mountain road this morning and accompanied me on my third attempt to meet the mayor. He has now deferred our meeting three times. On this occasion, he looks at me with despair while heading out the door:

— *Please treat me as a psychiatrist for stress, rather than as a journalist. I have no time, no time.* And he disappears, white rabbit-like, down the stairs. It does not matter. His work is infectious, and similar associations and projects have sprung up in the surrounding villages, all with the aim of housing and integrating migrants of all ages. Rosemarie's Civil Protection Association, for example, assists migrants with the entire process of documentation and education. She has just helped six students learn Italian in two months and is initiating a diploma course for adults in math, history and geography.

Not everyone is happy. I meet a West African man on the bus who has been in the project for eighteen months. His contract ends in January, and he does not know where he is going to go. *Where can I go? I have a wife and baby?*

The projects offer training for six months, and some of the most vulnerable, particularly women with children in school, are offered longer-term work. Others, like Daniel, succeed in finding local jobs. But still there are not enough opportunities for everyone and most are encouraged to move on once they have documents, to look for work elsewhere, and this is not easy. But, even if these villages in Calabria cannot solve the employment issue, by providing housing, training, and most importantly, welcoming migrants, they have addressed the more fundamental issue of hostility and fear of the other. Rosemarie is clear:

– *Life has definitely changed for the better. The boys play football together in the park and children play together. There is no fear. It's fantastic. We have many more people and the possibility to exchange ideas. Before, we knew nothing. Now, our children are citizens of the world.*

Riace, Thursday 17 November

On my last day, Stella takes me up to Stignano, another medieval mountain village two ridges across from Riace. We bump into Francesco Candia, the local mayor, in the town square. He is charming and welcoming and tells me that giving homes to migrants is a humanitarian necessity. He is from a centrist party, and on his fourth term (so his electors clearly agree). Simonetta, Stella's closest friend, insists on cooking me lunch. She takes me back to the home she has inherited from her mother: a narrow medieval building at the top of the town. While she cooks, I chat to her partner. He is from Pakistan. They have lived happily together for two years. *I am Muslim, she is Christian, it's not a problem. I go to church festivals. They are good people in this town. First you are a human—then comes religion.*

We sit around the table, eating Simonetta's delicious food. From her windows, I can see the Mediterranean in the distance, beyond the grey-green folds of hills. Around the table, we are people from three continents with far more in common than separates us. Why does it have to be complicated?

Siva's Story

Siva comes from Nigeria. She was eighteen years old when she told me this story in November 2016, while visiting friends in Riace, Calabria, Italy.

I lived with my father and mother in Nigeria. When I was eight, my father died and my mother married another man. He wanted to take advantage of me, and he treated me badly. I did not want to stay there, so when I was ten, I left there and stayed with some friends, Christian friends. At first, it was OK. We went to school, but when I was thirteen, my friend (she was older than me) started going with boys. Then, she took me to a place where there were many boys and they raped me. She took me many times, so I got pregnant. That's why I don't like making friends.

But then, I met another girl, so she told me to call my mum. So I called her and my mum told me to come home, and I gave birth to my baby there. She is called Blessing. That is because, when I was pregnant, I had an accident: while crossing the road, a car hit me, so they had to take me to the hospital. I was really bruised, but I had an ultrasound and the baby was OK. I had Blessing when I was fourteen.

But then, my stepfather decided to take my baby from me when she was four months old because I had no money. So, I went to live with another woman. She made alcohol and I helped her, and many men came to drink there. But I was not comfortable because the men were looking at me. I wanted to leave. My friend said—*Let's travel*—and I said—*I cannot travel because I have no money. How can I cope? I have no clothes, I have no means, I have no one.* But my mother decided to borrow money; she got 300,000 Nigerian dollars, and my friend said—*Don't worry, after you travel, you will meet Christian friends.*
She said—*I will take you somewhere you can meet people, and they will help you.* She took me to this park where there were many people,

and I got a bus to Agadez. But I had no idea where I was going and no one helped me. People are so wicked. I went to three countries with different buses—I don't know which countries. But on the way to Sabratha (Libya), I was kidnapped. The bus took us to some people—some men with guns—who stopped us and took us off and put us in a container. In there, they were raping some girls, but I said I was pregnant, and they said OK and gave me some water. Then they told me I should ask someone to come and bail me, and I said—*But I don't have any money.* Then a girl helped me. She called her brother and he brought 200,000 for me and for her. They let both of us go, but we were not going in the same direction.

An Arab guy took me to Sabratha. I waited five days on the beach without food because I had no money to buy it. So I begged and asked people to give me one dinar to buy water.

Then I decided to go in the boat. There is a big hole in the boat, and the water is covering me, and I am thinking I will die there. I am thinking: what made me leave my country, because everything is bad in the sea. You have nothing, you look at the sky and you look at the sea and there is nothing. We don't have a captain or a driver. We are 150 people and I am in the middle, and it is so hot. There is nothing to eat or drink, and I am vomiting, but there is no toilet.

When the rescue came, I was so happy. But the rescue ship was already full, so they put us in the toilet. They gave me a shirt and a blanket to wrap myself. I spent two days on the rescue ship. Then, I got to Italy, and after I got here, I said—*God this is such a beautiful place.* In Nigeria, there is dirt and pain, but after I got here, I was so happy. We don't have lights in Nigeria, but here everything is good. It's perfect and nice.

They put us in a tent first. It was not so beautiful. Maria was in my tent. I made her my close friend. Then her sister came to take her, and I asked if I could visit, and I got permission. That's why I am here. I stay in a centre for girls in another place. I am eighteen now; I was seventeen when I arrived.

I miss Blessing. I would like to have her with me.

Ventimiglia

Rome

Mediterranean

Ventimiglia

Italy, November 2016

Ventimiglia, Tuesday 22 November

– *Five migrants got caught in a flash flood this morning*—Lucia tells me when she picks me up at the station and drives me across the river to the old medieval town perched on the hill. The water is thick, muddy and raging. Four of them were rescued, but one is missing. A helicopter hovers, still searching. There is an ambulance parked in the green fields near where the river hits the sea in a murky, turbulent tide.

Welcome to Ventimiglia: the old city perches on a hill in a dramatic gorge where the Roia river cuts through from the snow-covered Alps to the sea. From my crow's nest up by the thousand-year-old cathedral, I can look in one direction towards Nice and Antibes in France, and in the other, down onto the beaches and the wider streets, lined with art nouveau style villas and public gardens, full of succulents and palm trees.

This is the end of the road for migrants in Italy. The ones who have come this far are all trying to leave and get to France. In the old days, it was not too hard to do, but around spring of this year, the French started getting more choosy. Then they shut the border completely, and migrants piled up in the town. They did not stop trying to cross, but now, it is either by hoping to slip through unnoticed on a train or bus, or by walking through the mountains with the help of smugglers at night. So, there is still a constant influx of people. Initially, the authorities provided some housing around the station but then closed it in a panic, as they were overwhelmed and feared a Calais 'Jungle' developing. They issued edicts that people were forbidden to assist migrants and would be fined for doing so. Needless to say, that did not stop migrants coming and sleeping rough on the streets. So at the end of May this year, Don Rito, a local Catholic priest, opened his church and let people sleep there, both inside the church itself and in the rooms underneath. He started with two hundred.

227

By summer, there were more than one thousand, many sleeping around the church. I asked him why.

– *It's very easy to do nothing in life and thus avoid making any mistakes. Helping migrants creates problems and criticism, but not helping does not solve the problem and creates more suffering. It's a humanitarian necessity. And when you look into the eyes of these children and see how they have seen the world, what they have seen.... you must respond. You have no choice. I opened the church because they arrived in Ventimiglia and were refused everywhere, so I had to.*

A Red Cross camp was opened for adult males a couple of kilometres away and the church shelter, supported by Caritas, became a protective transit camp for women, families and unaccompanied children. Many of Don Rito's parishioners help, and volunteers come from as far away as Nice to do shifts and cook meals. But other locals are not so happy. They are collecting signatures in town in a bid to have the shelter closed.

– *Strictly speaking, we are not legal. The building is a church; it is supposed to be a church, not a shelter, but the mayor has not offered an alternative solution. He keeps telling me to close so that it looks like he is doing his job and responding to pressure, but he could not come to the church and just close it—that would be unacceptable. If we decided to close the Church and send the children out, where would they go? I tell him, 'Give us a solution for these families, and I will close it.' But the Comune and the police send families to me!*

And it's still not enough. That is why there are people sleeping under bridges and getting caught in flash floods. Lucia, who works for Terre des Hommes, takes me down to the shelter. There are two large rooms packed with bunk beds, one for women and children, one for accompanying boys and men. A group of volunteers are serving dinner for around one hundred people from a small, very clean looking kitchen, and a midwife employed by MSF is running a clinic.

Small children are rioting around, women sit gossiping. Some Nigerian girls are plaiting and braiding each other's hair. Lucia appears to know everyone; they all regard her as an intimate friend, embracing her and chatting away. Many of them have spent months, even years, in Italy and speak some Italian. I sit chatting to Bridget, an Ethiopian woman with the most entrancing three-month-old infant who does nothing but smile and gurgle. She has been in Italy for seven years. She actually has asylum here, but after a boyfriend abandoned her and left her pregnant, she tried to go to Finland. Her baby was born there, then they deported her back to Italy, and she has lost her papers. Don Rito has given her a room, while she gets her documents sorted out again.

Ventimiglia, Wednesday 23 November

Today, I have learned that there are dolphins helping migrants in the Mediterranean, and that a night of prostitution in Italy, servicing five men, will allow you to pay off 1800 euros worth of debt. This is from Julie, another Nigerian caught up in a prostitution scam. Julie managed to escape from the woman who organised her trip.

– *But she is still doing Juju on my family to get to me!*

Julie initially told Lucia she was sixteen, but now she says she is twenty—either could be true. The interesting thing is that, while some young men claim to be younger than they are in order to meet the criteria for humanitarian protection as a minor, many young women I have met exaggerate their age in order to escape the restrictive living conditions which are imposed on female minors. This is obviously for their protection, but they still hate it.

Julie tells me a now familiar West African story: she was orphaned young, brought up by relatives who abused and exploited her, never went to school, but sold bottled water in the streets of Lagos. A woman offered to pay for her journey to Europe, so she travelled to Libya where, like so many, she was imprisoned for five months, beaten, threatened with rape, and finally released because her patron sent money to get her out. The boat journey was terrifying because it leaked and started to sink. But, apparently, they were saved by big fishes!

– *Fishes?* I ask Julie. This is certainly an interesting variation on being rescued by Frontex, MSF or the Italian navy.

– *Yes! They were swimming around us and showing us the way!*

– Were they very big fishes? Did they have a fin on their back and look like this? I draw a rough picture of a dolphin.

– That's it exactly! Julie smiles. *They came and showed us the way!*

She did not like the emergency camp at the port in Sicily because they would not let her out, so she ran away and connected with her sponsor. She was told to come to Torino. *I did one day's work with five men! But then I said NO. That lady collects the money. One night's work is 1800 euros. Then I ran away to Perugia.* She found a boyfriend and spent some time in various parts of Northern Italy. *But then, I decided to leave and start a real life. Someone gave me money to go to France. But I have decided to stay here. I want to study. I like Italy. I want a real life.*

What I still don't understand is why we create a hierarchy of suffering? Research done with children in Afghanistan and the Balkans shows that intimate family violence and abuse is more distressing and causes as much long-term mental suffering as war.[12] Almost all the children and young people I have met from Gambia, Senegal, Nigeria, Mali or Ghana, have experienced it. What continues to astonish me is the courage, intelligence and resilience they have shown in escaping and then enduring nightmare imprisonments in Libya and terrifying sea journeys. But still, they are regarded as less deserving of care, protection and support than those escaping war or political persecution. In addition, they are in danger of being sent home if they cannot find a way to integrate by the time they are eighteen. And how do you integrate if you are stuck in an emergency shelter for a year? It is not surprising that so many run away and try to make it to France or Germany.

I spend all morning in the shelter. Lucia wants me to meet another woman she is supporting and discuss her with me: an East African woman who has been raped twice on her journey and now has periods of odd, unusual behaviour. She talks about her experiences in a loud, disinhibited way. There are other times when she does not know what she is doing, taking things out of other people's bags. In spite of all this, she has tried to cross the border twice on foot and has come back in tears. Some of the other women bully and tease her, putting powder on her face, making her dance, and then laughing at her. In some ways, this is surprising. What is most striking about the shelter, given the crowded and stressful situation, is the easy camaraderie between people and the absence of fights. The woman's symptoms appear dissociative or possibly psychotic. We both agree she needs a local psychiatric assessment and should be encouraged to stay, not travel.

By lunchtime, the rain has stopped, and, in the sunlight, Ventimiglia is the colour of autumn. The reds, yellows and browns of the medieval houses echo the trees on the surrounding hills. I walk down to the beach which is empty except for scattered groups of young Afghan men, sleeping in the sun or playing cards. One smiles at me. He is sitting alone as he skims stones, so I sit beside him. He left Kunduz two years ago. He has a wife and child there; the son is five. He travelled all through Greece and the Balkans and got to Austria before being sent to Italy. He has no documents at all. He tries the border every night and sleeps on the beach. He has no money. It is no worse and no better than so many of the stories that now fill my heart, my head and my dreams, but there is a deep despairing sadness in him that is palpable, and he looks utterly exhausted. I don't know what to do. I pull 20 euros from my purse and ask him at least to buy a good meal. He refuses to take the money. I insist. Then I walk back to the shelter, feeling useless and horrible.

I spend the afternoon talking with Isabel and her family. They have come from Libya. They tried to cross the border to France on a bus yesterday along with a Syrian family. The Syrians made it. They got taken off at the French Border and sent back. Their plan is to stay here a few nights and try the train on Friday. This is market day, when loads of French pop across the border to shop in the market in Ventimiglia and then head home in the afternoon. So, the trains are less policed and it is easier to hide in the crowd, especially if, like Isabel and her sister with their pale skins and long wavy dark hair, you can easily pass as French.

Isabel is seventeen. She was about to go to medical school, but her mother had been a writer during Gaddafi's regime and supported him. The family survived the fighting, but life became impossible.

Afghan man sitting on the beach
Ventimiglia, November 2016

Her sister had been threatened with kidnap and her brother had been physically attacked.

They made it to Italy, but they want to join friends in Germany. They don't want to seek asylum here because they feel many Italians do not respect or like them.

Ventimiglia, Thursday 24 November

There is a storm warning today, and all the schools are closed. Lucia insists on picking me up. When we get to the shelter, we find Almaz, tense and tearful in wet clothes. She has just spent two days trying to walk into France. Then she got picked up by French police and was handed to Italian police who sent her to a camp in Taranto. (Think: heel-side of the instep of Italy's foot, the other end of the country). Lucia tells me that deportation back to Southern Italy is now common practice, and that the French police are increasingly unpleasant:

— *They cut off the soles of the shoes and then say to the migrant, 'Now walk back!' Sometimes, they hide behind bushes and throw rocks or chase the migrant with dogs. And even if you do get across, that is not the end of your problems in France.*

In Taranto, the camp was run by soldiers in a military barracks, Almaz tells us. She escaped and spent two days travelling back and is absolutely determined to try again.

— *The first thing is you need to eat*—says Lucia. But Almaz is so agitated, and we have difficulty persuading her even to sit and chat with us.

— *I am NOT staying in Italy! I want to go to Paris. Italy is no good.*

— *Do you know people in Paris?* I ask. *You know they have cleared the camps in the town.*

— *I know people, I know people, and Italy is no good! I have been here four months. They put me in a shelter, but they did not give me anything—no underwear, not even a bra, no pocket money, no phone card. They help Eritrean women but not Ethiopian women? Why? Don't they know what is happening in Ethiopia?*

She has my sympathy. No western government appears to want to acknowledge that Ethiopia, far from being a development success story, is killing protesters and students who object to land grabs and authoritarian rule. They've imposed a state of emergency and are on the brink of civil war.

– No one is helping us. We are abandoned and no one cares. That is why I am going to France. I tried for four days on foot. If they had given me a good place here, I would not go. I need peace. In Milan, I slept on the street! I walked through a desert. I was locked in a closed house for a year in Libya because I had no money. I lost my baby, it died. I have no one. I have no family. I am alone. I want peace. Eritreans and Ethiopians—our problems are the same. Don't people realise Ethiopia is in a war? We just came here to find peace. We went through a lot to get here…

She cannot get over the unfairness of her treatment. Lucia and I sit with her, just letting her talk until she winds down out of exhaustion.

– First, I want to apologise. We have not treated you in the way you deserve, and I am truly sorry—Lucia says. *I want to help, and I am sure we can.*

– I have just come from France—I tell Almaz—*and I am afraid it is not better there. Possibly, it's worse, and as you have been fingerprinted here, you risk being sent back.*

Lucia emphasises that the choice is Almaz's but asks her to think through the risks and consequences. We beg her to at least rest and eat over the weekend before trying again, and she appears to agree. There is a large new Iraqi family. Apparently, the Iraqis are a fairly new phenomenon—signs of the times and the effect of the closure of Greece. They want to go to England where they have close family ties. Lucia looks pleased. *There is a legal way for you to do this. It will take time, but while you wait, you have rights—to a lawyer and to pocket money, and all the children can go to school.*

I continue to accompany Lucia as she dispenses compassion, advice and comfort, all rolled into one. I am supposed to be teaching psychological first aid and stress management in the evening. I think I will simply ask Lucia to describe her daily routine, as she provides a perfect example.

As it happens, the lecture is postponed because of the rain. So, I hang out with the volunteer cooks. An elderly Italian man walks in with worn shoes and a too thin coat. He has a backpack. He says he has been sent here by the police. The Italian volunteer in charge is kind, but firm:

— We are full. This is for migrant women and children, I am so sorry but we cannot help.

The man, who has the hollowed out pallid face of a man with a malignant illness, bows his head, shifts his pack and heads back to the exit gate. *Where will he go?* I ask my new friend Maureen, a British expat living on an olive farm in the mountains and volunteering here three nights a week.

— I am not sure, probably the station. The trouble is, the volunteer feels that, if she says yes, it will open a floodgate. We are not legal, and we are not a homeless shelter.

So, we too are categorising vulnerable people into 'deserving' and 'less deserving.'

Ventimiglia, Friday 25 November

At least the rain has stopped. The sun is out, but Don Rito's other church is flooded. Maureen and I go up the road to see if we can help and find him in a football t-shirt and shorts, wading in and out of the lake filling his church basement, waiting for the civil protection people to come and help him pump it out. It is not a mop and bucket job, so there is nothing we can do but sit in the sun and wait.

I ask Don Rito for his solution to the migrant crisis. He tells me a story:

— Imagine there is a poor boy, and under his bed is a large gold nugget. He does not know it is there, but the neighbour does because he has seen it. So he says to the boy, 'Let me buy your old bed from you, and I will give you a nice new bed.' And he takes everything, including the gold nugget. Then the boy begins to understand what has happened, that he has been robbed, and he asks the neighbour questions, so the neighbour burns down the boy's house and hopes he will run away. This is the story of the relationship between Europe and Africa. The rich countries went there, they stole everything, and then they sold arms to create chaos, and in the meantime, they still reap benefits. They don't want poor countries

236

to know they are rich.

– But the secret is out, and the poor are running from the burning house in our direction—I say.

Don Rito goes indoors to print off a newspaper article—a recent piece that Antonio Maria Costa, former Under-Secretary-General at the United Nations Office on Drugs and Crime, wrote for La Stampa at the time of the Calais evictions in late October. It excoriates Europe for "the greatest crime in human history," the exploitation of Africa that has gone on since the fifteenth century, and continues to this day, "A crime that caused, says ex UN chief Kofi Annan, more than 250 million (black) deaths: [...] double the (white) deaths in the two world wars."[13]

Costa argues that "the African people have a miserable choice: to die of violence and poverty at home, or risk their lives in the Mediterranean in an exodus of biblical proportions—tens of thousands of people in recent months, tens of millions for years to come." The world needs to recognise that "London, Paris and Brussels have caused the African tragedy, stealing dignity and resources from already poor people. It's time for compensation—as happened after World War II, after the Holocaust, and after natural disasters. Compensation in terms of development assistance (to stop the migration) and in terms of integration (to assist immigrants)."

– If you are going to talk about global justice, we have to start to give back what we took away—Don Rito says. *I am in touch with priests in France, in Monaco and Nice. In Advent, we are having a meeting at the church. We invite everyone. We will meditate together and then go to the cathedral to celebrate Advent. Christmas is very important. It starts with Mary and Joseph having nowhere to go and everyone closing their doors against them. Jesus himself is then born in a stable.*

– And then he and his parents flee persecution into Egypt.

– Exactly. We need to reflect that we are all human beings, and we are the lucky ones.

Ventimiglia, Saturday 26 November

There was a French train strike yesterday, so there was no possibility of sneaking through on market day. Isabel and her sister Diana have spent all morning making themselves look French. Diana is dressed in a fashionable short kilt and sweater. Isabel is in her padded waistcoat and jeans. When I arrive, they are stuffing their luggage into shopping bags and doing their mum's hair. We all agree mum has to forgo her beloved woolly bobble-hat that she wears low on her forehead.

They are hopeful because an Eritrean family made it across the border two days ago. I promise to accompany them as far as Menton, simply to observe what happens. We head off to the station with another Libyan family who arrived two days ago. There are two little girls and one small boy, and both mum and dad are so nervous they appear unable to keep a grip on the children, who run off in all directions. I worry about how they will manage on the train.

At the station, the two families agree they will sit in different carriages, not to stand out. The train arrives, and Isabel and her family all get on the upper deck and settle themselves in. There is a French Algerian Man and his son sitting across from Diana. Isabel's mum chats away to him in Arabic, which seems a bit rash to me. Diana is reading an English language children's story. I sit one set of chairs down from them to observe, and the train pulls out.

The short journey is spectacular, as the train goes through a tunnel and then winds along the edge of the sea. We pass lovely, honey-coloured villas with palm tree-filled gardens. I have no idea where the actual frontier is, but we have obviously crossed because, at Menton Garavan, half a dozen uniformed French police climb aboard. The train remains standing as they walk through the carriages. Mum has put her bobble hat back on. Better to be bobble-hatted than nervous, I think to myself. Isabel and Diana are both deep in their books. The policeman asks the Algerian man for his passport but ignores the girls and women, and myself. They pass on. I see them climbing off the train. I see a crowd of about twelve young black African men on the platform. The train moves off. Isabel grins broadly at me.

– *We've made it!*

Then, the other Libyan woman appears with her daughters; she is in tears. They took her husband and son off! In five minutes I will be in Central Menton, and I have to get off the train. I promise to connect with the father as soon as I am back in Ventimiglia. There are hugs all around. I don't know when I will see any of them again. I am off the train, and they are on their way to Nice.

Menton Garavan is completely empty when I pass through, and I go back to Ventimiglia. Coming out of the station I bump into Bridget with her baby in a pushchair, half a dozen other migrants and their children, and a handful of the younger volunteers. They are having a small protest march. They are going down to the place where the signatures for closing the shelter are being collected. Will I join them?

We walk on through town. There is a banner attached to Bridget's pushchair: "If you close the Shelter, we will have to sleep in the river." The petition stand is a very small affair with a table and two rather bored looking Italians sitting there. No one else is around. "Close the Shelter! The situation is out of control" says the poster. But, surely, women and children sleeping on the streets again is even more out of control?

A man in a red jacket walks up to us and starts talking loudly. He wants the shelter closed. He has nothing against us personally, but it is a question of priorities. He is Italian. He has been homeless, and for him, it's *Italians first!* Then, a woman with a pushchair and infant joins us. She does not agree.

– *We are all the same*—she says.

It is time to take the children to the swings; they are getting bored. In the park, the police are clearing out the Afghans. They do it every day, but we are ignored, and the children get to play on slides and seesaws—a small moment of normality.

Back in the shelter in the evening, I meet the Libyan man and his son. We sit together at dinner, which, on this occasion, is served by a group of French Tunisian volunteers who have popped across that same border with a prepared meal, as they do every week.

– *My wife and daughters have made it to Nice*—he says. He is going to try again as soon as possible. He is weeping as he talks.

– *Not tonight*—I beg him—*you and your boy are exhausted. And you*

239

need to look a little less like an exhausted migrant. Adam, an Afghan friend who volunteers here, agrees. He tells the man he is going to give him a shave and sort out better clothes from the store in the morning. The man looks slightly comforted. Not how I feel myself.

On the train to Calais, Sunday 27 November

A long time ago, I was married to a Slovene philosopher. In those days, we still had a Cold War. He was a Yugoslav citizen, and many of our life choices were determined by where he could or could not travel.

– *There is one simple division in the world*—he said. *Between those who have a Western passport, and those who do not.*

Nothing has changed in thirty years. I take the train across France. I am reminded once again, as I travel so easily across the frontier and along the Cote d' Azur, with its blue sea and autumnal trees glistening in the sunlight, how astonishingly varied and beautiful Europe is, and that it is only luck that I am a citizen of this part of the continent, which, at the moment, is free of war and starvation, and that I can cross these frontiers so easily.

On my way from Riace to Ventimiglia, I stopped in Rome to go to a conference on Mental Health and Migration. One of the keynote speakers, Joseba Achotegui, secretary of the transcultural section of the World Psychiatric Association, pointed out that our mitochondrial DNA shows that we are all migrants, separated by only a few thousand generations from our common mother in East Africa. Our capacity to cooperate, move and adapt is what has enabled the survival of the species. I find myself wondering if becoming sedentary and building walls is a new adaptation, now that we have spread to five continents, or part of what will bring us to an evolutionary dead end?

Jamal, my young Somali friend from Calais, texts from the 'home' to which he was bussed from Calais, on the French-Spanish border. He's been interviewed by the British, but no one has told him what will happen. They do nothing all day long. Eloise tells me that our Afghan friend with PTSD has disappeared from the apartment in

Rouen where she thought he was happily settled. She had sent pictures of him with visiting volunteers showing off his new boots. But then, a few days later when a volunteer called, the flat was empty. He took his documents, clothes and phone charger, which suggests it was a planned move, not a suicide attempt, but I cannot get a response to my texts. We have lost him. Meanwhile, my Catholic worker friend, Johannes, has taken six young adult migrants from the Jungle into his house in Calais. Two of them seem stressed and unwell, and he wants me to drop in on my way back and give them advice on managing. Housam texts from Greece: Jafra has moved to Athens, where they are now helping urban refugees. Eleni, my psychologist colleague in Greece, tells me Majd and his family are getting accommodation in Thessaloniki. Maria and her family have been relocated to Holland, and she is already learning Dutch. The news from Syria grows more horrifying by the day. I am glad they are out of it.

I read the Guardian and learn that one small town in Northern Nigeria, with a population of 60,000, is currently hosting more than 140,000 displaced people, more or less the same number that have come to Italy this year. 1.5 million have been displaced by war and famine in Borno state alone. That is half a million more than the number of people who migrated to Europe in the entirety of last year. Meanwhile the nearby city of Maiduguri (with a population just over one million) has taken in 600,000 IDPs over three years, turning over new schools and housing projects for their use. As Toby Lanzer, the UN's Assistant Secretary General for the Sahel and the Lake Chad region, explains in the piece: "The local community has in effect said, 'We built that as a school, but you [IDPs can] have it. And we built that as a new neighbourhood, but we will put you lot in it. How's that for generosity, Europe?'"[14]

Postscript, Tuesday 27 December

I write this in the shadow of the complete destruction and 'liberation' of Eastern Aleppo, the assassination of the Russian Ambassador in Ankara, and the bombing in the German Christmas Market. What got much less coverage was the drowning of one hundred more migrants off the coast of Sicily four days ago, bringing the total number of drownings in the Mediterranean this year to 5000—the highest figure yet.

"You have to understand,
no one puts their children in a boat
unless the water is safer than the land."
   —Somali British poet Warsan Shire[15]

There is no such thing as complete safety. We can build ever-higher walls, and bomb with impunity, but terror will multiply and tunnel its way through, as ISIS does in Mosul today. Or, we can, as Don Rito said, start to give back what we took away, beginning with offering refuge to those children who, like us, are alone and afraid.

Isabel's Story

Isabel comes from Libya. At the time she told this story (November 2016) she was seventeen years old and staying in the family transit shelter in Ventimiglia, Italy.

We come from a town near Sabratha in Libya. My father is a businessman and my mother is a writer. I have a younger brother and sister. When I was little, our life in Libya was good. The best times were when we were together as a family. We went to funfairs and travelled on holiday together. We went to Egypt to see the Great Pyramid and the museum. We lived in an apartment, and we had a small house by the sea. Both my sister and I went to a good school and we had a lot of friends. I learned English from listening to songs and watching movies. I love to write poems and to sing. My sister is the same. She had a radio programme with other children who made it together. It was called 'Love Children.'

My parents divorced when I was seven years old, and my father married someone else. But we did not mind. My mother would not let us feel bad about it. She did everything to make us happy; she was like mother and father at the same time.

Our family liked Gaddafi. Maybe he was not so good, but people could go out at 4am on the street and be safe. There were no killers, no guns, and food was much cheaper. He was in control. He was a strong man. I met him when I was ten years old at a festival. I had written a poem for him and recited it at the festival. Then I went to see him, and the bodyguard tried to stop me. But he said to come over, and he put me on his knee and told me how beautiful I was. He was playing with my hair and he asked—*Do you want something from me? Tell me*—and I said—*No. I am too young.* Then I said—*I love you*—and he responded—*I love you too.*

In my opinion, Gaddafi was good. All of Africa loved him, and all of Africa lived in Libya because we had food and no one was poor. Nigerians, Gambians, Senegalese—they all lived in Libya. On the journey here, I met a Moroccan man. He told me—*Ten years ago, I said to everyone, I won't leave Libya, it's a beautiful life.* But after the war, he wanted to go. It is the same with Sudanese people. They wanted to stay in Libya because they were living a beautiful life. Libyan people respect all the religions of the world. And my mother liked Gaddafi. She told me he made schools and he gave her and other women an education and made them open-minded. She had a chance because of Gaddafi.

I liked high school. I had so many friends. Sometimes, we sneaked out of class and sat in the garden. I did well because I was clever. I did not need to study too much.

I was twelve when the war began. We saw it with our own eyes. At the beginning, we thought guns were just something you saw in movies. But that first night, people were protesting. They were shouting in the street—*No Gaddafi, No Gaddafi!* Then the police came with tear gas. But they did not want to stop. They broke everything there, and then they made a fire in the police station. The schools closed at that time, and the fighting began. There were bombs. We heard and saw everything. There were bullets coming into our apartment. The bullets went everywhere. One time, we were at home and we heard a really loud noise. We were really scared. Two bombs had hit the apartment building on the other side. We were in a corner room, so we were OK, but we were scared. You could not go in the street. We saw people killed in the street, so we could not go out. For one month, the house had no water and no electricity. We just had a small amount of food and water we got from a well in the yard. There were many people in the neighbourhood that I knew that died. Although, a lot of people left their houses. We did not have anywhere else to go. Father did not call to see if we were OK.

After that month, we went back to school for a short period. We had missed a lot, so we had to work hard to catch up. Then Gaddafi died and the new government came. I don't remember a lot of things—it is really complicated. We moved to Tripoli to a friend's house because there was so much fighting in our area. My mother decided to return home to get some important documents: our passports and papers, and on her way back a bomb hit the bus and injured her in the stomach. My mother's friend did not tell us because she did not want us to be sad. Every day we asked her—*When is she coming? When is she coming?* So she told us—*It's just that she is in hospital, don't worry.* But she lied, because she did not know where my mother was. They were all trying to find her. And then, my uncle found her in a hospital in Tripoli. It was empty. There were no doctors, no medicines. It was empty—just dying people. She was there six days without doctors or medicines and her stomach wound was open. They had to cut off a bit of her gut. They took her to Tunisia to a hospital there, and she was there for a very long time.

First, we went to our grandmother. Then my father came and took us, and we stayed with him for three years. We did not like it when Mum was away from us. My mother is my best friend. She knows everything about me. My stepmother was not kind; she said stupid things. School was the only thing that made me happy. It was a new school, but I made a lot of close friends. When I was at home, I stayed alone in my room.

Then my mum came home. Our aunt made a surprise for us. She invited us to her house—it was empty. Then my mum appeared, and it was the best moment of my life. We stayed in my grandmother's house in our old town together. It was a new school again, so new friends, new things, and I missed the old friends, but I had a boyfriend. Sometimes there was a bomb. Sometimes we heard that someone died. There were always voices saying this person died or that person… It became a normal thing.

But my whole family had supported the Gaddafi regime, and after he died, people started following my mother and wanted to put her in prison. There was no war, but people were dying every day. It was really strange. There was fighting and killing all the time, and every three to four months, the school closed for a bit. They even came into our school with guns on one occasion. We just heard the guns firing. We were sitting in class and when we heard shooting we went down, and we saw people with guns shooting in the air. They just wanted to frighten people and had taken refuge in the school. They did not shoot at the children, but one girl got hit in the arm and one boy died. The police came and took them, and I called Mum to come and get me.

It got so unsafe, you could not go out. Mum stopped work. My grandparents had money in the bank, so we used that. We decided to leave last year. We went to Tunisia to try to get a visa for France, and we went to Egypt to try to get a visa for Germany, but they both said no. So, we decided to go across the sea. That was a hard decision. This year, I would have been in medical school—my first year. I had a place to study. And I have a boyfriend in Libya; he is so sad that I came here.

But we had to go. People tried to kidnap my sister. They followed her on her way to school in a black car. She ran from them and went to a neighbour's house and told him what happened. He took her to school and told my mother to take her to school by car. Then some people captured my brother, some boys. They made a cut on his leg with a knife, but he ran away. And we thought, we cannot live like this, with something happening every day—no police, no government. The country is a mess. So my mum did everything. She had contact with people, and she gave them a lot of money.

The boat trip is another story. It was much too small and there were too many people. There were two Libyan families, one from Morocco and two families from Niger, and so many Africans from Nigeria, Gambia and Sudan. Maybe there were more than fifty people, and after about an hour, water started to come in, and we were scared. The man who drove the boat did not know how to drive, and we were following a star to show the way, but it was so dark, and the sea was so black, and there was nothing near us. Then, there was something like a ghost in the water, and it was the Libyan police boat. They came and just took the Libyan families and the Moroccans and left the Africans on the boat. So, we were all vomiting and crying, and they gave us medicine. We begged them—*Please, we gave all our money, please don't take us back to Libya.* Then I fell asleep, and when I woke up, I was on an EU boat! My mother told us what happened.

She was thinking that the people who caught us were opposed to Gaddafi, and so she was very scared, and she had us—all three children—on her lap. The police asked her why she did not get a visa, and she said she tried. She told them she had an operation and needed treatment. Then the police said—*These children are not yours, you kidnapped them.* And she said—*No, they are mine.* And, after all this, while talking, she saw the EU boat, and the policeman said—*You want Italy. Go on, go to Italy*—and they put us all on that EU boat!

We were really lucky. They gave us food and covered us not to be cold. We picked up many other people. But, twenty-five people drowned that day. There were helicopters dropping rescue boats to save people from drowning. And a fast boat came to rescue people and bring them to our boat. I took photos of Eva, a Spanish woman, saving people. And then they took us all to a much bigger ship, which had two thousand people. On that big ship, they scanned us and they took the belts off of all the Africans and put them in a waste-bin. I don't know why. On that big boat there was no food, just water for two days, and it was really cold. I could not feel my fingers.

The boat took us to Augusta in Sicily, and they put us in a big tent with one thousand people. We had to sleep on the floor. We stayed there for four days. They took our fingerprints. They gave us bread, cheese and an apple three times a day. On the third day there, the Africans and the Libyans had a fight. The Africans hate the Libyans because some had taken their money. So, when my sister was walking, an African man threw a bottle of water in her face. Then, a boy in another Libyan family was fighting with an African man, and suddenly, there was a big fight between the Arabs and the Africans. We told the police and they just stood and watched and did nothing. The Libyan boy had to go to hospital, and my arm was bruised by someone grabbing me. So we slept outside the tent for two nights. It was not safe because the Africans were angry and beating everyone and swearing. And we told them—*You must make a solution for this.* Then, on the 9th of October, they brought a bus and took us to Vicenza police station. They asked for our fingerprints again. They said it's just for 'identification.' But later, we found it was for 'protection.'[16] They lied to us, and we didn't want protection in Italy.

Then, because we are a family, they put us in a good apartment with a kitchen and a toilet, and they gave us clothes, toothbrushes and shampoo. And there were two Libyan families, a Moroccan family and four pregnant Nigerian women. But the women made the bathroom dirty all the time. We had discussions about keeping it clean many times, but they just laughed at us and didn't respect us.

Some people came and asked us if we wanted to get asylum in Italy, but we said we did not want to do that. Then they invited us to come to the centre to get clothes, and when we got there, a bad Italian woman was shouting at everyone. She said to the Africans—*Don't speak! Take what I give you!* And when my mother came up, she screamed at her:

– *Sit on the floor, respect Italy! You are in Italy! You should kiss our hands and say, 'Thank you Italy,' because you were poor, and your country had nothing, and you came to Italy. So sit on the floor, and do not speak!*

So my mother said—*Keep your clothes!* And she said to us—*You can stay and take the clothes, but I will not*—and we all went outside. We had a little money, and mother bought us clothes.

There was also a boy called Daniel. He was a real humanitarian. He was good and respected everyone. We all loved him. My mum told him—*You are like my son. You are the good face of Italy.* At this time, my sister got very sick with a fever. We don't know why. I went back to the centre at 3am and told them—*She has a fever of forty degrees*—and they said—*It is not dangerous, so don't worry.* Mum got angry and said—*It is not your daughter, you don't care. This is my daughter.* Then, a young man from Ghana said he would take her to a hospital. She stayed there one week. The doctors said it was a virus, and even in the hospital, it was up and down. So, that is why we stayed a month there.

Then we bought tickets for the bus and the train. We went to Verona and then took a bus for Nice. The man charged us 60 euros, and we saw later that it was only 37 euros—we did not realise he was tricking us. So, we got that bus and after five or six hours, we got to the Italian border. The Italian controller came on and asked for our passports. We had passports; mum had paid one thousand dollars for each of us in Libya to obtain them. They checked the passports, took them, got off the bus, came back, and said everything is OK. Then we went two miles more, and we could see the French border. At that control, we gave our passports again. This time, they told us to get off the bus, but they let the Syrians who were travelling with us continue. It was raining, and we were soaking wet. The French police took us to the police office and they were all laughing and saying—*I love my job when we catch someone.* My brother and sister were crying, and they put us in a room for a few hours, then they said—*Go back this way to Italy.* And we walked two hundred metres to the Italian Border Police. There was a woman inside. She was a doctor and she was kind. They gave us some sandwiches and some chocolate and water. We were all crying—all of us. We did not want to go back to Italy. They caught many Africans—young men—and they let them go in the rain. But because we were women and children, they brought us here to the Church yesterday morning.

We will try again. We want to go to Germany. We have family and friends there. My mother's friends are there. They left two years ago. They live a good life now in Germany—a normal life. I want to live a normal life again. I am tired of all these changes. I live with my mother…then my father…then back with my mother…then we cross a sea…then we go to Vicenza. It is so complicated. I want to live a normal life. I want to complete my studies. I want to be a doctor someday. I want to achieve my dreams. I want a normal life. I had a place in medical school, but I don't want to live without my family. I don't like leaving my country either. I left everyone I love, including my boyfriend. I knew him for eighteen months and he misses me and wants me to come back.

We will try on Friday. People say it is possible to cross on the train on Fridays because tourists come from France to go to the market and go back in the evening. So if we wear good clothes and make up and just sit on the train, we hope to arrive.

2017

Athens

Greece, February 2017

Athens, Tuesday 14 February

The cold has lifted a little, and I am down from four layers to three, but inside the building we are still hugging the small electric fan heaters I purchased Monday. I live in an Airbnb room in Exarchia in one of the grids of narrow hilly streets between two mountains. The larger one on the other side of the valley has a cliff face and a church on top. The smaller one is a block from where I live. In the mornings, I make my way along narrow, broken pavements beside badly parked cars. Every house has graffitied walls, and there is a small neglected park full of cats, uncut vegetation, plastic bottles, cans and other rubbish. There's a handful of small campfires and shelters—people are clearly living here. I have the sense that the whole area is at a tipping point—a marker for what happens when public money runs out. But there are cheerful local people walking their dogs and chatting. And the streets are full of coffee shops, book shops and small stores. Yesterday, I got my boots fixed for 15 euros. The boot mender is Albanian, and his wife is Bulgarian. The other lady in the shop was an elderly Greek woman with a botoxed face, smooth as a doll, short skirt and a white leather cap (circa 1965), who was happily trying on platform gold sandals that he had just fixed for her. He was delighted to hear I had spent some time in Albania, and we briefly discussed the beauties of Himare and the Albanian coast.

I walk to work. Housam and Jafra have rented a three-story villa in a neighbouring district. Jafra are turning downstairs into an office and meeting rooms, and the two large self-contained apartments upstairs into accommodation for vulnerable women. It's a good space. Each apartment has three bedrooms, a communal area, kitchen and bathroom. Jafra have spent some weeks cleaning and repainting. There are wooden floors and large windows. You can house up to twenty five people comfortably, and it feels friendly. They got the bunk beds, some bedding and basic food supplies from a large warehouse with

Man combing through rubbish in Exarchia district
Athens, February 2017

its own van that distributes to the refugee community—a bit like L'Auberge in Calais. But I have to admit to a slight feeling of panic when they showed me around on Monday morning. Two women, one with an infant, were arriving that afternoon, and as far as I could see, the apartment had a dangerous dysfunctional gas stove, there were no mattresses for the new bunk beds, the doors did not lock, half the lights did not work, and it was freezing. But, by mid-afternoon, a lovely Palestinian refugee, who had already checked and fixed all the electric wiring, had fixed the lights and switched the bad stove for a good electric one. We had put in a new request to the warehouse for crockery, cutlery and chairs, and I made an executive decision to use some foundation funds to buy the mattresses, heaters and padlocks. Jafra have already agreed that one of them will sleep downstairs every night so that there is someone available 24 hours for security.

When I went upstairs in the early evening, Maya and Sura had already put a blanket on the floor where two-year-old Fatima was playing. The heater and lights were on, and Maya wanted to make me tea.

Her story is another heart-breaking one. Last September, she was living in Yamouk in Damascus. Her husband went off to buy bread, and he never came back. She was pregnant and had 18-month-old Fatima. So, she decided to escape. Smugglers got her all the way to one of the islands. She was treated alright in the camps. She began the asylum process and was given a date for an interview. But then, she discovered her pregnancy was ectopic, yet the doctor who saw her, rather bizarrely, told her to return in two weeks—or so she understood. She was frightened and ran away on a ferry to Athens, where she was admitted to a hospital and had an abortion. Then she camped out with various friends in the city. The problem being that, if she stayed with them, they lost their housing because they were legal and she was not. So, she has come to Jafra, who want to support women like her—the ones that are falling between the cracks.

Athens, Wednesday 15 February
This is the big divide in the migrant community now: between mi-

grants like Maya and Sura and those who are in some kind of legal process, whether seeking asylum in Greece or waiting for relocation elsewhere. As long as they have documents, they can get a 'cashcard,' which allows them to draw a living allowance and survive. The size of the allowance depends on whether you have been put in a hotel with meals or in an apartment where you cook for yourself.

Ahmed and his family are in the latter group. I went with Naya (who is helping me with translation) to visit them this morning. They have a large sunny apartment in Galatia. They were moved here by a Greek NGO last August, shortly after we met in Vasiliki. They are halfway through the relocation process and waiting to hear which country might accept them. The rent is paid, and the whole family gets an allowance of 500 euros a month—not a lot to feed a family of nine. But they were glad to move. There was too much fighting with knives and drinking in the camp up north, and it felt really danger-ous, Ahmed told me.

— *They were saying things like, 'I am Kurd, you are Syrian, you are Arab.' Me and my family, we were afraid.*

He is not sure about Athens.

— *Some are good, some are bad. There were a lot of volunteers in the school in Athens. They helped us to make food and to learn languages—things like that. But when I walk in the street, and I ask someone for the way, he pulls away and won't tell me. We see that all the time.*

But he has discovered the mountains in the city and just been up to the Acropolis.

— *Nature is beautiful up there. We could see everything. It was amazing.*

He and his sisters were going to school four times a week to learn English, but it was forty minutes away, the classes were crowded, and they did not feel comfortable there, so now, they try to do some classes at home. The morning turns into a drawing group. The chil-dren want to make pictures and tell me what they are about. This leads to conversations about the good things they remember and what they hope will happen. Two of the girls said they want to write stories for me, so we go out to buy exercise books. Meanwhile, a beautiful lunch is spread out on the floor—Kurdish hospitality never

257

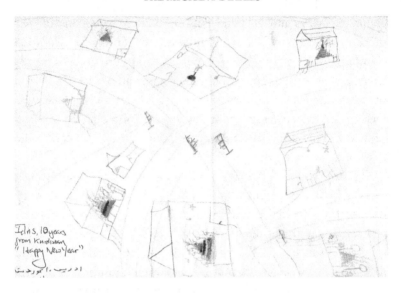

'Happy New Year' by Idris, age 10:
These are houses and inside there is a cake, a special one that we have at New Year. It has candles and six years. It is made in a shop but sometimes we make it at home. When I was in Iraq, we had cake in the house every day. The last 'Happy New Year' was in Iraq. It's at night, and we have a party. We have a special Kurdish dance called Dabkeh, the men and women do it. All my friends came and the family was there. At midnight, we saw the fireworks. This time we were in Athens. We made the cake in the house. We spent New Year in the house with the family, we had dinner and the cake. It was beautiful. I was very happy, but I miss Iraq. I want to be a policeman in Germany, and I want to go to school and learn English and Greek. But the school here was far away and crowded, and it was very cold.

258

fails in any circumstances, and we sit to eat beans and salad.

Back in the office, I do a training on ethnographic assessment methods for the Jafra volunteers—six of whom are off to live in a refugee camp for a week, at UNHCR invitation, to see if they can set up a psychosocial programme there. They will live there as fellow refugees. It seems likely that they will get much better insight into people's real needs than any external assessor like myself, dropping in like an alien from outer space. So, we discuss some of the methods that might help them get even more information, and I roleplay some of the most difficult people whose answer to every inquiry is: *Get me out of here.*

My other most useful function here appears to be connecting dots. The Jafra team moved here in the autumn, following most of the families who were moving from Lagkadikia. They started by doing psychosocial activities in the anarchist squats in the area, particularly, music and dance. But, Housam told me they felt increasingly uncomfortable with the way the anarchists appeared to use the migrants, demanding that they go on demonstrations, and the lack of real care. Drugs and alcohol were common in the squats; many were not secure.

They decided to rent their own building and embark on the shelter project. They have been in touch with a friendly lawyer to help them start the process of registration as an NGO in Greece. But that takes six months, meanwhile, they don't have a legal way to accept the money people want to donate, and as Housam freely admits:

– *We are great at just getting on and doing things, we are not so good at paperwork and administration and finance.*

So, I write to Help Refugees for their Greek contact, Pan, who has turned out to be incredibly supportive. He's helped establish the Khora Community Centre in Exarcheia—a five story building which now houses a wealth of activities for the migrant community, such as free meals, language classes, yoga and self-defence. It also has a women's space and a child-friendly space, where Fatima is already happily spending hours each day, a free dental clinic and legal aid. We went to the general coordination meeting on Monday where, after briefing everyone on hand signals to expedite discussion (an upward wave for assent, a downward one for disagree, pointing for a direct response, L-sign for don't understand language, P for point of order, etc.), plans are made, rotas are agreed upon, and new ideas are discussed. It felt like a much more organised version of the Park Hotel near Idomeni or Better Days for Moria and the Jungle, which is not surprising, as a large number of the volunteers have passed through those places.

I continue to be fascinated by this self-organised humanitarianism. The volunteers come from all over Europe. I have met Dutch, Spanish, Catalan and Swiss here so far—not so many Greeks. Pan tells me the Anarchists are not comfortable with the fact that Khora are renting, not squatting. Housam is not completely comfortable either. He points out that Khora don't appear to have involved migrants themselves in the organisation. As far as we could see, the coordination meeting was held in English with only three migrants present (apart from Housam).

Nevertheless, I am now in the messaging group, which means my phone beeps constantly with messages and updates about cleaning and cooking and classes and locking up and unlocking, etc. etc. They are definitely doing some good: they serve 500-600 meals a day to a dining room packed with migrants, and their classes are fully booked, as is the dental clinic and the lawyer.

Then there are the cracks in the old order of things—contrast the agency for whom I did the assessment last summer. They have just packed up and gone. They spent much of last year establishing themselves and getting considerable support to do both water and sanitation, and gender-based violence programming in a number of camps. I did the child psychosocial assessment for them in the North and hoped a programme would follow. But the agency decided the Greek programme was not financially viable and terminated it at short notice, using considerable amounts of donated funds to pay off their Greek staff.

So much for helping Syrian refugees.

Dina and a number of other good international staff have resigned.

Now they have set up an independent consultancy which works for free, helping volunteers and groups like Jafra get their act together, training them in things like finance, project development, protection and so on. So, I introduced Dina to Jafra and they are setting up some training.

Athens, Friday 17 February

Majd runs down the stairs to give me a hug and a kiss, followed by his brother Abou. I have not seen them since the summer in Lagkadikia. They are both taller and fit looking, wearing new tracksuits. They show Naya and me around the new apartment: five bunk beds and a rather bare living room, but it's enough. They now know for sure that they are on their way to Germany, and they don't care. And now there is a baby cousin, 25 days old and crowing with delight. Her sister is no longer a toddler but a determined little girl.

I ask Abou if he would like to do a photo story of their current home, and over the next hour, he and Majd run about with my mobile phone, producing some beautiful family portraits. We all look at the Migrantchild website, and Majd is delighted to find his pictures and film there, and his story. They had not seen it before.

Then I sit with their father while he smokes his hookah, perched on the bottom bunk in their rather crowded bedroom. He offers me some, but I explain I don't smoke. How does he feel about finally being on his way to Germany?

– *If you asked me, do I want to go to Germany rather than be in Syria? The answer is no, I have to learn a new language at fifty! But it's not in my hands. It will take another twenty years to sort out Syria. Life is impossible there now for everyone.*

He puffs gloomily. Then he looks up and gives me a big smile.

– *My second home will be Germany! We are going to learn the language, and we are going to open a shop and a restaurant. We will celebrate Syrian traditions and inform German people about our famous food in Syria and our culture, and the Germans will see we are not just about work. I know German people work all the time and don't relax much.*

– *So you will help Germans relax?*

– *Exactly! Merkel knew Syrians are smart people. We will make money and improve the economy.*

We have to head back to the office. I am supposed to be teaching 'case management,' because this is what all the individual women here need. But the 'cashcard' team from CARE just turned up, and that's more important. They review both women's documents. Both are out of date, and so, until they update them and get some legal standing as asylum-seekers, they are not eligible for the cash card. At least some of the Jafra team are.

An Iraqi family is coming—a mother and child. And on Monday, three generations—a grandmother of 75 and a mother and her three children. We need stair gates. The curved marble staircase is a death trap. I watched Fatima try to follow her mother up them yesterday morning. I let her try three steps and then picked her up, terrified she would tumble on the narrow shiny white steps. I also notice Maya is exhausted with Fatima. She pulls on her arm quite roughly when we go out for a walk, and Fatima stumbles trying to keep up. Naya and I take turns giving her rides and swing her between us (to her complete delight), and, coming home, Maya carries her affectionately.

Naya and I go for a coffee. I want to know her plans because on Monday she tried to leave with the smugglers. She is in her mid-twenties, and all her family left for Germany some years ago. She stayed in Syria because she liked her job. Then, when she tried to leave, she was told she was too old for family reunification. So, she did the usual illegal route: Turkey, Samos, then Athens, where she heard about Jafra and decided to join in and help. But her family ring her daily, pressing her to join them. So far, she has spent 6000 euros of her family's money. This was her sixth attempt. The smugglers had given her a Belgian passport. She was with another man, also being smuggled. At passport control, he went straight through, but they stopped her.

— *They asked me, 'What is the capital of Belgium?' I said 'Bruxelles.' They turned me back.*

— *They probably have a record of your face by now, after so many failed attempts*—I say.

— *I know, and actually I have decided that I want to apply for asylum here in Greece. I can work here and help people, like in Jafra. The trouble is, my mum keeps calling and calling for me to come.*

Naya told me her escape from Syria had increased her cynicism about all the groups. It was obvious on her way out with the smugglers that Assad's men had good relations with ISIS, as she passed through different checkpoints where they communicated easily with each other. All she had to do was cover herself and pay the money. As for the Free Syrian Army:

– They were not the ones dying in Aleppo—just civilians like me.

Athens, Saturday 18 February

Housam, Daniela, Bashar and I spent all day wandering through the Acropolis. They have been here since October and still had not visited, so I insisted they come with me. I have been here twice before. Once when I was fourteen with my older sister and my newly divorced mother. My grandmother had dispatched all three of us on a classical cruise thinking it would be educational for us two girls and a distraction for my miserable mother. I remember the whiteness of the rock, the astonishing grace of the buildings through which you could wander at will, and the emptiness. I came back seven years later when I was twenty-one, having hitchhiked across Europe with my (then) boyfriend. He was on his way to wash earth off Minoan skulls for an anatomy tutor doing physical anthropology research in Crete, and I was on my way to explore Turkey alone. Except, I missed the boyfriend so much that, after taking the Magic Bus to Istanbul, I turned around and followed him to Crete, turning up unannounced at the villa and asking if I could join the bone washing team. I was given a space to sleep on the roof and my own set of small brushes with which to delicately remove earth from bones. It certainly gave me an intimate acquaintance with the fragility and beauty of the human skull. Then suddenly, there were jets roaring over our heads and young men clambering onto military trucks in local villages while their mothers wept. Greece and Turkey had gone to war. It was my first experience of conflict. 'Direct' would be the wrong word because in Crete, although young men were sent off to

263

war, it did not touch us personally. We ignored all embassy warnings about Greece no longer being a safe holiday destination and kept on bone-washing and hiking in the mountains during our weekends off. But I digress. The war from which Housam and Bashar have escaped is conflict on another scale. Housam told me that a new law was issued in Syria last week, and that all men, regardless of religion, must now take two wives because there are so many widows. We decided not to talk about war or work and wandered, entranced, around the sunlit ruins. At one point, sitting on some stone steps, I could see people from every single continent relaxing in the sun.

We ate lunch sitting beside the Roma Agora. Our waiter asked where we were all from and was delighted to hear Slovakia, Syria and Britain. I could not help thinking that, at least during that time of empire, the ethnic mix in this area would have been just as diverse.

Lavriou Camp, Tuesday 21 February

— I'm a naval officer, I fix helicopters. When I came here, I had to start from scratch. But I am not a stupid man, I think I grasped the problems quite quickly. Most camp managers change every two months, and I have been here six months. I have tried to get the refugees to participate, but they don't want to do anything.

The lieutenant commander is a very friendly man. He has green-framed glasses and an easy-going manner. Through UNHCR, he has invited Housam to come and discuss what Jafra could do to get the refugee community more engaged and active, as his own attempts have failed so far. For a start, there is the old story with the food.

— Eighty percent of the food brought in is wasted. I know they don't like it, and I know they are cooking in their houses, which is not allowed. The houses are wood; they can burn down easily. I want everyone to be happy. Being hungry is not good. But they cannot cook in their houses.

He wanted to open a kitchen, but he wanted it to be a proper professional kitchen, which needed a regular commitment from the refugee community to staff it at the same times every day, which no one would do.

Housam has a suggestion for that, explaining how they built communal points with hot plates in Lagkadikia and lowered the voltage to the tents so that people could not use these stoves inside. The commander is interested and asks for a more detailed email.

He has already done a lot. There are agencies in the camp providing legal support and medical care. IOM transports the children to school and back, UNHCR does protection, and there is a WASH programme. But the passivity gets him down.

– *I tried to get them to help with cleaning. I pointed out that it's not good for them, and it's not good for us if there is rubbish everywhere. We could have a clean-up squad or clean-up days. We do it in the military. There are regular days when every single person is out in the field looking for foreign objects. We know they are lethal, so we all join in. But after this request, the next thing is there is a post on social media. Someone has written, 'The military has forced us to clean the camp.'*

I think of Jafra doing clean-ups in Lagkadikia and others joining in because they made it look like fun. Housam and the lieutenant commander agree—Housam can send some of the Jafra team down to stay in the camp and assess needs.

– *Come up with some good ideas! Don't just tell me the problems.*

We head back to Athens, giving a lift to a friend who lives in the camp, first stopping to wander around the beautiful Temple of Poseidon at Sounio on the Cape and eat lunch in a deserted restaurant by an empty beach. I get back in the evening in time to teach a session on stress and PTSD at Khora. Last week, I did grief and loss. There are even more people tonight, so I suppose it must have been OK, and they are a friendly and responsive audience. It has been a year since I started doing these basic talks in France. I no longer need notes or teaching aids at all and teach much better for it because everyone can draw on personal experience. Tomorrow, it will be taking care of ourselves and others.

Athens, Wednesday 22 February

I am making friends with the new Syrian family upstairs in the shelter—Lara, age nine and Rasha, age ten—who arrived on Monday with their older sister, their mother and grandmother. Their father is already in Germany, but they did not have the means to go with him. They were refugees in Lebanon for two years, but then went back a few months ago to Syria to escape to Greece, illegally, through Turkey. They hope they can apply for family reunification. Yesterday, we did some developmental movement games for all the children in the shelter and Lara, Rasha and Fatima all loved it. Today, I brought some crayons and drawing books for each of them. They want to draw picture stories for me. I am delighted.

Then I headed off to do a developmental movement session with Crista at Khora. I met Crista in Calais when we were both looking after Wasim—*I know he is alive because he is sending me daily jokes on text messages.* Crista tells me he is back in Scandinavia, living in a country that has already turned down his asylum application.

She has decided to stay in Greece for the long haul. We start the Movement session. There is one volunteer per child, which is ideal. Initially, five of the super lively boys show no interest, but, as the group progresses, and we move from rocking and rowboats to crawling through human tunnels, they become more and more curious, and by the end, all the children are completely engaged. They are all patient with one another and take turns. There is one small incident when one child gets upset with another, but we have enough volunteers that someone can be with her. I love this method of working with children. No toys, just using our bodies, even in the tiniest space. By the end of the session, all the children are both physically tired and calm.

Then I sit in the café area and talk to a Syrian man about the situation in his home. He has a son who is still in Damascus and a small daughter who was playing with us downstairs.

– *It is very bad now. Bashir al Assad destroyed everything. The living situation is terrible. My son is unhappy because there is no power, no water... He did not leave with us because his wife did not want to leave. But the army may ask him to join, and he does not want to, so he is trying to leave. I am very afraid for my son. Syria is a game for the big countries. Russia has complete control of Bashir Assad and Syria and everything. We have resources, so Russia wants Syria. I am very sad that Arab countries*

266

have not helped us, even when Europe did.

I am very confused about the situation. It will take twenty years to fix everything. Everyone fights everyone else in Syria. I don't support the government or the Free Army. I just want my family to be safe. The government offered me work: they asked me to get information and offered to pay me, but I refused. I won't sell myself, my country, or my religion.

The lecture on helping others and ourselves is the most crowded so far. We end with two sessions on slow breathing and physical relaxation. I am delighted when another volunteer takes over conducting the second group, using what she has learned from me. She does really well, and I get home exhausted.

Athens, Thursday 23 February

Rasha is very cross with me. She sits on the lower bunk in the bedroom that she shares with her mother and two sisters. While she was downstairs, I lent her drawing book and crayons to Muna, the 5-year-old girl from Iraq.

— *But she cannot draw, and she will scribble on my drawings!*

— *She has not done that, and I am so sorry, but I have only two drawing books at the moment. I will bring another tomorrow, but meanwhile, look, let her have three pages from each of you.*

I tear them out of the back of each book, along with a box of crayons. I hand these to Muna.

— *Now you two have your books and can share this box of crayons until tomorrow.*

Rasha still has her arms folded and a pout on her face. Her mother says something to her in Arabic.

— *I'm sorry*—she says somewhat reluctantly.

— *Thank you, Rasha, for sharing. That is very kind!*

I follow Muna into the living room, which has three sofas and a blanket on the floor. She has taken the crayons out of the box and clutches them like a bunch of flowers in one hand. She clearly is uncertain of what to do.

— *She cannot draw*—Fatima's mother says.

— *But she can enjoy colouring*—I say putting the paper on the floor. Muna gets down to join me, watching with pleasure as I draw an elephant and a cat. Fatima and her mother are already scribbling and drawing fishes.

A 5-year-old who never had a chance to draw. A 10-year-old who is scared to lose a drawing book because all she has left is a small hold-all with some clothes inside. This morning, I took Majd and Abou to the nearest small park to play. I wanted them to learn the way to their nearest green space, and they loved it. I bought them a football, and we played with a small, shy Russian boy who had come with his mum. Then we had coke and crisps. On the way back, Majd wanted a picture of himself standing in front of a large vegetable shop because it reminded him of home. Then, swings and ice cream with my Kurdish friends in the playground near their house.

We all had fun. But I have such a strong sense of all these children's lives being on hold. It matters. It won't be easy to restart school if you have been out for three years, forgotten how to read and write and are muddled over which language to use.

Athens, Friday 24 February

I am standing near the entrance of Hadrian's Library, when two African men in shabby clothes rush down the stairs and run towards the pillars. The Greek lady in the ticket booth calls out to them—*Tickets! Tickets!* And they turn, bewildered.

— *I want to see the Acropolis!* says one with greying hair and beard and a wool cap pulled down low on his forehead.

— *I am really sorry, they will want you to get a ticket. But this is not the Acropolis. It is up there*—I say, pointing to the craggy crest above us. As I come closer, I realise both are slightly inebriated. We walk out of the entrance gate together.

— *Where are you from?*

— *Sudan, and you?*

— *England.*

— *We want to see the Acropolis.*

— *Well, you can get a wonderful view for free if you go up there, it's not far.* I point to the hill visible beyond the Agora.

They head off somewhat unsteadily, and I stop being a tour guide and spend the rest of the morning wandering the ancient Agora in the sunlight. I am wearing too many clothes! These last few days of Mediterranean spring have been amazing—warm sunlight and blossom everywhere, the ground covered in yellow flowers. At least, the migrant crisis is reintroducing me to the loveliness of Greece and reminding me of the enduring relevance of classical history. I stand by the circular space where the Boule, or council, once met around two thousand years ago—fifty representatives of the different Athenian tribes who gave way every thirty five days to others, so that all tribes took their share in administration of the state. But democracy gives way to empire and empire to tyranny and barbarism, and then we start all over again.

In Greece, every taxi ride involves a rant about the lack of democracy today, or about the corruption and taxation imposed by the current regime, or against Germany for its arrogant imposition of austerity. This is always combined with extraordinary courtesy to Naya and myself when the driver has established who we are and what we do. We were taking taxis yesterday because there was a metro strike. I wanted to take the subway today, but I made the mistake of pausing to watch break-dancers in Monastiraki Square, and in thirty seconds, my wallet was lifted from my bag.

I suddenly felt the lightness and emptiness. So, I am standing penniless and credit cardless in the middle of Athens. This is a good way of reminding myself of how so many of my new friends feel. At least I still a have phone and passport. I decide to take a taxi, but I make the mistake (in my somewhat distressed state) of telling the driver *no money.* He slows down and indicates I should get out.

– *No no, I will pay you at office.* He shakes his head. I ring Pan, who amazingly picks up instantly.

– *Pan, please explain to this taxi driver my wallet was just stolen, I am returning to my office and will pay him immediately when I arrive.*

Pan, cool and friendly as ever, asks for no further explanation and explains everything in Greek. Taxi driver, all smiles, takes me to Jafra,

'The Long Grass' by Lara, age 9, from Syria.
This is my big sister, me and my sister and
my mother and my grandmother all walking
in the long grass to Turkey. It was very tall,
and I was very tired, and it was difficult. And
there were a lot of planes in the sky, and I
was scared because my mother was saying
the police could catch us, so we should go
quickly. When the planes came, the smuggler
told us to stay still in the grass and not walk,
so the planes could not see us. We kept
walking until morning, then we stopped. A
police car came to take people back to Syria,
but they did not see us. They took another
group and we kept walking to Turkey.

where I run in, asking if anyone has any cash. I am saved by an impoverished refugee. So wonderful to have friends.

The Syrian girls upstairs have let the Iraqi girl continue to use their crayons. Meanwhile, I have brought more drawing books and crayons so everyone has one. They spend an hour sitting with me explaining their pictures: there is the journey through the long grass at the border; the small boat across the sea; the ferry to Athens; and the meal their mother cooked them. I ask Lara for a picture of her happiest memory in Lebanon, and she comes back with a picture of two sisters on the balcony of a lovely house, but then explains they are calling their sister indoors because there is shooting and bombs.

Afterwards, one of the Khora volunteers wants me to meet with a refugee friend he is worried about because the young man appears to be 'making up stories' about his life, like saying he is married when he is not, or that he is a working for a press agency when he is not. The young man is extremely stressed and has been living off a diet of tobacco, tea, coffee and less than enough food. He says he has talked about his experiences with a psychologist and didn't find it helpful. The most helpful thing is helping others. That's why he likes working at Khora. As we chat away over coffee, I can see no evidence of psychosis, and I have no way to check the veracity of the stories he tells about his own experiences.

*— But exaggerating our importance within relationships and work is one way of making ourselves feel better when we feel fragile and lost. The more security, friends and rootedness he can find in this community in Athens, the less need there will be to do it—*I explain to the volunteer. *You can give him that, at the same time as gently challenging inconsistencies to let him know you know when he is exaggerating. And he needs sleep, food and regular exercise—boring remedies but so essential.*

It is a big ask, but the amazing thing about the volunteers out here is that so many of them are prepared to give this intensive support to the refugees that need it. Yesterday, I met with another volunteer who is trying to help a single mother with five children. Each of the three youngest boys are troubled in different ways, and mum is understandably overwhelmed and finding parenting difficult. The volunteer speaks the same language, so I suggest she spend regular time with mum, modelling some positive parenting, and she is happy to do this.

In the evening, Pan, Housam, Daniela and I go out to eat. Pan is sure there will be a general election soon, and he predicts a resurgent Right.

– *How can that happen here when people tell you it is the greed and corruption of the Right that brought about this crisis in the first place?* I ask.

– *They promise lower taxes and the left is split by the betrayal of Tsipras.*

– *So how will anything function?*

– *More privatisation...*

My heart sinks. How have we lost the idea which dominated my early life—that it was worth paying for the common good?

– *A resurgent right is not good for migrants.*

– *That's why it's good we are all acting legally—renting properties. They will crack down on all the squats.*

Housam had his relocation interview yesterday at the French Embassy, an exhausting seven-hour affair with one break for a snack. They grilled him on every aspect of his life: in Yamouk, in Lebanon, here in Greece. Overall, he felt it went well. They asked him where he wanted to go, and he said—*Send me to a small town or an island. I just need to rest and get away from everything.*

Athens, Sunday 26 February

Yesterday was full of small, last minute dramas. Crista wanted to discuss autism with me, as she thought one of the children who comes to the child-friendly space might be autistic. It sounded more like developmental delay to me, so I went through the key features of both. While we sat there chatting, another boy sharply pulled the hair of a little girl. When admonished, he went and hid under the stairs, hiding under two big cushions, and then rushed out of the space. Crista told me he was very physically aggressive much of the time, and they had not found a way to contain him, as he just became more destructive. His parent just left him there, which made it difficult to exclude him.

– *Accompanied exclusion*—I suggest. *You cannot ignore the destructive behaviour if he is hurting others, so, he has to be taken out of the situation by someone who sticks with him. He comes back when he is prepared to behave.* In fact, this was just what had happened today when another volunteer had followed the boy out. And, he was one of the boys that had enthusiastically joined in the developmental movement session. So, I suggest more of that as a way of both using energy and building relationships, because he had actually taken care of other children in that session.

When I got back to Jafra, I found Rasha had fainted and was complaining of severe stomach pain. The Jafra volunteer had already called an ambulance which had just arrived. Meanwhile, her illness had set something off in Sura, who became more and more dramatically unwell while waiting for the ambulance. By the time it arrived, Sura was bent over, clutching her stomach and moaning, so the kind ambulance man agreed to take both.

Housam went down to the hospital to meet them. It all turned out well. The attention given at the hospital appeared to allow Sura's recovery and for her to start talking about some difficulties that were happening in her life at the moment. Rasha just has a sore throat, which can give you stomach pain. But, Housam was astounded to discover that many migrants were sitting for hours and hours in the hospital without any care because there were no translators. He wants to find a way to address this.

Today was my last afternoon here. Housam, Daniela and I climbed the lovely wooded hills across from the Acropolis—Athens spread around and below us. The endless white buildings have a bony appearance from a distance, like a dried out coral reef, edged by mist and a grey sea. We wanted to visit the Philopappos Monument. Philopappos was a Syrian, and an Athenian and Roman Citizen, living here in the 1st and 2nd centuries AD. He appears to have been much loved by the Athenians for his generosity, so it seemed like an appropriate place to go.

Majd's Story

Majd comes from Syria. At the time that he told the first part of this story (August 2016) he was eleven years old and living in a refugee camp in Northern Greece. He told the final part in Athens in 2017.

I cannot remember anything from before the war. My first memory is bombing and being scattered around. War came suddenly. We started hearing boom, boom, boom, boom, and we ran away immediately, we jumped into our basement. There were snipers shooting into houses and we had to hide. It was my grandfather's house, but we lived there. My cousins in another town were injured. I was in second grade when I heard about them. Their mother was staying with us, and a bomb dropped in front of them and they got fragments in them. They were badly injured. They were in 5th and 8th grade.

I do remember school before the war. I was seven when I first went to school. We were living happily, we played a lot, and it was peaceful. I used to play and study. Football was my favourite thing. There were two schools next to each other. And when I was in fourth grade, we could not go to school because there was shooting there, and they were dropping bombs on the schools, and there were snipers everywhere, and we had to sit in the corridors. The teachers never told us anything because they did not want us to be sad. The teachers said—
Don't leave your houses.

I don't know why there is a war. When I asked Father the reason, he would just cry. Any time I asked him, he immediately started crying. I asked my aunts—they all just cried. They are the ones who suffered most. We were OK because they loved us so much, but I was scared. Our house had bombing all around it. We were actually going to die. Actually, I kept going to school. I missed one week. School was right next door to our house, so I could easily run home. The other school building right beside us was bombed, and this massive wall collapsed, so our entire building was shaking. We went to the basement straight away because snipers were shooting the injured in the other school, they were in 7th to 10th grade. None of them died. Stuff did not fall on their heads. The bombs did not come from a plane. The guns were nearby; they scattered metal which was very very hot. This one area was Free Syrian Army, and the other was Bashir Al Assad. We were in the Assad area, and these bombs could land anywhere, and if you were not lucky, you died. If our side did not send bombs back, the Free Syrian Army would keep bombing us. We just wanted to live in peace. We would pray and read the Koran. Then, Grandfather and Grandmother died. I think Grandfather had blood clots. Father inherited their house and sold it, and we bought a house in the countryside. But when we had been there one week, they dropped a bomb on our new house, and it was flattened. We arrived by car and were just going to put in the furniture, but the bomb fell, so, we pulled away. The house was completely destroyed. We went back to the city. It was OK there. There was no bombing. But I did not go to school. We were there just a week while Father got money and papers, and we left.

We travelled in a luxurious car belonging to some cousins. It had fourteen people in it. We escaped from the Free Syrian Army straight away, but when we got to the border, Bashir Al Assad's snipers were shooting at us to scare us. They did not want us to leave. We stayed two days, hiding in the mountains on the border until the snipers left. They were just trying to scare us to make us go back. Of course, I was terrified. I thought they would kill us. How would you feel? God helped us to leave. And, it was the smuggler who helped us. We did not know him, but later he became friends with Father.

I am not scared right now. I just want you to write these stories, so everyone knows. The worst thing was the bombing because they destroyed our house, and we lost everything, and we could not play. And I did think I might die with the sniper at the border.

I used to cry. I had bad dreams—not every night—just very scary dreams. Sometimes when I was really really scared, I would get bad fevers. I sometimes dreamed they would take everyone into prison except me, and then they would kill them and leave me.

I knew some people who were kidnapped. When I was five years old, there were a lot of events, and they were taking a lot of people to prison. My father's friend went to prison. I loved this man like my second father. And when he went to prison, I took a chair, and I sat outside his house, and refused to go until he returned. It went on for twenty days. I would get a sandwich from a stand. There was a market nearby with a bathroom. I sat there at night as well. Then he was released. He is in Syria now.

We stayed in Turkey for two days and then left on a boat. One of our friends was told to be the captain. He was really good. We had to pay. It was the first time I had been on a boat; I had never seen the sea. The boat was really crowded with a lot of people, but I could breathe, and I was not scared. The water was calm. I was wearing a life jacket. After about five hours, a boat came and took us. We stayed on an island for about two hours and then we went on another boat and we got to Greece.

Then we walked for around five hours. We got really, really tired. And then we got in a taxi and came to Idomeni. I remember you in the camp, you played the spoons. Then we tried to cross the border, but the Syrians were not allowed to cross, so we went back. Jafra was in Idomeni—they played with us most days. But here is better. The UN brought us here. There, if it rained, everything would be soaked. I got completely wet every time it rained. Living here is so much better. I don't know why, it just is. We play, we have fun, and there is school where we learn English, Arabic and music. It is not a real school. There is no sport. But there is a field where we go with the Spanish.

There is nothing I don't like here. The only bad thing is the food. Living in tents is OK—a house would be better—but a tent is OK. But my father is very fed up now. We dream of going home, but they won't let us. We would like to go back to Syria even though there is war. Here, we are humiliated even more than in Syria. If we went back, we would have a roof over our heads and Father would work and we would live better than we live here. I am happy to be in the camp, but not deep in my heart.

If God does not let us back to Syria, he will decide where we go—but I would prefer Syria. My cousins would not be able to come to me, and I want to be in a house with my cousins and be happy. My mother is much skinnier now, but she looks after me and she helps me in every way. God does not hold anything back from us. We are not a religious family. My mother prayed in Syria but not here. Father and I pray five times a day; we don't go to Mosque, we pray on our own. I sleep OK now. I am not feeling sick. I play and sing. What I miss most is my friends and relatives. None have died. When I grow up, I want to be a doctor or a dentist. When I have children, I won't tell them about this war, I don't want them to be sad.

Athens, February 2017

The camp was very boring; there was nothing to do. Jafra tried to teach the children English and Greek and to teach us how to read. We liked that, but we did not like the Spanish because they shouted at us. Jafra was always friendly. I did learn a bit, and I went to classes every day. I wanted to learn English, not Greek, because, if I walk on the streets, people understand English. We had football. Sometimes, I took Father's mobile to play on it. There were so many fights, especially the Iraqi people. They were fighting with knives. We still went to the village, just to walk and play in that garden.

Then it got cold in the camp. It snowed. We stayed in our tents all the time, but there was so much water in the tents. We went to the UN to get some more blankets, but we got no answer. If it rained, we tried to make a fire in the tent. We got wood from the forest (we tried to get dry wood), and we used cartons for the fire. The food was still very bad. If you asked Jafra, they always tried to help. If there had been no Jafra, we would have been much worse off. They gave us plastic to cover the tents.

I made friends, they still keep in touch. My friend sent this video because he misses me a lot. He is still in the hotel. I like to have lots of friends, but I hate to be too close, because then, if I travel, I will miss them. I don't want to miss people. I miss a lot of people in Syria.

It was better in the hotel. We moved there three months ago. The hotel was good. It was five people in one room, just like here. I was with Mother and Father and my brothers. The food was delicious! Better than the camp. And in the hotel, there was a big room for studying with a lot of books. I had English classes every day; the teacher was an old Syrian woman. There were lots of children. We all played together on bikes—that was how I hurt my toe. I was really happy to come to Athens because I know we are going to Germany, and I will see my brothers.

My brother in Syria is OK. He is in Damascus, and there is not a lot of fighting there. He has his work, and he does not want to leave Syria. Syria is not good now, especially in Aleppo because the president went there and was fighting with ISIS. Bashir is not good. The Free Syrian Army is not good. I don't like any of them. I don't know who the good people are. I just love my brothers. I don't know how we can make peace there. If we did, of course, I would want to go back. I want to sell vegetables like my father.

Tapachula and Tijuana

Mexico, April 2017

Ciudad Hidalgo, Guatemalan-Mexican border, Sunday 9th April
When I ask the tall woman with the tiny baby why she left El Salvador, she answers in five words:
— *Because they killed my husband.*
The tiny baby is 27 days old. She holds him close against her chest, with a cloth pulled over to protect him from the sun as she walks along. Her two daughters, aged four and sixteen, are walking along in front, following the banner held up by two other Salvadorans. It says: "Don't Hate Migrants." This is the start of the Via Crucis, and they are heading for Tijuana and the US border.

We got up at 5am to join in. Jeff and Heather, two doctor friends who work in Tapachula, picked us up and took us to Cristobal's house. Cristobal is a Mexican anthropologist who has been involved in organising the Via Crucis marches for a number of years. The idea is simple: Central American migrants marching the length of Mexico will draw attention to their right:

"To safely escape persecution in their countries, exercise their right to seek refuge through asylum, and raise awareness of the violence, human rights violations, and legal challenges they face, at home in Central America, in transit through Mexico, and upon arrival to the United States of America."

Cristobal gave us a small lecture about our roles as international observers. Article 33 of the Constitution of Mexico forbids participation in political actions, but we could come as observers to help ensure the safety of the marchers.

Marta, a Colombian researcher on migration, and three Salvadorans joined us, and we took two taxis down to Ciudad Hidalgo, jumped on one of the innumerable rafts made from rubber tyres and planks of wood, and were punted across to Tecun Uman—as the town is called in Guatemala. As simple as that, no signs that this was an international border—no police, no wires, no walls—just a very busy,

Crossing the Guatemala/Mexico border with
the Via Crucis Caravan April 2017

shallow river with rafts punting back and forth, laden with families and traders carrying goods in both directions. There is a formal border crossing on the bridge, but I did not see many going that way.

Our group weren't carrying much: a cross, a banner and a bunch of palms and flowers that were being sold in the market to mark Palm Sunday. The point of crossing was to make a symbolic start on the Guatemalan side. And that's what we did. At this point, journalists and observers outnumbered marchers, but there was something very moving watching Raul plant the wooden cross at the river's edge and then walk back along the Guatemalan bank barefoot. Crossing back to Mexico, we all walked through sandy shallows, and then Jose read the press release, while Global TV from Brazil, Reuters and a few others I did not know, filmed and recorded. Here it is in full:

"Central America is bleeding. Massive numbers of its people are fleeing for their lives on a daily basis. Our region's governments—the governments of Honduras, El Salvador, Guatemala, Mexico and the United States of America—are failing us. They are denying the existence of a refugee crisis in Central America, and they are violently repressing the people caught in its vicious cycle. It's time to take action to call attention to this emergency situation. On April 9th, refugees, migrants and allies will set foot from the edge of Central America and head north.

Caravan participants will be living proof of the dire situation in Central America. El Salvador has the highest homicide rate in the world. In Guatemala, a case of sexual violence was reported every 46 minutes in 2015. That same year, there were 174,000 Hondurans internally displaced due to conflict.

On the way to the US border we will speak out against Mexico's Southern Border Plan, which criminalizes migrants, militarizes the border regions, and has resulted in a massive increase in the detention and deportation of Central American refugees as well as instances of human rights abuses.

We demand that Mexico improve its capacity to grant refuge to Central Americans. Mexico's asylum system, despite recent advances, falls alarmingly short of addressing the current refugee crisis.

We demand that the US Government respect refugees' right to seek asylum. The US administration is leading a regional attack on the asylum process by drastically restricting access to safety. Rampant cases of US immigration officers illegally banning asylum seekers at our southern border, plus immigration courts rife with racism and due process violations, amount to a systematic subversion of refugee protections."

Elise is one of those caught up in this misery. Her 16-year-old daughter tells me the whole story as we walk along. She was happy in El Salvador, studying hard and hoping to be a doctor. Her father drove a bus. A criminal gang got on his bus and demanded the earnings, he refused, so they shot him. That was seven months ago. Then they started harassing his wife who ran a small business, saying—*Give us 100 dollars or we will take your children.* So, the family packed their bags and fled. When they got to the Mexican border, they had no idea how to plead for asylum or demand their rights, so they were instantly deported—as are many. They went back to El Salvador but tried again a short while later. This time, Elise was better informed and asked for asylum on the basis of the violence and terror she had experienced and the direct threat to their lives. It was refused. The Mexican Commission to Assist Refugees (COMAR) has a lengthy, impenetrable and seemingly arbitrary decision-making system. Cristobal knows many who have been accepted with far less justification. That is why the Via Crucis march this year is focussing particularly on the needs of families like Elise. Lawyers from the US are joining them, and they will plead their case at the US border.

– I just want a place to bring my son up safely. I will tell him the story of our country and how the violence forced us to leave.

By now, we are on the highway back to Tapachula. It is shade-less and baking hot. Elise and her family take refuge in Jeremiah's truck. Jeremiah is a refugee from Guatemala. He would love to go back there. He had been working in construction in the US since he was eighteen years old. He met his Mexican wife there and had two children. But, as Obama's government tightened the screws, they decided that they should go home and make a life in Guatemala. They tried. They had a nice house and some animals. They farmed and sold cheese and cream. The trouble is that, if you show any sign of stability or success, you immediately become a target for extortion. Gangs came to his house and said—*Pay 3000 quetzals or we will kill your children*—so they fled to Hidalgo.

– But Mexico is impossible. The Maras came here as well and threatened me with a gun. I sent my wife to another city. I followed her, but it was very racist. They kept saying, 'No you are Guatemalan,' so we tried Puebla, but they said, 'You are Christians (meaning protestant), and we are Catholics. We don't want you,' so we came back to Hidalgo. Then the gangs came again this December and said they will kidnap my children. So now, we are leaving. We have to escape. I told Cristobal my story and he said, 'Join the March. We have lawyers who can help you at the US border,' because our children are US citizens. I am very glad I can help with my truck.

His truck slowly brings up the rear. The local police have joined us and are leading in a pick-up from the front. Jeff jokes at me accompanying a protest on my first days in the country, but I point out that I am following the law every step of the way. Cristobal says we will stop at the checkpoint on the highway. People can cross the actual frontier, easily enough, as we all did this morning.

– But these checkpoints are where the immigration police stop you and ask for your papers. If you say you are a refugee, they are obliged to take you to the office in town, from where you are sent to a detention centre while your plea is judged. They cannot send you straight back. But many people just don't know enough to ask and they get sent back.

I can't believe I am looking forward to seeing a police checkpoint, but I am so hot and exhausted after some two hours of walking, I would welcome any excuse for a break. I envy Carlos, on his skateboard. He sails along, stops, and takes the banner for a bit, then skates some more. He's a 23-year-old who left his wife, 5-year-old son and 3-month-old baby behind in El Salvador a few weeks ago:

– Because I don't want to join a gang. I will stay anywhere I can get a job.

– Are your wife and children OK?

— They are with my mother. We don't talk except on public telephones, it is safer. I did start the asylum process here, but I don't want to stay, there's too much discrimination. I will go north with the Via Crucis.

Carlos explains that the Mexican police put him in prison for skateboarding, using anti-terrorist legislation to do so. While in jail, they told him to find a lawyer, but he had no money. The police let him go after they had failed to find any evidence against him and discovered he was in the process of claiming asylum, but it left him feeling very afraid.

— I am not a criminal. I just like to skateboard. They actually brought in a lawyer and told me to phone my family for the money to pay him. I refused, and the next day they let me go free. They are 'mala gente,' bad people, rats.

We arrive at a service station. The municipal police turn around and head home. The icy cool inside the shop is like heaven. The checkpoint police are also hanging out here having refrescos. They seem quite uninterested in us.

Everyone grabs drinks, and we all pile into the back of Jeremiah's truck to do the last bit to Tapachula, where we stop outside Casa Belen, one of the larger shelters on the edge of the town. Cristobal speaks to the crowd who gather outside the door, inviting the compañeros to join. Some twenty people do, carrying bags and backpacks, following the banner into the central park where they sleep the night.

Tapachula, Monday 10 April

— You are good people, you are hardworking people. Do not ask anyone for anything, do not say bad words, do not permit bandits among us. If there are any bad people among us, we will not allow them. We will report them to the authorities. We are our own security and we should all walk together, leaving no one behind. We will look after one another…

It is 8am. Cristobal is making a speech to some 250 assembled marchers, many of whom have slept the night under the shelter of the performance area in the central park. I am particularly taken with the LGBT group, who, in spite of sleeping all night on cardboard, are immaculately dressed and made up.

I am glad to see Cristina here. She came into the clinic I was doing in a shelter a few days ago, sat down and started crying, speaking in rushed sentences between sobs.

— *I am very scared of being found…that's why we are here. They want to kill us, me and my mother. They found us at home. They told my mum they will cut off her head and they will kill me by dropping me in a river… I have nightmares every night, I cannot sleep. I am terrified all the time… And the shelter manager says we must leave in five days because we have been here five days already, and we are only allowed ten days.*

As she was gulping air and chest-breathing rapidly in a way that foretold a panic attack, I begged her to stop for a minute and breathe slowly, while I looked for the shelter manager, and her mother, Dolores, to try and understand the whole situation. The manager confirmed the eviction notice:

— *We have a new policy. This shelter is only for sick migrants without papers, and they have their papers, so they can only stay ten days.*

Cristina started sobbing again. Dolores took her hand and explained. She is divorced and lived in Guatemala with her daughter. She worked hard as a cleaner and managed to feed her family.

— *But the gangs saw that I earned something and was without a husband. One day, they came to my house and said if I did not give them money, they would kill me. I was terrified, but neighbours called the police, who rescued us.*

But it was too dangerous to go home. A year ago, the whole family fled to Mexico. Cristina and Dolores obtained residency, rented a place to live, and Dolores found work as a cleaner. However, the gangs found them.

— *We called the police, who brought us to this shelter for safety, but they said there was nothing else they could do. I don't know what to do. We cannot live here. The gangs are present in the other shelters. I know we should leave. I have relatives in northern Mexico, but we have nothing, how should we get there?* Dolores said.

We spent an hour doing some stress relaxation and breathing, just to help Cristina calm down. Then we talked through what options they had. One possibility was to travel freely and immediately by joining the Via Crucis de Refugiado—lawyers and international observers accompany the march. There would be transport, food, and shelter along the way and a chance to connect with others who could give advice and assistance. It was not free of risk, but nor was being homeless in Tapachula. I emphasised that it was their decision. All I could do was help them think through the advantages and disadvantages of different courses of action.

They are here today to join the marchers. As she gives me a hug, Cristina tells me that she is crying inside, but she knows they should leave.

I think Dolores and Cristina have made the right decision. But, once again, I find myself agonising over whether I have acted appropriately as her doctor by supporting her choice to join a march that might further expose her to violence. Remaining in the medical domain, providing individual psychological or biological treatments, is less complicated than helping your patients think through the consequences of engaging in political action. But if you are fleeing for your life, every action to save it is political.

The March heads off to COMAR, where the marchers pause in front of the closed gates.

– *Migrants are not criminals!* they shout. *Migrants are international workers!*

We head out onto the highway and walk along with the march for the next hour, before heading back to Tapachula in a combi. We have promised to cover Jeff's clinic for the week he is away. We give Cristina and Dolores a hug.

– *We'll see you in Tijuana in a month*—I promise.[17]

Tapachula, Tuesday 11 April

In fact, the shelter is completely quiet today, as most people went on the march, but I have promised to see a young woman I first saw a few days ago. Beatriz is from Honduras. It is another terrible story. She was abused repeatedly by her father as a small child and then thrown out by her mother, who accused her of trying to *steal my husband.* She was sold into prostitution, but she somehow managed to escape and start her life again, meeting a nice man, marrying him, finding a job, and starting to study in night school. But the gangs came and told her she belonged to them, and he belonged to another territory so they could not marry, and both would be killed. So they escaped to Mexico and are applying for asylum here. They like Tapachula and would like to stay. Except, Beatriz misses her friends and her job and the life she made. She has nightmares every night about what happened as a child, and sometimes, she feels quite suicidal.

– I am afraid all the time these days, of dark places, of people following me at night, of anyone who has a tattoo.

At least her papers are in process. Everyone I have talked to in this shelter has a similar tale: abuse as a child and then trying to make a life amid murderous violence. Any sign that you are doing well in any conventional manner immediately makes you a target for extortion, and so you are left with no choice but to flee. The stories are as horrifying as any I have heard in any war zone, worse in some way because of the resigned acceptance with which rape and threats of execution are discussed as facts of life that must be endured. UNHCR and IOM apparently changed their terminology some years back. They no longer distinguish between economic and forced migration; they talk about mixed movement, acknowledging the vulnerability and structural violence that is driving people to move. But this has not affected the apparent arbitrariness of decision-making at COMAR.

I could not do much in that first session. We talked about how horrible it was to be uprooted from home and dumped among strangers with no connections and no identity. I explained that I thought it was quite normal to grieve in such a situation, and that such sadness could stir up older, more painful, memories. This made sense to her. She is also a devout Catholic, so I gave her some homework: to ask the priest who visits this shelter weekly where the nearest church was so she could actually go out and join the community there. And I brought a local friend, a Salvadoran woman, who has been here a while and could give her advice about restarting in another country.

We have not even started on the nightmares, but she came to see me this morning and seems transformed. She had found out about the nearest church—a ten-minute walk away and had decided to join a dance class she saw advertised. She had met my friend, and they had talked a lot, and were meeting again for coffee. Meanwhile, she and her husband plan more outings together, like going to the park and a movie. She is sleeping better, and the nightmares are less. Friendship and connection, what a difference they make!

Union Juarez, Thursday 13 April

What a difference 40 kilometres makes. We escaped the choking humidity of the city by taking a cab up into the mountains yesterday. We walked up the skirts of the volcano on a dirt road through deep green forest, climbing to sit and read beside a waterfall and series of rock pools—bird songs and water the only sounds. Today we take another path. A steep zigzagging rocky route that leads from the village of Talquian to 'the Line.' The Line is a series of white concrete bollards, some one hundred metres apart, stretching up the other side of the volcano. The footpath leading up to it on the Mexican side is a busy highway—mothers and children carrying shopping, young men with satchels, older men carrying enormous heavy loads. Manuel joins us with his loaded mule. He carries three boxes of eggs strung together in one hand. For an hour, he walks along besides us, chatting away about his life. He lives in a Guatemalan village an hour from the border with his wife. They have a small farm. He worked in the US in construction for five years. That's how he earned the money to build a home, but he never learned English because all his workmates were Spanish. Now, his children are grown and have left home. One of them, a daughter, works in a restaurant in Tapachula. She buys supplies for him every week, and he walks over the border to collect them. He has never had any problems doing so. Everyone does it.

We have reached the concrete bollards—a dead straight line cut through the forest, beyond a cluster of cafés and a bus stop and a small road on the Guatemalan side. When you look across the forested mountains to the ridge that resembles a woman lying on her back and the volcano beyond and see the small settlements identical to those on the Mexican side, what strikes you is the commonality. Much of the Chiapas did once belong to Guatemala after all. There is an old boundary stone in Union Juarez. The border moves around; the people remain the same.

Manuel drinks a couple of cans of beer—the only payment he requested for acting as our guide. We head back down the steep, busy path.

– *No one in Tapachula minds Guatemalans coming shopping*—our friend Enrique tells us. Enrique is a lecturer and researcher at the Grupo de Estudios de Migración y Procesos Transfronterizos at El Colegio de la Frontera Sur. He has organised the mental health course I am teaching next week.

– *But they are not welcome to stay. One of our prominent local politicians recently said that Tapachula is 'toxic' with migrants, and any who try to go further north will be stopped. Of course, you can apply for asylum, but the majority get turned down. They get deported back, and then they get killed. Do you know that, since the clamp down by the US in 2014, Mexico now sends more people back to Central America than the US? Three to four buses a day going to El Salvador or Honduras, and at least one plane load.*

But that has not stopped the number of asylum applications to Mexico increasing dramatically since Trump's election, Enrique tells us.

– *People's ideas about their future and what is possible have all changed. The price of Coyotes*[18] *has gone up, as have the chances of being deported straight back to Central America. So it's better to try and stay here.*

In fact, there is a process of regularisation going on. If you have been here since 2012 and can prove it with phone bills or rent payments or such, or show that you have a child born here, then you can regularise your position.

– *The trouble is people are still afraid to come forward because, if their paperwork is found to be unsatisfactory, they may be instantly deported. So living under the radar is preferable.*

Guatemala-Mexico border in the Chiapas,
April 2017

Tapachula, Friday 14 April

The trouble with living illegally is that you have no access to any kind of health care. In the clinic at the shelter this morning, along with some coughs and aches and pains, there was a homeless Salvadoran man who was caught in a gun fight here in Mexico and shot in the leg. He had been in a hospital for a couple of weeks but had been discharged and told he had to wait for the operation until the Red Cross donated the appropriate materials:

– *By which they mean never*—the man said. *I begged them to amputate, but they threw me out. I felt worse than an animal.*

He had been living on the streets for some years after being deported from the US, where he had had a small business. The wound was suppurating and smelling through poorly applied bandages and splint, but there was no response to calls to the hospital that had seen him, so Asmamaw did his best to clean the wound, organise the dressing, and start him on antibiotics—not enough, but all that he could do.

Meantime I go out to find Sodium Valproate for a woman who has been taking it for fifteen years to effectively control her epilepsy. A Mexican doctor had switched it to another drug without discussion, as a result of which she was sleeping all the time and having two fits a day. As she assured me that she was not going to get pregnant, and knew all the risks,[19] I agreed to find the drug and give it to her. All I can do for her as she is moving on tomorrow.

Tapachula, Thursday 20 April

I learned today that Mexicans have at least twelve words for sad states. I particularly like chipiliento, apparently used for a crying child who is jealous of a baby sibling, and cabizbajo, literally having your head down. I have been teaching mental health related to migration: six hours a day for the last four days to some thirty people—psychologists, NGO workers, UNHCR and ten medical students. When I explained during my lecture on acute stress that WHO guidelines make a strong recommendation against prescribing benzodiazepines, one of them said they could not believe they were listening to a psychiatrist who was against prescribing pills for everything.

293

At the end when we had a feedback session on what they liked about the course and what could be improved, one of them told me I was 'eclectic and unorthodox' and unlike any psychiatrist he had ever met. I thought this might be meant to go under the 'room for improvement' column, but he was kind enough to clarify that it was intended as a compliment and added that I was humane as well. I do hope so.

A small news item from Reuters says that asylum applications to Mexico have increased by 150% since Trump's election. Between November and March 2017, 5421 have applied to stay, compared to 2148 in the same period last year. They expect perhaps 22,000 this year, and COMAR and UNHCR say they are better at identifying who is eligible for asylum.

Let's hope that means Elise and her children can stay—if they don't make it across the US border, that is.

Tijuana, Saturday 29 April

Charles has a very nice bed. It's king-sized and the mattress looks firm. The trouble is he does not get to share it with his wife. She sleeps on a similar mattress with their 2-year-old daughter in the room next door, in a row of mattresses for other migrant women and children. Charles sleeps alongside half a dozen other Haitian men on the edge of the large, echoing room. Personal space is delineated by chairs and suitcases. He and his family have been living in this temporary shelter for three months.

We brought him back here after our parent and baby workshop this morning. He was attending as both a parent and translator. He was a Spanish teacher in Port Aux Prince, Haiti. It was a good job, but the school was destroyed in the 2010 earthquake, as was his home.

– *Luckily, I did not lose anyone*—he told me. But he ended up camping out at the airport for almost a year. We might have bumped into one another in the first half of 2010, me on my way to a humanitarian cluster meeting in the air-conditioned containers ringed by security fences and UN troops, him to a collapsing tent in the IDP camp next door. After a year of waiting for the humanitarian community to 'build back better,' as promised, Charles still had no job and no home. So, in 2011 he left for Brazil, which was making Haitians welcome.

– I worked hard, I learnt how to paint cars.

Unfortunately, as Brazil's economy began to fail so did the welcome. In September of last year, along with many other Haitians, Charles and his wife and daughter decided to flee north, hoping to make it into the US before Trump's election.

They made it up to the US border. The trouble was that, by the time they arrived in Tijuana, the US was trying to stem the flow by giving asylum applicants precise dates for crossing. He was allocated 11 March 2017. He did not cross.

– Because the US has started deporting people directly back to Haiti. People who crossed before the beginning of January were fine. But those crossing after, unless they were unaccompanied mothers with babies, the US just rejected them. I won't take the risk. We are going to stay here. I want to find a job and earn some money so we can get out of this place.

The shelter is perched on the side of a large gully at the end of a dirt road. Like the houses around it, it looks quickly put up, and one gets the feeling that, with the next big flood, it could simply slide down the hill. In the bottom of the gully, three large pigs are mud bathing. This area, with its ramshackle housing crowded onto the sides of steep, dry hills looks a bit like Port Aux Prince (as do many parts of Tijuana). It is the freeways, the size of cars, and the presence of Walmart's and Costco's that remind you that you are right next to the US.

There are nicer parts. Our short-term rental is in one: Playas, the beach area of town where villas of all shapes, sizes and colours jostle along the Pacific edge. Adrianna drops us off after leaving Charles' shelter, and we decide to walk home along the wall. This is the end section, predating Trump. On the Mexican side, it is mostly corrugated iron covered in graffiti, and you can see over it to the spotlights and more solid-looking fence on the US side. Here in Playas, about three blocks from the ocean, the Mexican wall turns into a proper metal fence made of closely set posts and heavy metal mesh, topped with flat sheets that have made a perfect base for graffiti artists.

We walk the section from the small community garden to 'Friend-ship Park,' where it plunges into the sea at the beach end. A friend told us that when she was a child, families could meet freely in this border zone and even picnic together. These days, the only contact is the touch of fingers through the metal fence on Saturday and Sunday mornings, when the gate is opened on the US side.

The gate is closed now, but on this side, there are still crowds of happy Mexicans eating, playing music, and taking selfies of them-selves in front of the wall. It is a holiday weekend after all. Over on the other side, there is one parked jeep, flowery dunes and marsh stretching all the way to the towers of distant San Diego. Seagulls perch and fly freely back and forth, bringing home the silliness of the whole enterprise.

Then we walk home along the Malecón, past the snack vendors, the musicians, the dancers, the man blowing what looked like a didg-eridoo, a Guatemalan tuba player, Jehovah's Witnesses, and a whole team of cheering young people with t-shirts telling you to "Be sur-prised by the love of God." Every café is full, and at the water's edge, happy families paddle.

We are running the parent and baby groups at the invitation of the Comité Estratégico de Ayuda Humanitaria. The Comité was formed by volunteers last year to deal with the sudden rush of migrants flooding north. The traditional shelters run by some churches and by the Salvation Army were overwhelmed. In the past, they had mainly housed Mexicans deported from the US, while they made up their minds whether to try again or go home. But starting last summer, more and more migrants were passing through—Haitians, Cubans, Africans, Venezuelans and Ukrainians, as well as Central Americans.

– *They did not have enough places, so new shelters opened—mostly in churches—and our group has tried to organise infrastructure and support.* Lourdes is a social worker and does all this work unpaid in her spare time. She explains there are now about 36 shelters in the town, and at any one point, there might be 3000 migrants. The numbers change all the time. Sometimes 100-150 arrive in a day. There has been a reduction in those heading north since January, post Trump inauguration. On the other hand, deportations have increased and large numbers of Haitian families, like Charles', have decided to stay. Ella, for example—another mother in the group—has a six-month-old baby who was born by emergency caesarean section in Costa Rica. Her husband is a doctor and has a job here in a Mexican hospital. They are staying, as are the two other mothers in the group. All of them have come from Brazil.

Tijuana, Monday 1 May

Toy making this morning. This is my favourite parent and baby group session because everyone always gets completely engaged. And today, we have four fathers. At the beginning, the infants are rioting around as usual, and I am trying to sort out my box of rubbish: old juice and milk cartons to make bricks, empty plastic bottles for rattles, needles and thread to make simple puppets. One child grabs the scissors or the needles, and another hits a smaller child with the wooden spoon that I brought, along with saucepans and tin cups, to demonstrate that your kitchen is full of toys, and the smaller one starts yelling. But then there is always that magical moment when something catches everyone's attention and they become happy and focussed. Today, it is making jigsaws out of pieces of cardboard box. I demonstrate 'one I prepared earlier' (just like a good TV chef), and all the parents present immediately grab cardboard and magic markers and start drawing pictures with their children who are completely engrossed.

Blessed and her husband draw a picture of a mountain range—it looks just like Haiti—and then cut out the mountains as jigsaw pieces. Matthieu carefully replaces them, propping the jigsaw up on boxes so that the whole thing is upright.

Afterwards, Arriana and Soraya from the Comité, want us to visit another shelter with them. The pastor in charge sent a message saying one of the Haitian women had been diagnosed with terminal cancer. We all drive up there. I am getting accustomed to rows of mattresses crowded together in untidy basements—the usual church furniture

The parent and baby group,
Tijuana, May 2017

of plastic chairs and tables pushed into the middle of the room—the cobwebs in the high corners because it's hard to clean those places when beds cover the floor—the hold-alls, plastic bags and cardboard boxes that contain all that is left of a previous life—the men sleeping in the middle of the day because there is nothing to do.

The woman is on a day bed in the courtyard. She is clearly in some pain and has one grossly swollen leg, but she does not have the look of someone in the terminal phase of cancer. Her husband gives us the medical notes from the public hospital. We read through them. No mention of terminal, no mention of cancer. A lump discovered on her leg requiring biopsy and further investigation, but nothing else. A doctor saw her at speed at the public hospital and discharged her. The woman begs not to be sent back there. I think of my homeless Guatemalan friend in Tapachula. This is what happens if you are outside anyone's health system: rapid consultations, muddled communications, and discharge. Soraya is already making calls to friends, with effect. A colleague working privately agrees to see the woman and hopefully arrange the necessary investigations.

– *Please understand that there is no evidence here that this woman either has cancer or is dying, so there is no need to describe her in this way*—we say to the pastor's wife, a kind woman who tells us this was what a visiting doctor implied.

– *Perhaps he did not have much time to read her notes, but it is alarming for her and her husband to hear those words, and they are not true.*

We sit later with the pastor and his wife in their living room. The pastor tells us he opened the dining room of his church up a few months ago when people were pouring through:

– *Africans, Haitians, Syrians, Muslims, Christians... Everyone said it was the United Nations. It is quieter now. But we still have problems and a lot of stress. For example, everyone wants to cook their own food in their own way!* The pastor tells us he is used to living with all sorts of different people. He is ex-Mexican army and that taught him a lot.

Adam is one of the Africans sheltering here, a Ghanaian farmer in his thirties. He went bankrupt when all his cattle died because they ate something poisonous in the forest.

— I could not even sell the meat because the vet said it would poison people. So I looked for work, but there was none. So I had to leave.

He has five children, and he wanted to find a way to support them. A friend who he had helped out in the past gave him the money to fly from Ghana to Ecuador, which allows Ghanaians to enter without a visa. Once he got to Ecuador, he met some other Ghanaians

— They said, 'We are going to America,' so I thought, Ok, I'll go too! My dream was to get to Canada.

He had a nightmare journey. Adam poured out the details as we sat in the courtyard of the church:

— In Colombia, all the passports were spoiled because we were in the forest and we were crossing rivers, and there were so many to cross! We crossed and crossed and crossed. Then we found someone to help us. He took twenty dollars from each of us and then walked with us for ten hours. Each smuggler has his own patch, and you are passed from person to person. Then you see the frontier of Panama. It's a very big mountain. It took two hours to climb. People look like lizards on that mountain. Then you climb down, and they say follow the water and you will get to Panama. We had to leave one girl by the road because she had problems with her leg. We tried to help her for some miles but she told us to leave her.

In Panama, the police were helpful, giving them water and taking them to a camp. In Nicaragua they were tricked, their money was stolen and they were deported back to Costa Rica. By now, Adam had run out of money. So, he persuaded a supermarket manager to allow him to beg outside.

— I got one thousand dollars in a week, people are very kind in Costa Rica.

They bribed and bargained their way back across Nicaragua, slept on the streets in Honduras, begged outside a supermarket again, and finally got on a bus to Guatemala and then Mexico.

— In Mexico, people welcomed us. The immigration man looked at our legs and took us to hospital. Then they took us to a camp, but it was full. Then a woman called Mama Africa let us sleep on the floor of her hotel. Then I asked a policeman for help and he wrote 'I am African' in Spanish and I copied it on a board and stood by the exit door of a supermarket again, and I got some money, and immigration gave me a paper so I could

travel to Tijuana.

He got here in November of last year. He has not crossed. He fears the US will deport him back to Africa. He has been to the Canadian Embassy twice, but they have not helped. He has asked for asylum in Mexico but worries about how to send enough money home.

– I did find work in a car wash but I left the job because the other workers, if they found anything in the car, they stole it. I did not want anything to do with that. So I left. But now when I call home, they are angry with me. I have sent everything I can. I am the first traveller in my family.

He was going for another job interview at a construction site the next day.

Tijuana, Wednesday 3 May

The Haitian woman does not have cancer I am glad to say. It's osteomyelitis and treatable. She has gone back to the public hospital; we are hoping she will get the antibiotics she needs and not be summarily discharged. I learned all this from the Comité members who arrived late and apologetic for my training workshop. At least they all got the relaxation and-self-care bit.

Amparo, an amazing woman in charge of binational education for the whole state of Baja California (at whose invitation we are in Tijuana), asked me to do a workshop for teachers to give them some idea of what it feels like to be a migrant. I love teaching in Latin America because people really want to share their own ideas and experiences. One woman discussed what it was like to move away from all her family and friends in another state when she married:

– It took ten years to adjust. I missed my family and friends so much.

– And you moved out of choice and because of love?

– Exactly!

– So imagine what it is like when you are forced to move?

Another man talked of suddenly having to flee across the border because of the threat of violence and not knowing how to tell his children what was happening or why. Another talked of the grief of losing his father. He was near tears but insisted on sharing. One thing the workshop brings home is that it is not us and them. No one has an unscarred life, many of us have been uprooted, even if by choice, and most of us have lost someone, so we can draw on how it felt and what helped at the time. It is the basis of understanding.

Asmamaw and I walk along the Malecón every evening now. It's empty after the bustle of the weekend, and we stop to drink mojitos, watch the sun set into the Pacific, and to gaze entranced at the pelicans flying low in formation skimming the surf. Beyond, there are dolphins heading south. They must be common here. Asmamaw and I are the only ones who stand and stare and point.

In the mornings, I get up early to run the same stretch and use the exercise machines kindly donated by OXXO, a local chain store. I suppose, if you fill your shelves with sugary drinks and two thousand varieties of Doritos, the least you can do is provide a means to work it off. And this must be the best view I have ever had for a workout.

Tijuana, Thursday 4 May

The problem with making any plans to work with migrant children is that they migrate. Amparo had also asked me to do a camera/storytelling workshop with a group of Haitian children living in a shelter here in Tijuana. But four days ago, she discovered that they have all gone north to the US. Never mind. Two days ago, we started the workshop in a local school with six entirely new participants, all of whom were slightly bewildered at being invited to skip classes for a few hours without much further explanation. Not surprisingly, they were somewhat shy, but when we went round asking them to introduce themselves and explain why and how long they had been in Mexico each said:

– *I did not choose to be here.*

All the participants, except one, are from families that have been deported from the US. Some, a few years ago. Others, last year. One, just two weeks ago.

– *So if you would like to take a camera for a day and show us something about your life here, anything at all, we would love to see it—I explained. We want people to hear directly from you what it is like to suddenly be forced to move home and country. To see what you see.*

303

I shared the website and some of the Syrian children's pictures and stories. Fifteen-year-old Noah gave a sharp intake of breath as I read a 9-year-old girl's description of her house being bombed, losing her Barbie doll, and her grandfather dying. We did a short training with the cameras. I don't call it training any more. I know if I just give them the cameras, they can work it out for themselves in less than two minutes. Then we sent them out in the schoolyard to practice. Everyone was happy. Amparo expressed some surprise when I said I was letting the children take the cameras home with them. *Our risk*—I explained, and, as in Greece, they all came back the next day, with cameras and pictures. Amazing Alex, the son of one of the Comité members, who we have made technical assistant/translator/general project assistant, downloaded all the pictures at speed. Meanwhile, Noah trained two new participants on how to use the camera, and all the rules, which all the children can now recite:

– *Ask permission of your subjects.*
– *Keep the wristband on so you don't drop the camera.*
– *Don't lend your camera to anyone else.*
– *Don't photograph fights or policemen.*

Today we sat with each one and asked them to select their favourite pictures and tell us about them.

As with the Syrian children in Greece, it was all about love, friendship, family connection, nature, and beauty. I never cease to be astounded and moved that, if you give a young person a choice of what to show, they will usually choose to share what makes them happy.

And that's not because everything is wonderful. While 15-year-old Emily was showing us her pictures of her best friends here in Mexico, she burst into tears, saying:

– *I miss the US, I grew up there and everything I knew was there. I really wanted to go to university there. I always worked really hard in school. I had such big dreams. I was promoted and about to be a freshman. I really want to be a doctor. Then, just after I was promoted, I heard we did not get the visa, and I was so sad.*

Thank goodness for Alex, nineteen years old, Mexican, and on his way to Toronto to do media studies. He sits there explaining to Emily how good the medical schools are in Mexico, and that it is not difficult for Mexicans to go to the US and Canada to study.

– *You don't have to give up your dreams*—he assures her.

For Kefrem on the other hand, Mexico is an improvement from El Salvador, where they tried to recruit him into a gang, and then threatened kidnap and death when he refused. He thinks it is safer and more secure here. This, in spite of the fact that last week on the way to school he was robbed of his phone and money at gunpoint! How bad can it have been in El Salvador?

I met his mother in the office a few days ago. They have asylum here, but she is worrying about the rent. She earns eight dollars a day for cleaning, and it is too little. Kefrem dreams of becoming a mechanical engineer and enjoys body building. He wanted to give us a selfie of himself looking handsome and tough, but I had to say we could not use it. His headmaster has told him not to reveal that he is a migrant to other children, because the same gang that was after him in El Salvador is present here. So, if we put his actual photo on a migrant child website, that rather gives the game away, whereas, we can anonymise his other contributions, as I have done.

Tijuana, Friday 5 May

– *Information is a human right. We want you to know your rights. It does not matter what your status is, your religion, your skin colour, you have rights because you are human. We have dignity because we are rational thinking beings. It is important to understand this because it makes us more secure. The Universal Declaration of Human Rights is incorporated into Mexican law. So any person in Mexico has these rights.*

Soraya is giving a lecture to a packed room full of Haitians in yet another shelter dining room, in another church, on another hillside. They have brought audio so that everyone can have simultaneous translation. Charles is doing Spanish/Creole and Paulina is doing Spanish/English. Soraya is explaining that the Comité see their job as explaining to the people of Tijuana what Haitians have been through since the earthquake and why so many came last year (20,000 in September alone). They do these talks every night in different

I was in my room at home and saw a lot of birds outside, just sitting there, so I decided to capture them. You can see one bird is flying. Emma, age 13, Tijuana

shelters, explaining to Haitians what their rights are now that the temporary protection scheme in the US is closed and many of them are thinking about staying in Mexico.

— *We know what risks and difficulties you have suffered to get here. We know you had a dream and now you are stuck. We want you to feel welcome. We like it that you are here. Tijuana is a city of migrants. That's why people have supported you with food and shelter. But now, most of you have to think how to make yourselves regular. It does not mean you have to stay here forever, but you do need to think about what you will do.*

She is encouraging them to regularise their status and explaining the different options: seeking asylum or permission to remain on humanitarian grounds. Both take time and involve various bureaucratic steps, but Soraya emphasises that without this they are irregular and risk deportation. She explains that getting permission on humanitarian grounds gives them time to decide.

— *If you regularise your status, you can draw breath and make a new plan. You won't be persecuted, you have the right not just to work but to have employment rights and benefits. School is free for 4 to 15-year-olds. You have the right to health care…*

It's not an easy choice. Wages are low and in pesos, and rents are high and, in many cases, in dollars.

— *I have been looking for somewhere for two months. I have surgery in a few days and really need a place*—a woman says.

A man gets up:

— *I want to thank you for receiving us with open arms. God always does things at the right time. We were very worried when we arrived, but people started helping us and we thank you very much for your support. We want to fix our status, but it takes a long time and meanwhile, we have to go and sign every week.*

Soraya acknowledges the problems. The Comité are advocating changes and will try and help individual cases like these. She finishes by encouraging people to enjoy the city, to visit the art galleries and the parks, to feel at home.

— *They belong to you!*

Soraya is speaking the truth. Tijuana is a welcoming city. Many of the

Uber drivers think Asmamaw is a Cuban, or African, migrant with his Cuban-accented Spanish, but we have experienced no hostility. When we say we are here to volunteer, people are enthusiastic.

A few days ago, Anne Coulter, the Republican writer, tweeted, "Perhaps a workable compromise on North Korea would be: We allow Kim to develop only warheads capable of reaching Tijuana." She should come visit and learn something from Mexicans about living with people different from herself. When did it become OK to suggest the nuclear annihilation of whole cities that you do not like?

Tijuana, Saturday 6 May

It's the last parent and babies group, and there are two new mothers whom I met at last night's meeting. One of them has a 2-year-old who scarcely speaks. Part of the problem is that all these parents and babies live scattered across the city in different shelters—one here, two there—so there is little company or encouragement to play and communicate. The group went really well. Children and parents loved the movement work. At one point, I had four small children sitting on me using me as a boat. At another, they were all crawling through the tunnel we made with our bodies, and then turning their parents into horses to ride. Toys are not required, one happy adult can become a fabulous horse or rock or climbing frame, ending up as a safe armchair for rocking. At the end of today's group, everyone agreed they wanted to continue to meet once a fortnight; Lourdes and Ella are going to try to organise that. I am so happy that we have started something. Charles could not come because he had an interview for a job. He is being considered as a Spanish teacher in a local school.

Alexandra's father has not been so lucky. He tried for a translator job at a company yesterday but did not get it. He is trying with a bathroom company on Monday. He tells me he had a good job in the US, doing house reconstruction. They had been living in Idaho for a number of years. They decided to move to Las Vegas after Trump was nominated because the atmosphere towards Mexicans became quite hostile in Idaho. They liked it there and things were going well. But, two weeks ago, he was picked up by the police for driving without a licence.

— They took me straight to jail and then to the ICE police. Then I got sent back to Mexico. The children are all US citizens because they were born there, but of course they did not want to stay without me. They all followed me. My wife left everything in our apartment. All we brought were our clothes and a few bags. I imagine the landlord will take everything.

His wife got a job in the local supermarket straight away. She works six days a week and earns a thousand pesos (approximately fifty dollars) a week. Half of that goes to rent, the rest to utilities and food for all the family. It's not enough.

— I was so sad and scared when my dad was deported—Alexandra tells me. *I thought it could happen to Mum and the government would take us into care! That's why we all decided to join my dad. So we could be together. I felt good about the decision because I want my family to be together.*

She likes it in Tijuana. The house they live in is bigger than the flat they had in Las Vegas, and she has already made local friends.

— I don't feel a big effect. I feel normal and happy. I am with my family. I am a bit worried about school, but I want to go and I want to finish. Then, as I am a US citizen, I can go to college in the US.

I asked her what she wanted to do when she grew up.

— Join the immigration police. I will treat people well.

Tijuana, Sunday 7 May

Dolores sits behind a cloth-covered table in the upstairs room of the Café Caracol next to three other marchers; Cristina sits beside her. Dolores is telling the assembled international media her story and demanding better treatment for all Central American refugees with moving articulacy. The tearful, troubled mother and daughter of a month ago have been replaced by striking and powerful activists who have travelled four thousand kilometers and appear to have befriended the entire march. Others at the table share their stories.[16]

— We did not leave for adventure, we were pushed by violence and corruption. There are no work opportunities because of homophobia. People think we are coming for prostitution, but there are dignified jobs

I took this picture to have fun. It's my
brothers' and my sister's feet here in our
house. That is our floor. I like living here.
This is my aunt's house. I like it, it has lots
of windows and light. It is better than
Las Vegas, there is a lot more space. I share a
room with my three brothers and one sister,
but that is not a problem, we all get on well.
We moved from the US two weeks ago.
I don't feel a big effect. I feel normal and
happy because I am with my family, and
I want us to be together.
Alexandra, age 13, Tijuana

here. We can work as cooks, maids, cleaners…
– They killed my pregnant wife…
– The gangs own Guatemala, El Salvador and Honduras. The government is powerless. The authorities are caught up in the corruption. They are better armed than the police. No institutions function. They cannot help.
– The gangs follow you everywhere.
– They killed my brother because he would not join them. They sent part of the ear and finger to my mother. She told me to get out, so I did.

Here is the tragedy. The peace treaties that ended decades of government-sponsored death squads and civil wars in Central America did not bring peace. What has happened in these countries is a warning to us all. They demonstrate what happens when the State collapses because the rich have exempted themselves from taxation and public responsibility. They plunder the remaining natural resources with impunity, protect themselves with private security firms, fly by helicopter between beautiful heavily guarded fincas and private apartments, and leave the rest to struggle with environmental destruction, abject poverty, and the death threats and extortions of gangs and petty warlords. And if you do manage to escape:

– The immigration process in Tapachula is a trap. They make you do fifty pages of paperwork, then, after six months, they come and tell you no, and you can appeal in 115 days or leave the country. It's a trap.
– But the Mexican people are good, helping us fight for our rights.

That is certainly true here. Crowds came down to Friendship Park to welcome the Via Crucis March this morning, including many who had crossed from the US just to accompany this last stage. But then, the heavens opened with a heavy unprecedented rainstorm. So everyone has taken refuge here while we wait for other marchers—mostly the men and boys who rode 'La Bestia' (the train on which many migrants hitch a ride) to get here. There was some trouble. Police were asking migrants for documents. Cristobal told them it was not their right to do so as they were not immigration police, so he was armlocked and beaten up. We understand he is OK now.

Jeremiah is here with his wife and children, so is Elise and her baby son and daughters—all looking cheerful and well. They are part of the group that intends to cross to the US. While we wait for the others to join us, the lawyers and observers explain carefully what is required if people want to seek asylum in the US.

— *You need to state clearly: 'I have a fear to go back. I have a right to an asylum interview.' Insist. You are entitled to that interview and border guards cannot refuse it.*

Unfortunately, these days it is increasingly common for asylum seekers to just be turned back. One Mexican woman explains to the group how she did not know what to say and the immigration police bullied and intimidated her into saying that she was not afraid by threatening to take her children from her. Later, she tells me the whole story. She was trying to escape from a violent and abusive husband:

— *He raped me. I was crying and anxious when I crossed with my two children, and they came and said, 'Are you a crazy woman or what?' I told them that I don't want to go back, I am terrified. And they said:*

— *Stop the show. You have nothing to fear in your country.*

— *It's not a show! It's true!*

— *Then they made me lie on the ground and said, 'If you don't stop this show we will send you back, and we will chain you in front of your children,' and at the same time they were pushing me back across the frontier, and I was shouting that I wanted political asylum, and they were saying you are joking. They said, 'We are not giving you asylum. Our President has removed all these rights, especially for Mexicans!'*

The other marchers finally arrive, and the whole group (of some hundreds) marches across the complex series of walkways that lead to one of the US frontier crossing points. In the taxi pull up point before the white metal gates, those not crossing pause to say goodbye. There are tears and hugs and more tears, and the seventy eight go through.

Tijuana, Monday 8 May

Nicole, one of the US lawyers supporting the marchers posted the following on social media today:

"NONE of the families will be released on ankle monitor and humanitarian parole. ALL will remain INCARCERATED until their case is decided by a judge. THIS IS RETALIATION for so many asylum seekers EXERCISING THEIR LEGAL RIGHT to seek asylum through the port-of-entry. WE CANNOT ALLOW THIS TO CONTINUE."

But, the Haitian woman with osteomyelitis has crossed to the US and is in a hospital in California. Apparently, her sister, already living in the US, arranged it. So, some good news!   .

We had the picture show this morning. All the children came, and some brought their parents and friends. There were school staff, Amparo and her colleagues, some of the Comité, and a local TV station doing a story on deported children. This is my favourite moment in the project. Just like in Greece, I saw how showing the pictures individually and reading aloud the children's words in Spanish and English made the children light up with pride.

Doing storytelling projects here—and in Italy, Greece and France—has brought home to me that we all have a story to tell. Storytelling lets us decide what is important to keep and what to let go—what aspects of our identity we want others to understand. Storytelling helps us make sense of tragedy, grieve, mourn and memorialise loss. It helps us capture and celebrate love and beauty, and share it. When others see what matters to us, this gives significance and validity to our experiences. It is empowering.

Cornwall, Wednesday 24 May

Nonviolent collective action and international solidarity does work. The following has been posted on the Pueblo Sin Fronteras social media page:

"Seventy-eight asylum seekers of the Refugee Caravan entered the US on May 7th. Customs and Border Protection used intimidation to send one child back to Mexico, but seventy-seven refugees held their heads high, insisted their rights be respected, and withstood being separated from their families and incarcerated. Some have received positive determinations from the asylum office to continue their cases, and some have achieved release. Many, however, remain detained for no reason other than trying to save their lives."

314

Emily's Story

Emily returned to Mexico last year with her family. She was fifteen years old when she wrote this story in Spring 2017, while living in Tijuana, Mexico.

My name is Emily, I'm from the busy city of Tijuana, Mexico. I lived in Mexico for six years before I moved to California with my mom, dad, and my only brother. The only thing I remember about living in Mexico those six years is preschool. My mom and dad wanted my brother and I to have the best education we could get because they know how hard it is to survive and get a job without a good education. From what I've seen, most of the public schools in Mexico aren't good, so we were enrolled in a private school. I liked that school, every classroom was painted a different colour and it made the school look vivid. The playground was very small and it was inside a huge cage where the kids couldn't get out. There would always be special assemblies where the students would dance and sing and perform plays. The bell would ring, my brother and I would be picked up by my mom, and she would take us home. My family lived in a small house that my dad had built in a gated community. The living room was small, and I remember that my brother and I would be watching television, see our dad coming through the front door, and run to greet him.

One day, my dad started packing our things and crossed the border multiple times to bring our belongings to what would be our new home. I don't remember being excited to move, and I know that I didn't think much of moving. We moved because my dad had gotten a work visa. He took the opportunity because he wanted my brother and me to learn English and lead a better life, free of bad influences. We moved into a small but pretty one-bedroom apartment that I shared with my mom, dad, and brother. After a year or so, we moved into a bigger apartment in the same complex. My brother

317

and I were enrolled in kindergarten, and the years went by quickly. Elementary school was great, I loved my teachers and they loved me. My parents said that I learned English in a couple of months because my kindergarten teacher was bilingual and she focused on helping us with our English. My parents wanted me to be in extracurricular activities, so I was enrolled in soccer and softball, and since then, I have loved sports. I was always a shy person in school and it didn't help that it was around this age that I began to notice that I was different from most kids. Kids would ask me where I was from. It always made me uncomfortable when their expression showed pity when I told them I was an immigrant from Mexico. They would sometimes ask if I was an illegal immigrant. Some kids didn't understand what a work visa was and assumed my dad was the stereotypical Mexican immigrant that worked in the fields or cleaned houses. Even though my dad worked for a good company, they were partially right, it was hard for us to live in Woodside. We could barely afford the basic expenses. There was always food on the table, and I will forever be grateful for my parents' sacrifices to keep us above the water. It was because of this that I felt I couldn't be friends with some people. I wasn't like them, plus, I was scared of what they would think of my different lifestyle.

Middle school was better though. I got into all the honours classes, and I always tried my best to get good grades. I made amazing friendships throughout middle school; they were all people that accepted me for who I was and we encouraged each other to be great people. I kept playing soccer through middle school as well. I loved it because my teammates were awesome, and, even though we started off as a terrible team, we became County champions. We moved houses again, but this time to a somewhat isolated area where all the Mexicans lived. I hated it—it was small and ugly. I didn't want to tell anyone where I lived because everyone at my school referred to it as the ghetto, and it hurt to know how inconsiderate some people could be. Some people at school already made racist jokes, and I didn't want to give them another reason to keep making more. My brother and I shared a room, but this time, it was also part of the living and dining room. It was hard to get used to living in a tiny garage-sized 'house,' but my parents were always supportive and we all adapted to the change as best as we could. Even though eighth grade was the toughest year I had during my entire time in California, it was still the best in many ways. It was when I was really coming out of my shell, and I was starting to prepare to be a freshman in high school. I would regularly ice skate, go to the park, watch movies, and have the best times with my closest friends. I went to cross country practices and soccer try-outs at the high school I would attend that fall. Of course, that was before we found out we had to move.

It was a day in June when my dad called all of us into his room and told us that his work visa had been denied. I don't know why, but I had already felt that news coming weeks before. Even though I sort of already knew, it's not something you can prepare yourself for. Being forced to move in such a short period of time and leave behind everything you grew up with for nine years was pretty devastating to say the least. My family cried for what felt like the longest time. One of my friends was in a different country when I found out, so I couldn't tell him in person that I was going to move. It made it easier because I didn't want to say goodbye to anyone, I just wanted to pack my things and go because goodbyes are hard. I told my best friend that I was going to move when we were walking to the park together. Three of my friends were also there, and it was really hard to watch them cry over the news. I felt like my life was falling apart. Sure, I would make new friends and start a new life in Mexico, but I didn't want to move. It was July 23rd, 2016 when we got into our caravan and headed south to a new life, culture, and society.

When my family and I got to Mexico, our family came to the border to help us transfer our things and then we went to my grandma's house. We moved in with her, and we've been living with her still up until now. I like it here because it's bigger than the house we lived in at Woodside. Upon arriving, we had to look for schools; we went to three schools before enrolling in one. I liked how the school looked when we visited it over summer. Even though there are cons about living here, such as the poverty and different education, I feel like I

319

actually fit in. I'm treated differently than I was in the US. People are much friendlier to me and we have a lot more things in common. So, after nine months of being in Mexico, I would say that I'm coming to terms with it. There will always be new friends, new schools, and new opportunities no matter where I go.

I still have friends in the US. I have a tourist visa, so we can go over and visit. My brother and I take the train by ourselves and someone meets us. My friend there has a small plane and sometimes we fly back. I miss the US; I grew up there and everything I knew was there. I really wanted to go to university there. I always worked really hard in school. I had such big dreams. I was promoted and about to be a freshman. I really want to be a doctor. Then, just after I was promoted, I heard we did not get the visa and I was so sad.

This is taken in the garden behind the school. It is a nice quiet place. Sometimes, I just go there to be quiet. I have been at the school since 2016. I don't like it as much as my old school, but it's not terrible. In the US, kids move classes, here we stay in the same room with the same group of children all the time. I prefer moving because the five minutes we spend outside is kind of relaxing, and I like changing classes because you get a wider group of friends.
Emily, age 15, Tijuana

Calais

France, November 2017

Calais, Sunday 12 November

An icy wind blows as we walk up the canal to the bleak grassy corner. Johannes told us yesterday that this is where the young Oromo hang out—they are here now. Some twenty to thirty young men queue around a white van distributing food from the back. Some others are charging their phones. I get talking to one boy who speaks reasonable English. Dhaba tells me he is fifteen years old and from the Bale area, a mountainous region in the middle of Ethiopia. He's delighted when I tell him I have been there and think it is beautiful. He has been sleeping rough on the streets of Calais for the last eight months. He did make it into the back of a lorry once when he first arrived. It dropped him in Germany.

– Why not stay there?

– I don't want to, I have an uncle in the UK.

– So why not go the legal route and ask for family reunification?

– Because it takes too long.

– But you have already been here eight months. He shrugs. *Where are you sleeping?*

He points to under the bridge. The police come every night and take our sleeping bags.

We talk some more. He is not sure where this uncle is and does not have the phone number. He cannot get it from home because he has no credit left to call there. He has nothing. But he knows that he wants to be in England.

The rest of the group have gathered around Asmamaw and I. They want to know what we have brought for them. Asmamaw is translating from both Oromipha and Amharic.

– Why are you here? One asks. He looks and sounds angry.

– We are medics, we can attend to any first aid needs you have. I am afraid we are not carrying anything else.

– Thanks, we are healthy—the angry boy says.

– I am glad to hear it.

Dhaba and I talk more. He wants to phone Ethiopia to get his uncle's details. I know there is a social media page helping with credit for young people like him. I promise to meet him tomorrow when we have found out more.

The French Government thought that destroying the Jungle would solve the 'migrant problem' in the town. But all they have done is stamped on mercury. The community has scattered, but pepper spray and the nightly removal of sleeping bags has not stopped the procession of dreamers coming north. At any one time, there is an estimated population of around one thousand in the town, but, as it is constantly changing, the actual numbers passing through are much higher.

This bleak corner is just one of a number of distribution points. I spent part of yesterday afternoon standing at the main one on a piece of wasteland under an electricity pylon in the industrial zone, on Route des Gravelines, just down from the site of the old Jungle. At least two hundred young migrants had gathered for afternoon distribution. There was a van serving hot food out the back door. The Refugee Youth Service had set up another van with an awning and put out tables and chairs where young boys were playing chess. Further over, a group of Afghans were playing cricket. The School Bus was there offering English classes and social activities. Given that all the migrants here had spent the night sleeping in the surrounding hedges, the atmosphere was remarkably cheerful. There were also toilets and sinks, both stand-alone chemical ones and some in trucks.

Since the eviction at the end of last year, the policy of the Mayor of Calais and local police has been to crack down as heavily as possible on any volunteers or aid groups supporting migrants in order to discourage them from coming. When Secours Catholique tried to provide showers for migrants at its shelter, the government prosecuted them for 'change of use.' But this August, the French courts ruled that showers, fresh water and toilet facilities must be available to migrants on the streets of Calais. The Court case established that there have to be adequate services 'to maintain human dignity.'

— When I arrived here in 2005, there was one water tap that the homeless and migrants could use in the whole of Calais—Brother Johannes told me. *There are now fourteen open every day, and you get six minutes, or ten if you are a woman.*

Brother Johannes has adapted to changing times as well. He has always seen the necessity to be 'prayerfully present among refugees' and migrants, which is why he persuaded his order to let him establish a house in Calais some years ago. When I first met him two years ago, it housed some twenty volunteers working in the Jungle. Immediately after the eviction last year, they took in some of the sickest and most vulnerable migrants who had somehow been left behind. At one point, they were also trying to provide a shower, washing facilities and a meal for anyone dropping in.

— We had one hundred people coming in each week, and some were causing trouble. It was too exhausting and the volunteers gave up after a few weeks. So now he provides a safe house named after Maria Skobtsova, a Russian orthodox saint whose house in Paris in the second world war was open to refugees, migrants, the homeless and Jews. This house is a community for anyone medically or psychiatrically unwell or very young. At any one time, there may be fifteen living in the house. Some have been suicidal, others had alcohol problems. No one is forced to move on, but the population in the house has changed over time.

— Most of the Afghans have gone to Dunkirk, now it is mainly Ethiopians and Eritreans.

Asmamaw and I drove here last week, once again bringing donations from our small village in Cornwall: sleeping bags, warm jackets and backpacks, essential survival gear. When we dropped our load off on Friday, we found a handful of Habesha boys cheerfully making plasticine figures for an animated movie. Art Refuge comes over to do art therapy twice a week, both here and at the distribution points. The volunteer community that supports the migrants has also transformed. The ad hoc fluctuating networks of young volunteers who slept in donated caravans alongside migrants in the Jungle two years

The school bus
Calais, November 2017

ago has morphed into new professional NGOs closely connected with the longstanding French Associations like L'Auberge des Migrants. The professionalism allows them to mount legal challenges to the French and British Governments, but they have created structures that welcome and make use of a constantly changing population of volunteers. Annie was a law graduate who came for a few days two years ago. She is now the paid coordinator for Help Refugees and commutes between France and the UK.

When I wrote to Annie that I had time to come over, and was there anyway to be useful, she put me in touch with Luke, the 'volunteer welfare coordinator,' who asked me to do my usual training sessions on sources of stress in migrants, psychological first aid and self-care. I started yesterday and will do more in the next two days.

Asmamaw and I have also joined an ad hoc group of medics providing first aid. We are coordinated by a paramedic from Holland, Joram, who comes over regularly. It's not easy providing consistent care to a population that are both unwelcome in the local community and would themselves rather be elsewhere. We spent this morning treating sore and blistered feet at a distribution point in Dunkirk. Then we walked around a lake, right beside the site of the old 'official' camp in Grand Synthe that was burned down in a fight between Kurds and Afghans last April, leaving 1500 homeless. Now, in among the trees and bushes beside the water, you can find small tarpaulin shelters and fireplaces still smoking, a child's bike, a cooked meal… but no people. Joram told us that mostly women and children lived in this area. He was looking for one in particular who was heavily pregnant. Then we met a volunteer collecting rubbish. She told us the women all decided to go into official shelters last night—something they do regularly for a few days to get warm and dry. Then they leave again to keep trying to cross the channel.

The misery of the small encampments contrasted with the beauty of the lake. Crested grebe, moorhen and swans swam on the water. The occasional jogger passed. The notices beside the lake asking passers-by to respect the environment were in Arabic and Farsi as well as French.

— They appear not to have noticed that the majority of refugees in this area are Kurds—Housam commented.

Housam, my Syrian friend with whom I worked in Greece, is here with us in Calais as a volunteer. He is now an official refugee in France (who offered him relocation this March). He moved to Strasbourg and finally has a pink card, which allows him to work and study. It has not been easy. They put him in a shared house with Afghan, Kurdish and Sudanese refugees. He is learning French and plans to start intensive studies at university, so that he can go on and do a degree in political science. Meanwhile, he has found work in a restaurant and is looking for another house to rent. He gets 510 euros a month as financial support, and friends he met in Greece have connected him with new friends in France—although, that is also challenging:

— Some people, when they hear I am a refugee, they get scared... at a party for example... they run away. Or if you go to rent a house, they see you are a refugee and refuse. I cannot get a credit card, so I can only draw cash from a particular machine...

The other problem is time:

— Too much of it. I think too much. Initially, I just sat, and then you get depressed.

When I rang Housam two months ago he told me he wanted to go and work with the Rohingya refugees in Bangladesh. He needed to do something, so I asked him to join me in Calais and meet Johannes and the associations working here, thinking he might like to volunteer here himself in the future, if he had time. This evening Housam sits with Asmamaw and me and eleven Ethiopian and Eritrean refugees at the table in Johannes' house, eating pasta and lentils with chilli and talking animatedly in Arabic to two of them. He is explaining his own experiences in getting here, and how it is not so terrible to be a refugee in France.

The question is, given the miseries of life on the street and the difficulties and dangers of reaching the UK, why do so many persist in trying? The answers are varied. This morning, an Iranian man in Dunkirk told me he had already been deported twice from the UK, but he was determined to go back because he was a happier and safer living illegally in Britain than in France.

– *Refugee attitudes have hardened since the increase in police violence towards them. They cannot imagine living here. They want to work and study, which is almost impossible in France or Italy. Some Afghans and Sudanese have decided to stay, but the Eritreans and Ethiopians rarely change their minds*—Johannes tells us.

Another very sad man from Kirkuk told us he would happily seek asylum anywhere. His home was destroyed and his father had been killed, having been a leading officer in the fight with ISIS. He was then put on a wanted list and escaped via Turkey to Greece and then Serbia. But then, he had been arrested and fingerprinted in Romania, so when he reached Germany, they had sent him back there.

– *But there is nothing there, they cannot help you. I am afraid of being returned to jail there.*

It is a horrible situation. You are stuck and yet live in a constant state of anxiety about the threats faced every night. This is combined with hope that you might just make it onto the next unguarded lorry. And these fears and hopes come on top of all you have escaped in your home country, and all you have endured to get here. This creates some of the most difficult psychological states that I have encountered. You and your friends spend the day at a parking lot. The main sources of conflict these days are fights over access to the truck parking. This is because now that the port and access roads are so heavily guarded and fenced, the only other route is with the smugglers, and that can be anything between one and five thousand dollars. So, you need to hang out in the truck parks to keep ownership of your spot. Then someone makes it, on their first day in Calais, or in their first week, or their first month. And they post on social media: "We made it— here we are in Canterbury… or Birmingham… or Swindon." So, you keep trying, perhaps tomorrow it will be you… just a few more nights in the miserable bushes. The whole process has the addictive quality of a slot machine in a betting shop. Just one more go and you might win big.

Calais, Monday 13 November

I discuss this the next morning with some twenty volunteers attending training in a glass-walled office inside the large warehouse run by L'Auberge des Migrants. Outside in the kitchen area, volunteers are preparing the morning meal for distribution. In the other half, the endless process of organising donations for redistribution continues. This is the second group. As before, it is multinational. There is a combination of gap year students wanting to learn and be useful, an actress, a researcher, unemployed graduates, school teachers, youth workers, festival workers. One young woman told me she was here because both her parents were refugees, another because her grandparents were refugees from Germany.

– And I can cook, so I thought I would put it to good use.

A British undergraduate, studying French and politics, thought this would be a good place to spend her year abroad. A finance officer quit her job because she knew this was going on and wanted to help. Two art students have travelled from the US because they felt too detached from the real world.

At the outset, I ask them to brainstorm a list of the particular miseries they think migrants face in Calais:

– Hopelessness, loneliness, separation from loved ones, segregation and discrimination, chaos, misinformation, no information, loss of identity, dehumanisation, lack of respect, racism, feeling stuck, in a limbo, absence of state, absence of structure, gender imbalance, no recreation, no structure...

Then we make a second list of the things they are doing or want to do to help. As always, what I want to get across—or reinforce, because many know it already—is that the critical psychological support in this situation does not come from professional counselling to explore the horrors of the past. It comes from trying to address the stresses of the present. These are the things the volunteers are doing already—providing food, water, first aid, and information; listening without forcing talking; and helping people connect to loved ones. Yes, providing phone charging points helps. Of course, the big issues—lack of shelter, security, justice, a decent humane approach to the whole migration crisis—cannot be resolved so easily, but, empathy and solidarity count for a great deal.

When we get to self-care it is good to discover another change from two years ago. Everyone recognises the absolute necessity to take regular time off. Days off are actively encouraged and no one in the group is working till they drop.

Asmamaw and I go back to meet Dhaba in the afternoon. Stevie, from the Refugee Youth Service, has discovered that he is on the list to get phone credit from the Facebook site, but that is monthly, so I give him something to get credit now, and he will try to connect with a legal team next week. Meanwhile, he wants to tell me his story to put on the Migrantchild website. We sit at a café table in the afternoon sun while he tells us of fleeing Ethiopia because he was afraid of being imprisoned and tortured after demonstrating with other students and school children, of being beaten and imprisoned in Libya, and of finally getting to the Jungle just before it was evicted. He is courageous, intelligent and resilient. Why are we wasting the lives of these extraordinary young people?

Calais, Tuesday 14 November

We stopped at the main distribution site this morning looking for the school bus as Housam was planning to work with them. None of the vans were there, just a very angry crowd of young African men. One of them came up to ask me why, yesterday, I had given out jeans to Afghans but not Ethiopians. I explained that I had not been there yesterday and knew nothing about it. A rapid text exchange with Stevie told me another aid group had been doing distribution the night before. They were known for handing out on 'a first come first served' basis, which as usual, means the toughest get served and the most vulnerable go without.

We found the school bus with a punctured tire at L'Auberge and left Housam with the team sorting it out. Meanwhile, Asmamaw and I were invited to lunch at Secours Catholique. At least twice a week, they drive around collecting any women who want to spend a day in the shelter, doing activities, cooking or just resting in a dry warm place. Two women were deeply asleep lying on rugs when we arrived. The others had just finished cooking lunch.

– *Why is she asking questions?* One woman said to Asmamaw in Amharic, when I introduced myself and asked her name.

– *Everyone asks the same questions, we are so tired of questions... Journalists, young people doing research, they all come here...*

– *I am so sorry*—I replied. *I just wanted to introduce myself.*

But as lunch progressed, and the woman realised that we were not there to write an academic paper, she was happy to chat about Ethiopia with Asmamaw.

– *No one in Europe understands the situation in Ethiopia. It gets worse and worse. Angela Merkel went there and did nothing. The prime minister is a toy. There are no chances to be prosperous. They charge unpayable taxes—more than a thousand percent. I had a house, a garden, a car. I ran an infant school. They asked me to pay a bribe to lessen the tax. When I refused, they started to attack me. Then they put me in prison, I was beaten. When I got out, I knew I had to leave. I left my husband and four children. I hope I can bring them. You know, in 2005, a boy was killed in front of my house. The woman is crying now as she talks. They told me, if I said a word about it, they would kill me. I do think of staying here in France, but it is so difficult.*

– *You know they closed the asylum office in Calais when they destroyed the Jungle*—the volunteer from Secours Catholique explains. *Now you have to get to Lille and once there it can take two to four months just to get an invitation to give fingerprints, during which time you have no support and can still be deported. It's impossible.*

No wonder that Dhaba and others would rather put their energy into the daily gamble of the parking lots.

We spent the afternoon with Yonas, an Eritrean boy who is currently staying with Johannes because he is unwell. He escaped from Eritrea in 2014 after both his father and aunt were imprisoned. He was fourteen years old. Three years later—after a year in Ethiopia, nine months working in Sudan, and then almost nine months kidnapped and imprisoned in Libya—he had made it across the Mediterranean at the cost of almost seven thousand dollars, money paid by family

Young migrants in the
wasteland where they sleep
Calais, November 2017

to the extortioners.

He crossed in April. A month afterwards, in May, a boat with 800 aboard capsized, and more than 230 died.

— *I knew so many of them.* They were friends he had made in the previous nine months of captivity. *Now, when I hear about the death of someone, I am indifferent. Do you understand?*

He arrived in Calais with four friends.

— *Yes, we know it's bad, but we want to try. And in the first ten days that we were here, two of our group got into the UK. We are in touch with them by phone. The thing is, we were new, so we were not afraid. A truck came into the parking and opened the back. It was empty and they just jumped in. I was a bit further away and could not make it. There was no checking. When they got to London, they knocked, and the driver let them out. He shouted and was really angry, but they ran away. Then they went to the police and asked for asylum, and now it's in process, and they have a place to live in Birmingham. They are eighteen and nineteen years old.*

For the last five months I have been trying every day. We get beaten all the time if there are no white people around. They beat us and spray us with pepper. If foreigners are around, they don't do it, but otherwise they take your sleeping bag and pepper spray you. But then I got sick, so Brother Johannes has given me refuge here.

Another chilly late afternoon. We drive back to the main distribution to pick up Housam from the school bus. All of us are leaving Calais tomorrow. We find him on the lower deck of the bus. It is packed. Housam is leading an animated circle of drummers and musicians. In the middle of the circle, an Afghan and an Ethiopian are dancing together.

Dhaba's Story

Dhaba comes from the Oromo region of Ethiopia. He was fifteen years old and sleeping rough in Calais when he told me this story in November 2017. He told the final part when living in the UK in October 2018.

I lived a good life with my family. My father was a shopkeeper in the Oromia region. I have two sisters and a brother. We were happy. I love football, I support Manchester United, and I played for my school. I loved school. I started at five. It was a private school, and I studied hard. My favourite subjects were history, math and English. Everything was going well, and there were no problems until the day of the demonstrations, when I was caught on camera.

The demonstrations began at school when I was thirteen. Why? Because the government was bad and we demonstrated to show our unhappiness. There is a university near where we live. The university students came out, demonstrating about problems. We saw them kicked and taken to prison. And yet, our constitution says people have the right to demonstrate. So, we school students demonstrated to ask —*Why are they going to prison? Will the same thing happen to us?*

They tear gassed us and some students were killed. In my neighbourhood, a guy was injured. Some students from our school were killed. Then we demonstrated again. This time, I was right at the front holding a banner saying: "Stop killing Oromo students." University students were demonstrating, school students—not just our school—all of Oromia—it was very, very big.

The next day the police covered the country, and no one was allowed out of his house. But I didn't go home. I was hiding in the countryside. There were older people with us. We realised we would be tortured in prison if we were caught, so we decided to leave the country. We all went separately. I went to another city and prepared for a long journey, then I went to Northwest Ethiopia. I contacted my family from the border and they also helped.

The journey was really difficult. We crossed into Sudan. It is hard to walk in the desert. We walked for two nights and then stopped in a small village for two weeks until I got some assistance from my family. Smugglers took us to Khartoum, but it was not good there. There is no rule-of-law, people just abuse you and there are spies everywhere. So, we paid again for smugglers to take us to Libya. It took ten days to cross the desert. We travelled in a truck for three days, but, in some places, we had to walk because the sand was too deep. And then, before we got to Tripoli, we were kidnapped by bandits. They were armed, and in a land-cruiser. They started to exchange shots with the smugglers, but the smugglers were beaten and kicked, and the bandits took all of us from two lorries and put us in a container. Then they told us to ask our families for money—two thousand dollars each. We were given water once a day, and they asked us to call again and again, and they kicked us again and again. There was a big fence around the container. You could not get out. Males and females, adults and children, all crammed together. The women were abused. You shit, you ate, you slept, there was nothing else to do.

Then they took us to Tripoli. Those who could not pay remained. My family found money. But when we got to Tripoli, those bandits sold us to other smugglers, and these new smugglers asked for more money—one thousand dollars per head to cross the Mediterranean. They kept us in a warehouse, and we were taken to do heavy work carrying stones. I was there for about two months. Finally, we crossed. It was just a rubber boat with one hundred people on it. It was too small, and I was in the middle. I cannot swim and we had no lifejackets. I was just about to give up hope because the water was coming in, and I was sure we were going to sink, but the big rescue ships arrived.

When we got to Italy, they put us in a camp and gave us food and clothes. Then I moved to an adult shelter because I did not want to be separated from my friends. It was not very good, and the Italian workers told me, as I was young, I could go to another better place.

After one week, I left with my friend, and we took the train to Ventimiglia and tried to cross the border to France. We tried by foot through the mountains, and on the train. Each time they caught us they just sent us back to Italy. Finally, I hid under the seats in the train carriage and got across.

That was almost a year ago. I followed my friends here to Calais, and everyone said to go to the UK. The language is much easier. I was with four friends, and two have already succeeded. They are in England now.

When I got here, the Jungle was still standing. I lived there for two months. It was hard but so much better than now. At least you had a place that was your own. There were fights, yes, but people got on. I was not there when they dismantled it. By mistake, I went to Germany! What happened was that there was a lorry at a petrol station, and when my friends opened the back, I jumped on without checking. There was my friend and a Sudanese guy, and we did not know that it was not going to the UK. When we noticed, we shouted at the driver to stop, but he would not, and he took us to the police in Germany. They fingerprinted us and took us to camp. We were put in a dormitory. There were so many people from so many countries. They asked us where we were from and why and gave us language lessons and clothes, and I stayed for five months. But the language is really tough, and they put us in the remote countryside. I have an uncle in the UK, and I did not want to stay, so I just got on a train and crossed back to France.

This is not better. I have been living under a bridge for eight months. I try every day to cross. We survive on distributions. Sometimes at night, a dog urinates on us. The police take our sleeping bags, or, sometimes, they just take us to the police station and keep us there for an hour. I have been pepper sprayed several times. Sometimes, when walking along the street, a police car comes by and they just spray you in the face. It happened the day before yesterday. We had just taken our sleeping bags and were walking, and the policeman ran up and sprayed us. They take your clothes and everything.

Ethiopia? I could go back, if the government respected people and did not kill and imprison them. There is no conflict between people in Ethiopia. It is the government that is making problems. Amhara, Oromo, everyone is against the government; they are not against each other. People are killed in all regions of the country and we need to stop this. We need respect!

England, October 2018

There were some French people who sometimes came to Calais to the food distribution sites. They had an office in St. Omer. I told them about my uncle in the UK, but I did not have an address. So, a woman took my number, but she could not find him. I think he must have changed his name and address. But this woman called me and said she wanted to help and told me to come to St. Omer. So, I did. I stopped trying the illegal crossings as soon as I was in this process. They gave us a place to stay in St. Omer. It was definitely better than under the bridge. There were lots of children there, perhaps thirty/forty, all boys. I spent three to four months there while they were arranging for me to go to the UK. I arrived here in May. I came here by plane—it was my first time to fly. A woman accompanied me, and we were met by police because I had no visa. They allowed me in. First of all, they sent me to a town in the north and I lived with a man. He was very kind, but he asked me a lot of questions, especially whenever I was talking with my friends on social media, so I felt a little bit uncomfortable. I did not go to school at first, as it was already almost the end of term. But they sent me to conversation classes. There were two friends from Calais there.

And also, I have a social worker. I am not sure where she is based, but I see her often, almost once a week. I like her very much, she is easy to talk to and she understood my problem with this man. She changed my home to another town. My new family is Pakistani. The mother and father have taken in four refugees. Their own children are grown up. Now I go to school. I am in year eleven. There are many refugees in the school, and they give us language classes. They treat me very well. Some of the teachers from my school go to Calais to help. I still have two friends living there. My family in Ethiopia are very happy because they know I am safe.

I am happy about what is happening in Ethiopia. The new prime minister is good. We are eighty four different cultures and different languages, but we are one. For example, in Ethiopia we had Christian neighbours. What we need is tolerance. But it is not safe yet to go back.

I will do GCSE's next year, and I want to go to university. I want to get my education here. I like England. The British government cares for refugees. I don't see refugees on the street like in Calais. No one has been hostile to me. People are so friendly. I have two close friends here, one is from Eritrea and one from Kuwait. They are neighbours. I speak Arabic, Oromipha, English, Amharic and even some French, so there is no difficulty talking. I go to Mosque. The one in our area is a little different from the one in our country. They have different ways of praying. I found another Mosque. The people who go there are from everywhere, and it is more like my own country. In my spare time, I play football, both with the school and for a local group. I am going to play football this weekend, with a Sudanese team.

I am going for my interview soon. I have a solicitor as well as a social worker. I hope it goes well.

2019

Samos

Greece, June 2019

Vathy, Samos, Wednesday 12 June

It's unbearable.

I walk down a steep, winding, earth path between small tents and hovels made of plastic, scrap wood and blankets clustered around smoking fires. There is rubbish everywhere, and the smell of human faeces. At one point the path runs beside a high mesh fence, topped with razor wire and cameras. Inside are the familiar white containers and yet more filthy tents crammed in between.

– Don't take photos of the camp! Stijn yells at me as I raise my mobile phone to take pictures. *It's forbidden, they have cameras everywhere.* The 'camp' was once a military base, built to house 650. Now it is a Reception and Identification Centre (RIC) for more than 1500, while another 2500 people squat out here in what is appropriately called the 'Jungle'.

– Where do people wash or go the toilet? I ask.

– In the bushes—Stijn replies. There are no toilets, taps or showers out here, and those inside the camp are filthy, broken and with permanent queues. Aslam, whom I last saw working flat out in the Park Hotel near the Macedonian border, is now based on the island. Like Stijn, he now works for Help Refugees. He went to the police to get permission to put up porta-loos. They sent him to the environment agency—who sent him to the local authorities.

– We thought we had an agreement to put them on land that we rented, but the police took them down. There are some toilets and taps inside the camp. But if you are a woman, it is too dangerous to go out at night, it's a nightmare. Rates of sexual violence are really high.

– And you can't drink the water from the taps—Holly tells me. *They dish out two litres a day per person for everything*

Last November, UNHCR urged the Greek authorities to urgently address the situation for the 11,000 asylum seekers that have passed through Samos, describing the conditions as 'abhorrent.'

"New arrivals are left having to buy flimsy tents from local stores, which they are pitching on a steep slope in adjacent fields. This offers little protection from the cold weather, without electricity, running water or toilets. There are snakes in the area, and rats are thriving in the uncollected waste.

Many of the asylum-seekers arrive in Greece in a vulnerable state, but even those who turn up at the RIC in good condition soon find themselves suffering from health problems. A single doctor per shift provides medical care to the entire population and often only the most urgent cases get seen. Doctors at the local hospital are also overwhelmed. Many of the toilets and showers are broken, resulting in open sewage close to people's tents. Others are using nearby bushes as a toilet. Vulnerable asylum-seekers—including some 200 unaccompanied children, over 60 pregnant women, the disabled and survivors of sexual violence—are left at risk in the RIC as alternative accommodation places on the island are taken. A container with broken windows and doors for unaccompanied children is hosting three times its intended capacity of six."

It could not be clearer, but things have deteriorated rather than improved.

– *The NGOs have offered tents and blankets, but the Ministry won't collaborate*—Stijn tells me. I watch two grubby, barefoot children running between shelters. At least they are laughing, but scabies and lice are rampant, and when migrant children attended the local school, Greek parents withdrew their own children in protest, saying they feared infection.

– *Food is another problem*—Stijn explains. *You have to start queuing three hours ahead, which means you spend most of your day in line for food.* Meanwhile, the nutritional value has not improved since my time in Lagkadikia, so most of it gets thrown away, and there is not enough water, so everyone is dehydrated.

Standing above the Jungle we can look down across the scruffy tents to the horseshoe of buildings that make up Vathy town as it curves around the bay of bright blue water. Gold and white houses climb up to dark green wooded hillsides. Picture postcard loveliness, the width of one highway from the misery around us.

When I told friends at home I was coming out to work with asylum seekers on Samos, some raised a quizzical eyebrow, asking:

– *Is that still going on?*

The answer is unfortunately yes. Two small girls, four women and one man drowned yesterday when their boat capsized near Mytilene on Lesvos. The other 57 on board were rescued. They were just a few of the 10,749 people who have arrived in the Greek islands since the beginning of the year. Over 3194 of those have come to Samos. And although the Turkish coast guard stopped 30 boats, just in the last week, arrivals on the islands are increasing. There were some transfers to the mainland a month ago, but people keep coming—90 people arrived every day last week. Greece currently hosts over 70,000 refugees, including nearly 15,000 in these overcrowded Aegean island camps.

The illegal EU-Turkey Deal is not working. The closure of European borders has done nothing to end the conflicts in Central Asia and the Middle East, or mitigate the wars, poverty and desperation that drive the global migration crisis. What the deal has done is trapped people on the Greek islands indefinitely while they wait for their asylum applications to be processed. Many have been here as long as three years.

At least you can go swimming, whether migrant or volunteer. Holly and Stijn take me to a nearby beach, where they have a meeting. Holly is a high dependency paediatric nurse who has decided she can do more out here on the front line of the migrant crisis than at home. She runs Indigo Volunteers, which matches people who want to volunteer with those who need their help. She has already connected me with a number of NGOs in Samos who want more training in mental health and psychosocial support. We swim in glass clear water next to rows of holiday-makers lying on sun loungers. Besides the fancy hotel, with its balconies and restaurant by a bright blue pool, there is an empty boarded up café, and the skeleton of an older, ruined hotel on the cliff side. Young asylum seekers sit in the shade at this end of the beach. Some are just relaxing, others jumping

Migrant families relax by the sea in
Vathy, Samos, June 2019

and somersaulting into the sea from a small headland. It's a happy scene. The sea does provide some relief from the miseries and stresses of the camp.

Vathy, Thursday 13 June
— *Don't force talking, don't make anyone, of any age, talk about something if they don't want to do so. But, if they do want to talk, be able to listen.*
— *We cannot do that*—a young man in the audience says.
— *We don't have time.*
— *We have been told we need to cut them short if there are too many people with serious physical problems waiting.*
I was not expecting this. The twenty or so people gathered are mostly GPs, nursing and paramedical staff from one of the NGOs that provides primary healthcare. They have asked me to do my usual introductory session on the most important psychological issues around forced migration. This includes how we approach the sensitive issue of discussing their past experiences.
I ask one of the GPs what percentage of the problems she has encountered are somatic presentations of stress.
— *More than fifty percent.*
Throughout the talk, a stream of patients has banged on the clinic door (in spite of the fact that Thursday is known to be staff day off, and there is a notice up saying clearly that the clinic is closed).
— *I do understand the pressure that you are under. But if someone does want to open up to you, listening may be the most important and healing thing you can do, and it might actually save time. Because, if they have had an opportunity to share whatever distresses them, and if they have physical symptoms which you think are connected, you can then explain how their distress affects the body, causing palpitations for example. This might prevent the patient returning multiple times with other aches and pains, and also decrease the amount of medication you prescribe.*
A long time ago when I was a trainee GP, we had Balint groups, named after the famous Hungarian psychoanalyst who taught GPs (including my mother) that even in a time-limited setting, it was important to pay attention to their patients underlying anxieties, rather

than simply medicating the physical symptoms.

Our trainer role-played a patient who had come with a sore throat, been briefly examined and given a prescription. Then, as the patient left, he turned with his hand on the doorknob and said... *oh, by the way doctor, I forgot to mention ...*

– *What would you do?* I ask the audience, for whom I am replaying this scene.

– *Ask the patient to come back into the room and sit down*—one of the GP's says.

– *Of course, because, probably, that was why he came in the first place, it's just taken ten minutes to decide to share it with you.*

Some of my audience are nodding, and some shaking their heads, looking worried and unconvinced.

– *We just don't have time*—one says again. *There are children with chicken pox, people with injuries, they have to be prioritised.*

Vathy, Saturday 15 June

Lack of time to listen is not the only difficulty. All the guidelines for mental health and psychological support in humanitarian emergencies rightly tell you that helping people address their basic needs is a first step to both alleviating and preventing further mental health problems.

– *So, what do you do when it's impossible to address those basic needs, like for water and shelter, when whatever we do, refugees still have to return to these shitty, dangerous places?* One volunteer asks me.

Good question. And it is these present miseries that weigh most heavily on asylum seekers' lives. Yesterday, a young Afghan told me he shared one tent with ten others:

– *I have a mattress and a blanket, I cannot sleep. It was impossible in winter, it was too cold. Now it is too hot, it is filthy, there are rats and mice. I have been here almost two years, but I have no ID, so there is no possibility of moving. I worry about my family at home all the time. Now I have so many problems that I don't want to do anything—not work, not read, not teach, nothing...*

I have now been asked to do this introductory workshop three times in as many days. Just now, I am with a packed room of both international and refugee community volunteers from Action for Education (A4E). They provide a drop-in centre, education, showers and a community kitchen, for young people between eighteen and twenty three, as well as similar support to women and children on the weekends. Next door is the 'Nest,' where they work with infants. All this inside a normal house with a large kitchen, meeting room and a beautiful courtyard garden in the centre of town.

– *I have only been here a few days, but I can already see what a difference you make*—I say. *You cannot change the camp or the Jungle, but you are providing safe, clean spaces where people can go and feel normal, relax, make new connections, learn new skills, launder their clothes. It's not just a distraction from the awfulness of life in the Jungle. It also helps them prepare for the future. This is all good for their mental health.*

The humanitarians have professionalised, just like in France. The new NGOs are registered legal entities, but they retain the flexibility that allows them to adapt to the changing situation. I sat in their fortnightly coordination meeting on Wednesday, held at the Samos Hotel. The lack of duplication is also impressive. Refugees 4 Refugees helps orient new arrivals and provides essential items they need, like tents. Med'Equali provides primary health care, while MSF does public health and attends to sexual and gender-based violence. The Samos Legal Centre provides legal advice. Drop in the Ocean provides play-based education for children aged 7-12, while Still I Rise runs education and recreation for 12 to 19-year-olds, and Samos Volunteers at the Alpha centre does the same for young adults. Baobab provides a community space and 500 meals a day for families, and Movement on the Ground organises litter clean up's in the Jungle.

Yesterday afternoon, I watched some twenty, mostly Afghan and Iranian, women learning how to fix mobile phones and computer hardware—all clearly loving it. Alexandra, their teacher, drew diagrams on the board and set them to practice with the small toolboxes she had provided.

– *Fixing phones and computer hardware are some of the few technical skills you can use without certification, which means there are no barriers to employment*—Alexandra explained.

She is an American student in political science. She taught herself these skills and used them to support herself at different times in her life. She had suggested International Rescue Committee run this project with resettled refugees in the US when she interned there. They showed no interest, so she had approached a friend of her mother who was setting up a psychosocial support programme for women on Samos through Fearless Planet.

They came up with a three-week course for two groups of women, each doing three hours per day.

— *Most cannot come for longer because they spend so much time waiting in lines. But these women learn really fast, and it's enough to get the basic skills. You know why I want them to learn this? No one can take this from them. They can work anywhere. They can put a sign up at home, a neighbour can come by, and they can say, 'Yes, I can fix that for you if you pay me,' or they can get a job in a local shop, or maybe some will want to go on and get more technical skills, and this will help pay for their studies.*

— *I love it*—a 22-year-old tells me over tea and biscuits after class—*if someone brings a mobile, I can fix it, and I am useful.*

— *My husband had a shop with phones and laptops. He is so happy I am doing this. If we get another, I can work there.*

— *My field was artificial intelligence, I understood software, now I can fix hardware, so I am very happy.*

Vathy, Sunday 16 June

My landlady had a rant at me today. She asked me if I thought some crockery and towels, and some clothes and linen could be used by the refugees. Refugees 4 Refugees runs a free shop in town and distributes non-food items. I was sure they would take them.

— *You know when they first came, I was down there every day, making sandwiches.*

— *That is wonderful!*

— *Yes, we all wanted to help, they were making food in Samos Hotel. But the refugees said they didn't like the food. And now it is too much! Why Samos town? It is not fair. You know mothers and children don't go to*

The phone workshop
Vathy 2019

*the playground anymore? Because the refugees are there. And the hospital!
You cannot see a doctor; you must wait so long because there are so many
refugees. Why must we have them in Vathy, when the other towns won't
have them, and other countries won't either? It is not fair. It is too much,
the tourism is down, the cafés are empty...*
– The beach seemed crowded yesterday.
– Those are last year's bookings. They should take them off the island!
*– You know the refugees would be delighted if they could go to the
mainland.*
– I know it is not their fault, but it is not fair.
*– I completely agree, I am ashamed of my own country. We definitely do
not take our share, that's why I am here.*
It isn't fair. What is a town of 5000 people supposed to do when
4000 refugees arrive on their doorstep? Aslam and I sit discussing
it later over coffee—*To be honest, I feel really sad about how the locals
are affected*—Aslam says. *You must see it from the local point of view.
People have been arriving here for four years... There are a large number
of single men around, you cannot send your small child out to the bus
queue, your 16-year-old cannot walk home at 3am in the dark as she
used to do, nor can you leave your doors and windows open day and
night as was the custom. This was a safe country. You can't ignore the fact
that any population has a few criminals, but they don't get punished.
There are twenty two police reports on theft. That's not 9000 criminals,
just one or two, but they have not been deported. For example, when
some mobile phones were stolen, the shop owner did not even call the
police because he knew the guys would only get a couple of hours in jail...*
Luckily, many on Samos remain friendly. Vasilis has invited us to
a barbecue at his small cabin near a tiny cove. The mountainous
coast of Turkey is visible half a mile away. There is an empty gun
emplacement in the overgrown garden. *Sometimes they put the gun
there, sometimes they take it away.* Vasilis laughs and shrugs when I
ask about it.
He used to work for a food company—*A good job but too busy. I had
enough.* Now he works as a fixer for the NGO community, a middle-
man between them and Greek companies—*For example, if there is a*

need for food, I can make the orders with the company.

He likes helping—*It is not just now. I have lived my whole life trying to help if I can—people, dogs, cats....*

He thought the majority of islanders were sympathetic to the refugees—*ninety percent of people don't want them in the Jungle, they hate to see it, but they also don't want to change their lives. They want open doors and open windows. They say, 'We want to help, but it should be a small camp, they should be here a short time, get their papers and go.' They say tourism is down forty percent, but that is not because of refugees. It's because European weather is good, people have less money, and Turkey has become very cheap. Vathy never had that many tourists.*

Another long-standing volunteer points out to me that locals actually make more money from the refugee crisis than they do from tourists.

– All the volunteers are here year-round, renting rooms and cars, eating locally, and each refugee has 90 euros a month to spend on food.

I think about these discussions as I walk along the seafront in town in the evening. This is the best time of day. Young African men play football on the plaza under the statue. There are families with strollers, small children pushing bikes and playing football and tag. Couples sit together on the sea wall. Many of these people are not Greek, many of the women wear long robes and headscarves in various styles, but I do not sense any hostility. A young Cameroonian with dreadlocks sits next to an old Greek man on a bench. Both are smiling. Everyone is peacefully enjoying sitting or promenading, chatting and playing with friends, admiring the beauty of the light from the large red sun, setting into the sea in the west. We all want the same things: food, shelter, to feel useful, respected and loved, access to beauty and calm space for our children to grow and thrive.

Three Afghan women sitting on piles of fishing nets by the quay wave and smile at me. A small fishing boat bobs behind them. I know them because we have discussed having some mother and baby sessions.

– We want you to run the camp!

– Camp no good! You run it, camp no good.

— I am so sorry. I know it's hard. I would be useless. I think they are building a new camp…

The current camp manager does not appear to be popular with anyone. Last week, Still I Rise took the unprecedented step of suing the camp management on behalf of unaccompanied minors living in the camp. These young people were continually reporting various abuses: bruises from being hit by the police, bite marks from rats. So, Still I Rise started to systematically collect evidence and then filed an affidavit. Now the camp manager is suing back for defamation, and also suing the local press for reporting on the case.

There are plans for a new camp. It will be built some eight kilometres out of town inland and be designed to hold 1500 people. Whether it will be open or closed, what services will be allowed within the camp, or where the extra people will go, remains completely unclear. What is obvious is that the immediate relief of walking down to the sea to stare at the sunset will be unavailable.

Vathy, Monday 17 June

Swimming is already unavailable, at least from some public beaches. I was talking with a young man from the Congo this morning, who was telling me about the boredom and frustrations of his day to day life. I suggested swimming at the beach where I had seen the other young men the other day.

— It's not allowed. They stopped it. The police will not let you go down there.

— But it's a public beach. They are open to all!

The young man shrugged his shoulders.

I went down to check for myself in the evening. The beach was almost deserted. The white sun loungers were empty and the umbrellas folded. Just a few white people were there catching the evening sun. The crowd of happy darker-skinned young men that I had seen swimming and diving last week were absent.

— One of the restaurant owners cleared them off with dogs—a volunteer told me. *And now the police stop them coming down the road.*

I felt a bit sick, lowering myself into the crystal-clear water, snatching a guilty swim. So apparently, asylum seekers are allowed to drown in these waters but not enjoy them in any place where they might 'disturb the view.'

Vathy, Tuesday 18 June

At least everyone can still swim on the small beach below Baobab. There are families sitting beside shimmering water in the afternoon sun. A father swings his daughter through the waves, a young woman paddles, another shouts with delight as she balances on a large rock. Baobab is packed as usual. Lunch has just finished. In one corner of the large dining room, children are drawing and painting, in another, men play chess. The large, tree-filled, courtyard besides the sea has a brightly painted wooden picket fence keeping roaming children safe. It is filled with families chatting to one another in the shady areas. There are French lessons in the small classroom. Mahmoud, a Syrian haematologist, who now has asylum in Greece, set the Centre up with the support of Swiss Cross. He and Swiss Cross founder Michael had visited in January 2019 and been shocked at the needs.

— I saw that this café was closed and empty and had not been used for a long time, so I set up an appointment between Michael and the owner, and we rented it and refurbished it. Just fixing the electricity cost 5000 euros because it had seawater in it. We started with 35 people, and now, at least 450 come every day to eat and socialise. The refugees who volunteer are amazing, they smile every day. We have washing machines, activities, showers …

And I have a packed room of parents and infants attending my parent and baby session. It is the first time I have had equal numbers of fathers and mothers. We only have a tiny narrow classroom with long tables and chairs, so the parents let the infants play on the tables, forming a protective barrier by sitting close. These Afghan fathers are very loving and interactive with their children, and interested in the discussion, so the group goes really well. They all want to come back for more.

Alas, not every father is so wonderful. In the discussion group with the small children this morning at Drop in the Ocean, the most energetic and restless boy in the class told us his father beat him a lot for failing to read or do his homework. Other children told me that, although their parents never beat them in their home countries, they had started doing so here:

— *Since we moved here, my dad started hitting me. Once, I went to the Jungle and I cut myself on the back and it was bleeding. He got angry and said, 'I will hit you again.' Luckily, it's healed now.*

The small school is a sanctuary.

— *I love school more than home, we have nothing to do at home. Here there are lots of things to learn.*

In the evening I have coffee with two doctors from Med'Equali who want to discuss how to approach psychological issues in patients further.

— *My position is that we have to ask if there are any issues, physical or sexual violence. But if the patient starts to explain in detail what happened to them, we apologize, say 'I am very sorry this happened to you, but listening to the full story will not change anything that I can help you with. How do you feel physically or psychologically right now?' I ask about the symptoms they are having in the present time. I also have to protect the mental health of the volunteer staff and the translators. Mental health is a huge issue on Samos and we are the only medical NGO, it is too much.*

— *It must be really difficult.* Many GP's share this doctor's concern, that psychological issues take too much time. The paradox is that primary health care is usually the place where these difficulties will present. People feel safe talking to a GP or nurse in this setting, and it has no stigma attached. Moreover, because primary healthcare workers take a holistic approach, connecting the mental and physical, they can do a very good job. When I had to write an action sheet for some international guidelines,[20] I suggested one approach might be setting dedicated time aside—in the same way GP's do with antenatal care—and asking people who want to talk more to return at a particular time.

— *The refugees are crashing the system here*—her colleague explains. *We were seeing thirty reported rape cases a week, and we were sending HIV blood tests up to the hospital. They could not do them anymore; they ran out of the materials. So, we had to stop altogether for some time.*

360

I have been told repeatedly that rape is a major problem. The Jungle is not safe, and many women have been raped in Turkey, or in their country of origin. MSF has a sexual and gender-based violence specialist, but the numbers of historical rapes are so high they can only take on cases that occurred less than six months ago.

– You need to understand—the colleague continues—*a lot of patients tell you stories just to get the vulnerability status. In the first three seconds they tell you a story and ask for a psychiatrist. Some come in pretending to be psychotic, eating cardboard, talking to themselves.*

This was the problem Eleni had in Lagkadikia. Psychological complaints and stories of abuse are the easiest things to make up and the hardest things to check. One young man had already explained that everyone in the Jungle told him:

– If you have a statement saying you are sick, you get priority to leave. European people like sick people. If you are good in the camp, you will never go to Athens. If you feel bad, you will. Everyone tells us that.

I realise I am biased. During my junior hospital jobs in accident and emergency, and as a GP trainee, I always found the psychological world fascinating and was only too glad if my patients wanted to discuss it. My colleagues' frustration and distaste for these patients was perplexing, and I was delighted when they tended to pass them along to me. Indeed, in Britain, the stigma attached to anything remotely psychiatric has led to a completely unethical division of resources and care. But I could also see that, Med'Equali was stuck between a rock and a hard place with its heavy patient load. Faced with a screaming, feverish child or a broken limb, there is little time for the possibly made up story of mental distress.

Vathy, Thursday 20 June, World Refugee Day

BBC news today: The rate of melting for glaciers in the Himalayas has doubled in the last twenty years, putting the one billion people who depend upon it at risk of losing their water supply. The Iranians shoot down a US drone, and back in Britain we are about to have a prime minster imposed upon us who calls black children picaninnies and thinks Muslim women in hijabs look like letter boxes. I cannot

The School, Drop in the Ocean, Vathy

get rid of the tight feeling of despair in my stomach. While the planet as a whole hurtles towards catastrophe, the day to day acts of trying to bring comfort to a few migrants trapped in squalor on a tiny Greek island seem almost meaningless, and I cannot comfort myself with the astonishing beauties of this island.

It is the migrants themselves who continue to amaze me. Tonight, to celebrate World Refugee Day, they put on a wonderful talent show. Samos Volunteers had persuaded the town authorities to let them use the small classical amphitheatre above the town. So, for almost three hours, different groups and individuals danced, play acted, sang and made music. My favourite part was when a large group of young people from both Africa and Asia did break dancing together, followed by stunning individual performances by both Congolese boys and Afghan girls. The crowd cheered and cheered, as they did for the Kurdish singer and the African guitarists, the kick boxing team and the circus acts.

– *The girls almost did not perform*—Aboolfazl told me. He is an Iranian circus artist who teaches breakdancing and martial arts.

– *The girls were dancing in my classes, and I asked them if they would like to dance on the stage. They said no, 'Our fathers and brothers will kill us, we can dance in class, where our fathers cannot see us but not on stage.' So, I said, 'No they won't kill you, I will support you.'*

He had shown them films of other girls dancing and worked with them.

Then they said 'OK'—then 'no,' then 'OK…no…OK…no.' Finally, they decided to dance. But then, on the morning before the show, they came to me and said, 'no.' I said, 'Please, just come up to the theatre and look at the stage and hear the music. We may not get this opportunity again,' and they came and they saw it and they said, 'we want to dance.' Really, they were just shy. I said, 'I am your teacher, trust me. Dance with me. We are all equal, men and women, African, Arab, Iranian, Afghan—you have to trust. You came up here to dance, so dance, don't think about any problems. If you have any problems, bring them to me.

– *Then Benesh's father came to me and said, 'She cannot dance.' I said, 'Look, people are just watching her dance, nothing else.' He said, 'No, I am a Muslim,' and I said, 'So am I, but I dance. Please let Benesh dance. If someone says a single bad word about your daughter, I will go to the police and challenge them.' Then he said, 'Ok.' So, she danced, and everyone was watching and cheering, you saw. And then Benesh's father came to me after and said, 'Oh Abool, you were right, you were amazing, she was amazing, I am so happy.' And he hugged his daughter and kissed her a lot, and he said, 'I want to see you dance again in another place,' and she was crying and then she was really happy.*

Abool is inspiring, a 29-year-old Iranian who taught himself break-dancing from watching YouTube videos when he was fifteen. Then he learned kickboxing in Thailand and became a circus artist, even though in parts of Iran this was a tough thing to do.

– Someone wanted to kill me because I was breakdancing. Five or six men attacked me with knives. My city was very rigid about these things, so I moved to another city and got a job with another circus.

When he got the authorities to ban the use of animals in the circus there were further attacks on his life, so he fled the country. He arrived here two years ago, and even though he was living in the Jungle, he started working at the Alpha centre immediately. He had his asylum interview five months ago but is still waiting for a decision and cannot leave Samos. He shares an apartment with friends. They pool the 90 euros a month they each receive from UNHCR, to pay for rent and food—*We are really poor, but we manage*—The classes are his life.

– When I arrived here, I thought I have to open the minds of Muslim people. They say girls have to sit and men can move. That's wrong! Now I am in Europe, men and women are equal and we have to open girls' minds.

He taught kickboxing to help young people resolve conflicts. He told me about two boys who had been really angry with each other.

– They learned in class that you cannot fight well if you are angry, and after three or four bouts, they started to relax and now they have embraced and made up and are friends.

His ambition is to start his own circus in Europe, but first he wants to go to circus school.

365

— I love Samos, and I understand the Greeks. Sometimes they say, 'Don't sit here.' But then you see a refugee dropping litter. If this was my island, I would feel the same. Or the refugees play loud music at night, or some have stolen things. That's not good. You have to respect others and they will respect you. And they ask us: why don't we learn Greek? We should.

It is working and respect that have kept Abool sane. *If Samos Volunteers was not here, I would have gone crazy. Really, they are family.*

Mahmoud, the doctor who manages the Baobab centre, tells a similar story. He left Syria in 2016, arrived in Lesvos by boat, and got to Idomeni in early March 2016, just a few days before the border closed. Then he moved to a camp near Thessaloniki.

— I was just smoking in front of that camp. I never smoked in Syria, I started on the journey. Anyway, the logistics guy from Swiss Cross saw me, and he asked me, 'Can you help us change things a little bit here?' It was such a different request. I was so fed up of being asked, 'How are you?' When there is a queue of 1500 for the toilet! Or, they ask you about Daesh! But this was different. I felt respected for the first time. I still had the power to help. He had touched my secret key.

Mahmoud helped create the social programmes, liaising between camp authorities, police, army and Swiss Cross. Then, Greek authorities started moving people out of the camps. They put him in a seven-star hotel on the highest mountain in Greece. It snowed every day, and the luxury did not compensate for having nothing to do, and no ideas about his future. He felt deeply relieved when Swiss Cross asked him to go back to Mytiline on Lesvos and open a project.

— I sat in the same café where I had sat when I first arrived. But I felt so different, now I had a plan and a future in front of me. In that hotel on the mountain, I felt unstable. Now I felt stable. I had a life, and I decided it made no sense to move on, even if Switzerland were to offer me asylum. So, when they told me in Athens in March 2017 that I could go to France, I said no thanks. I will ask for asylum in Greece.

The Greeks could not believe it.

— They said, 'Are you serious? Have a coffee and a cigarette and take some time, we will come back in 30 minutes.' When they came back, I said yes, I want to stay in Greece. Then the French Embassy called, to see if I had

been forced to take that decision.

It did not end there. On the morning of Mahmoud's appointment to ask for asylum in Greece, the French Embassy called him again:

— Did you change your mind? If so, we can move your interview for Greek asylum to us if you would like that?

— I said no thank you. The Greek interview lasted an hour. I explained that I love France and want to visit, but it would take me five years to learn French, and adjust and fit in, whereas in Greece, I felt I fit, the culture had similarities to my own, and I had a project—important work helping others—that I knew I could do.

The Greeks accepted. Mahmoud has asylum. His documents must be renewed in three years. His travel document entitles him to travel anywhere in the Schengen area without a visa.

— I can go anywhere except home. I cannot go to Syria.

Meanwhile, Mahmoud decided he wanted to do more than volunteer. Fifteen months ago, he opened a small Syrian-Arabic restaurant, on Lesvos. He employs three refugees and everyone has a good salary.

— Local Greeks do not want to work for a refugee boss. That's fine, there are a lot of skilled people in the camp. I have a trustworthy manager. I think we have changed lives.

Vathy, Friday 21 June

Adults who can find meaningful work as volunteers, and small children who have the protective embrace of at least one parent, have an easier time than teenagers. I was just finishing some individual sessions at one of the centres, when one of the volunteers asked if I would come and help with a teenager from Pakistan who had got into an argument with a younger boy and hit him. The volunteer involved in the class had sat with him for over an hour, explaining that this was unacceptable behaviour and that he would have to be excluded for the next 48 hours.

This evening, he had been found in the street directly outside the centre, with numerous small self-inflicted cuts all down his arm and a couple on the side of his neck. There was quite a lot of blood, but, fortunately, all the wounds were superficial. After cleaning him up, we found a translator and sat him down to talk.

– *So, what made you cut yourself?* My colleagues asked.

– *I was so angry! After you sent me out, I found a bottle in the rubbish and broke it and used that. I wanted to die, but the glass was too blunt.* Thank goodness I thought, looking at the fine cuts he had made near the carotid artery.

– *And now?*

– *I don't want to die now, but in that moment, yes. Now, I suppose you might as well deport me back to Pakistan.*

– *We don't want to do that. We just want to understand things better so we can help.*

– *Is hitting another person respectful?* I ask.

– *No, I know it is not, and I did not want to but....* He pulls a face and shakes his head.

– *And does it show respect for yourself if you cut yourself?* I asked. He made a small rueful smile—*No.*

My colleagues asked more about his life in the camp. It was horrible and frustrating, but his parents were good people. There was no violence in the family.

The volunteer wanted to let his parents know and to meet with them the next day. He walked back to the camp with the boy who was, by now, quite calm and contrite.

Self-harm is becoming an issue here. Everyone recognises it is a method of both expressing and coping with frustration. Mostly, it is not about suicidal intent. One boy told me the whole class had self-harmed in his home country:

– *We did it in school together, with pencil sharpeners. It made us feel better.*

Here he uses a rock. He showed me the multiple fine scratches down his arm. Indeed, just before I left the UK, a colleague remarked that her 12-year-old daughter had told her—*Mum, self-harm is cool. All the cool kids do it.*

But how does one properly assess risk in a situation as frustrating and volatile as the Jungle? A child that at one moment says he is just feeling angry, says he wants to die at the next. It is a method of protest.

I cannot forget what happened in Idomeni.

We discuss what to do in these situations. If we exclude children who express anger as violence to someone else, they are the most likely to turn that anger on themselves. I make the same suggestion I did in Calais: accompanied exclusion. Yes, the boy has endangered someone else and has to leave that situation, but someone goes with him to discuss and support him, helping him first to calm down and then, when appropriate, to think about what happened, understand his feelings and how he might cope with them differently. Even better, the staff want to create a quiet staffed space where children can retreat to cool off when they don't feel in control, somewhere supportive rather than punitive, and introduce some anger management sessions. The boy told us he would happily attend.

Vathy, Monday 24 June

Nine-year-old Mia sat down this morning and drew her life story in fourteen pictures, starting with herself—*inside my mother's tummy.* Both parents stand outside their house, mother smiles happily, hand on stomach, father looks anxiously up at a rocket in the sky, heading their way. Mia coloured the rocket bright red.

She worked fast, each picture a simple dramatic sketch catching the moment, mostly with only one key point in colour. Here was someone threatening her father and him carrying his pregnant wife through the mountains to Lebanon. Here she was wrapped in a pink blanket with a knot of brown hair—the moment after birth. The most painful picture was a man with a bloody knife standing over a tangled mass of red, and a telephone cable stretching to a weeping woman:

– *Then someone called my mum and said someone got my dad.*

But the next picture was of them smiling outside their home in Lebanon along with a dog.

– *I was really happy because I had my dog. We named him Poochy.*

– *I want to do three more*—she announced after sketching their climb up the mountains to Turkey. *The sea, the camp and this school! But I need paint.* I gave her watercolours and she started on a picture

369

Everything was black in Yemen. In Yemen I
was still in my mummy's tummy, so I don't
remember, but my mum told me about it.
This is a picture of my mum and me in her
tummy, this is my dad. This is something
going to break the house and destroy it
because, in Yemen, all the houses are being
destroyed.
Mia from Yemen, age 9

This is a picture of one day in Afghanistan,
when we went out with my aunts and uncles
and father and brothers. We had so much
fun on that day. It was a children's park in
the city. The weather was so nice, although
there was not so much shade, so we had to
find another place for shade. Then we all
went to a restaurant for food. This is my
mum and dad in the picture. It was one of
my best days ever; it is such a happy memory.
We have not had any days like that here on
Samos. Sometimes we go out. We did find
a nice place yesterday, next to the sea. That
was beautiful.
Zeinab from Afghanistan, age 8

of the boat.

– *I need black!*

– *I am so sorry there is no black paint.* Mia experimented with brown.

– *It's not dark enough. It has to be black!* She started mixing colours to get black, finally settling on a murky purplish-brown. The series ends with Mia happy in school dreaming of going to America.

I love the way drawing provides the freedom to show both the imagined past and hoped for future. As usual, I started with sharing work by other children on the Migrantchild website, and then invited them to do anything they like.

– *Can I draw the happiest day in my life?* Zeinab, an 8-year-old Afghan girl asked.

– *Of course*—I replied and she settled down to draw a detailed picture of her family in the park at home.

In a workshop last week, another teenage boy from Afghanistan gave me a split picture. He had drawn a line across the page and left the top half blank, while the bottom half had intricate coloured pictures of intact buildings and a mosque.

– *The top half has nothing because I have forgotten everything, and I don't want to remember. I cannot draw that. The bottom half is peace. I never saw a peaceful country, so I imagined it.*

At the end of one workshop, one of the children glanced at the screensaver on my computer. It happened to be a picture of my Ethiopian husband sitting by a waterfall in Scotland.

– *Who is that?*

– *That's my husband.* The children (all of whom were from Iran, Iraq or Yemen) stared at me in amazed bewilderment. How could this be possible?

– *But, But…* one stammered.

– *Yes?* I asked. She could not bring herself to voice the imagined complaint.

There are the same racial divides here that I saw in Northern France. I have been doing regular play activities with some of the NGOs working up in the Jungle. Understandably, children tend to cluster with those most like themselves. Sometimes, it's more pronounced.

On one occasion, I was organising a game of 'knots' when a small Afghan girl refused to take the hands of a Congolese child.

– *They say we are dirty and don't wash*—a Ugandan refugee volunteer told me. *So, I have become tough, turned from a butterfly into a tiger.*

I was glad my computer screen challenged some of the stereotypes. One of the joys of the talent show last week was watching young people from the Middle East, Central Asia and Africa all doing break-dancing together. Audience members of every nationality cheered every act, and by the end, people of all nationalities were getting up to dance to each other's music. It was beautiful, moving and hopeful.

Vathy, Wednesday 26 June

I think, after almost three weeks, I finally understand the current process of seeking asylum in Greece. Lena, one of the law students from Germany who volunteers at the Refugee Law Centre (RLC), patiently explained it to me. The Law Centre provides orientation workshops to explain the general process and do casework to help asylum seekers prepare for interviews, supervised by a migration lawyer in Berlin. One problem is that the interviews are not just to decide whether they are eligible for asylum as refugees.

– *Many don't realise that, because of the EU-Turkey Deal, they will be asked about their lives in Turkey to see if they are 'admissible' here or can be sent back there. Also, they need to know their rights—to a translator and to have a transcript.*

So, even if you are eligible for refugee status, you can be 'inadmissible' to Greece if the authorities judge that you were safe in Turkey—perhaps because you have connections there, stayed longer than ten days, had work, access to health care, or did not suffer any discrimination.

– *We work to strict criteria*—my neighbour, who works for the European Asylum Support Office (EASO), explained. One part of his job was to interview applicants and write opinions for the Greek Asylum Service on admissibility and eligibility

– I went to them and said—'*Look, it is obvious they cannot live freely in Turkey.' And the Greeks told me not to worry, 'We will reject most of your opinions anyway.' So, most of the ones I have said are inadmissible are allowed to be admissible here. My opinion has to be based on particular criteria, but the real question that should be asked is: Can they live free from persecution and harm in Turkey? I don't think so, and Greek Asylum service does not think so either. I was really happy to hear they were rejecting my opinions.*

He had gone into this work because he is on the side of refugees. So are my Greek colleagues. He hoped that in interviews he could help asylum seekers make the best case possible.

Another interesting fact is that the more eligible you are for refugee status (because you are Syrian, Afghan or Iraqi), the more likely you are to be found inadmissible.

– *If the person comes from the DRC or another African country, their likelihood of being eligible for asylum here is much lower, so I am told don't worry about admissibility with these groups. That is EU politics.*

– *The EU-Turkey Deal is criminal*—my neighbour continued. *It's dysfunctional, it does not achieve its aims. Right now, Turkish citizens are getting refugee status in Germany at the same time that we in Greece are saying Turkey is a safe country to which we can return Syrians!*

So, this is how it goes: you arrive on Samos and the police give you a paper. This should be immediately followed by a 'small interview,' but it may not be until a month later. It only takes an hour to cover your biographical information, your health status, whether you are vulnerable, what happened to you in your home country and Turkey. After this, you are fingerprinted and given an 'Ausweis' (don't ask me why a German word is used), which will have an interview date for your 'big interview,' during which your right to asylum will be assessed. That may be as much as two, or even three years into the future. Most single young men get a closed Ausweis with a red stamp. This means they cannot leave Samos while they wait. No stamp, or a blue stamp, means you can travel around Greece. Unaccompanied minors, the elderly, and pregnant women should all be transferred to the mainland. So should victims of torture and rape. But these require a medical report by a psychiatrist, and, as there is only one on the island, there is an enormous backlog.

Oh, and another thing: the big interview can be suddenly brought forward and you might be told—*it is tonight*—when, theoretically, you should have at least 24 hours to prepare.

The big interview covers the same ground as the small one but in greater detail, so it takes all day. Then, you wait for the decision, which can be: 1. Refugee status, 2. Subsidiary protection, or 3. Refusal, which means you have five days to appeal. Some people had their 'big interview' sixteen months ago and still have not received a decision.

It was a 26-year-old Syrian translator at the Refugee Law Centre who brought home what this process means in reality and its emotional cost. Farid fled Aleppo to avoid being called up to do military service.

– I did not want to kill people I know. I have friends in the Syrian Army and friends in the Free Army, both have had terrible experiences. Their whole life is hell. I did not want to give up my dreams of being a geologist or civil engineer.

He travelled the usual routes to Izmir on the Turkish coast and looked for smugglers. *You don't know who is good, you just have to hope. If you go with the wrong person, you may end up with an organised gang who takes your body parts. So, many Syrians have disappeared.*

After a terrifying journey with a boat captain who had no idea how to drive, he got to Chios.

– I fell into a black hole—it was so dirty, there was not enough water to drink, rats everywhere, there were fights all the time. I had never had flashbacks before, but I started having them on Chios. You know, in some moments, you stop trusting yourself. I became physically and mentally unwell. You need someone to respect you, to let you think and feel you are important, that you are not just a rat, but a human being.

He was completely unprepared for his big interview and was rejected on the basis that he was safe in Turkey.

– You don't know anything. You think you just need to say you are Syrian and you will be allowed in.

The RLC helped him appeal and the rejection was revoked on health grounds. Then, as he had an open card, UNHCR sent him to wait in Lagkadikia Camp in Northern Greece, where conditions appear to have deteriorated—*mostly there was no water, the rain got into the containers and tents. There was no power, so you could not dry anything. There was nothing to do. So, I used the time to become fluent in English. I was determined not to die in those camps.*

He had his second big interview last August and was granted asylum. *But I wasted half my life in a war and two years waiting for this decision.*

Farid now works as a volunteer translator for the RLC, helping people by sharing his own experiences. He still feels that he is recovering his emotional stability:

– *They put you in a place for making monsters. If you want to turn a peaceful man into a monster just make him wait for things that he does not understand that he is waiting for. Make him swim in the flashbacks of his old life. Just let him lie and stare at the ceiling of the tent, remembering and thinking about every single bad moment through which he passed. You feel like there is a volcano inside you. I am in my twenties. This age is full of energy, and you are lying there doing nothing, so you get panic attacks and feel utterly changed. This is the way to make monsters.*

The irony is that Farid was lucky that his asylum application was not approved earlier. As of the end of March this year, anyone granted asylum before the 31st of July 2017 had to give up the allowance and accommodation provided by UNHCR. In addition, anyone getting asylum after January 2019 will only get six months of support. The idea is to free up space on the mainland, where jungle-like conditions are growing around many camps, to enable more transfers from the overcrowded islands.

The ESTIA programme set up by UNHCR to support refugees in Greece looks good on its website. It has provided accommodation for over 25,000 people outside the camps and cash support to more than 120,000 since April 2017. But, in spite of €722.9 million spent in the last three years on emergency support, the reintegration programme—mandatory language training, preparation for seeking employment, including getting a tax number, opening a bank account, registering at job centres so that refugees can actually find work or get state benefits and pay the rent—has not happened. There are finally plans to begin, but those who got asylum before 2018 will not be eligible. Meanwhile, many landlords remain hostile to refugees and find Airbnb rentals much more profitable. So, a possible 6000 refugees and asylum seekers, including those given accommodation because they were vulnerable through age or physical or mental infirmity, face eviction and homelessness in the very near future.

Vathy, Thursday 27 June

I spend my last morning doing litter inspection in the Jungle with Matthew from Movement on the Ground (MOTG). He used to pick up the trash with some fifteen international volunteers. After a lot of friendly tea drinking, he has found community volunteers to keep the public areas clean. He has also helped groups of four or five houses organise themselves to gather the litter up in their own area. He goes up every morning to see how things are going.

We walk down the main path where three empty dustbins are strategically placed. The volunteers empty them and leave the garbage sacks at the top of the road every night. MOTG has contracted a truck to come and take the sacks to the landfill. Matthew has also arranged to get the bushes where snakes lurk cut back.

I follow him into a small shady gully where a man is collecting water from a deep well. He says it is just for washing clothes. A large sign placed there by MSF warns people not to drink it.

– *The rubbish in this gulley was over our heads, Matthew explains. The trouble is, now we have removed most of it. It's a nice hidden place, so people use it as a latrine.*

Further up, I step over a pile of human excrement and find six dead rats lying on the ground. On the edge of the gully is a pit latrine built by the residents. Matthew got them buckets, so at least they have earth, but one rainstorm and everything—the rats, the shit, and the waste from the latrines—washes down through the camp into town. It's only 9:30am and it's astonishingly hot. What will this be like as the heat waves get more intense? At the coordination meeting yesterday, MSF said they wanted to install water points in the Jungle because they were seeing so much dehydration. We walk back up to

Rats and rubbish in the Jungle, Vathy

the road where the trash bags are waiting pick up and sit in the shade. Matthew likes solving problems. He got involved in Better Days for Moria on Lesvos when he came out to fix solar panels. He tells me I would not recognise the camp in the olive grove any more. With the help of the refugees themselves, they have terraced and organised the area, and put in toilets.

– I went to the local mayor and asked, 'What can we do for you?' He wept and told me, in two years, no one had asked him that. Now refugees pick up the litter between the camp and the village. People here in Vathy complain about all the young men just hanging around on the sea front. On Lesvos we have got a local football club to engage in training them and now they play football. I want to do the same here.

Vathy, Friday 28 June

– The authorities won't allow water taps in the Jungle. They don't want the responsibility. They asked me what if someone gets sick? Who would be responsible? Vasilis is late for coffee with me because he had been meeting with the authorities at the Town Hall to try and get permission for water points and toilets to be placed on land rented by Help Refugees. Apparently, there is one section of law that says you can only put up particular structures, and that does not include chemical toilets.

– But there is another section of law that does not say you cannot put up chemical toilets. So, they are going with the section that does not explicitly give permission for toilets. Our lawyer is going to argue using the section that does not explicitly forbid it.

My question is: why are the local authorities not concerned to protect both local population and asylum seekers from all the health hazards that follow from uncollected waste and denying access to toilets and clean water? There was a count yesterday. There are at least 3896 migrants living in the camp and jungle. But the attitude seems to be that pretending two thirds of them don't exist, and making life as miserable as possible will actively discourage asylum seekers from coming here, regardless of the risks to locals from rats and raw sewage.

And people still suffer daily dehumanising indignities. I was walking back to my room yesterday evening. Swifts wheeled through the air which smelt of ripe figs. I was just thinking about how beautiful Samos was, when I met two distressed-looking Somali women walking down the road by the hospital. I knew one, a lovely Somali volunteer who regularly translates at the hospital.

– *What's up?*

– *The policeman at the gate won't let us in to visit a friend, an elderly woman who is sick.*

– *Why not? It's visiting hour and you translate there all the time!*

She shrugged.

– *That's not acceptable. Let's go back!*

– *You can go in with one of them*—the policeman said to me.

– *I am sorry, that does not make sense. If two visitors are allowed, then why not these two women? Where does this rule come from?*

He had no answer and suddenly relented, saying we had five minutes. Of course, we stayed much longer, but I was furious that it had taken a 'stroppy white lady' act to gain entrance.

– *It was the deputy governor who had Aslam's toilets removed*—Matthew told me yesterday. The deputy governor's party, New Democracy, expect to make sweeping gains in the general elections in early July. If he wins, Samos will only have a small processing centre, and all new arrivals will be rapidly transferred to the mainland where they will have to live in closed camps. Then, if they have not been processed within six months, they will all be returned to Turkey anyway, regardless of their rights.

– *The EU-Turkey Deal does not allow that.*

– *He says that does not matter, there are ways around it.*

New Democracy is a Centre Right party, one of whose MP's, Thanos Plevris, once famously claimed that the use of deadly force against those trying to cross Greek borders would be an effective solution to the immigration crisis. In addition, he suggested that immigrants should be denied access to food, water and healthcare, until they realised that conditions in Greece were worse than those in their homelands.

381

– There is still this idea that, if conditions are humane, more people will come here—a colleague in UNHCR told me—but only a privileged person would think like that. There is absolutely no evidence supporting this. It completely ignores the desperation of the situations from which people are escaping. Everyone knows the conditions are getting worse and yet people are still coming.

Making the lives of asylum seekers hell on earth does not work. It does not work on the southern borders of the United States, where young single men are 'concentrated' in holding centres, and families would rather risk their children being separated and kept in cages than live with the violence in their own countries. It does not work in the Mediterranean, where people believe that extortion by smugglers, and the possibility of rape, death by drowning or through being kidnapped for your organs, are all preferable to continuing with the miseries they endure at home. Thanos Plevris should read Warsan Shire:

"You have to understand,
no one puts their children in a boat
unless the water is safer than the land."

If we want to stop people fleeing to Europe and North America, the fundamental changes required are in our own lives, not theirs, so that the wellbeing of every country on this tiny planet is equally protected and its resources equitably shared.

Pan, my friend in Athens, suggests this process could begin with taking the EU to the International Criminal Court for imposing the EU-Turkey Deal, and forcing Europe to share the burden of forced migration by reopening its borders. It is the poorest countries in the world, mostly in Africa, that take 85% of the 70 million forcibly displaced people in the world today. One in six people in Lebanon is a refugee, while Uganda, a country of 42 million, currently hosts more than a million. So, the idea that Europe is 'full' is laughable.

– Who decided that people have to stay in the camps? Mahmoud asked me this morning. *They have not committed a crime. They found them-*

*selves here. How come you have the right to fly from here to there to
anywhere, and because they look different, they do not have that right?*
It is Tawab's question again, and four years after meeting him in that
other Jungle in Calais, I still have no answer. Both of them are correct. The right to a dignified, happy life cannot rest on the accident
of geography at birth.

Cornwall, Thursday 25 July
New Democracy won the Greek elections on July 7th. Mitsotakis,
the new Prime Minister, immediately moved migration to the Ministry of Social Protection (the equivalent of our Home Office). He has
promised to improve conditions in the reception centres, particularly
on Samos, and focus on the needs of minors and unaccompanied
children. He also wants to overhaul and speed up the asylum and deportation process, police the sea borders more effectively, and properly implement the EU-Turkey Deal. It's not clear what this means in
practice, but my Greek friends were gloomy, predicting more illegal
returns and a clampdown on the solidarity movements that support
asylum seekers.
– *We will go the way of Italy and Hungary*—said one.
The tightening up has begun. On Samos, six doctors, three nurses
and an interpreter at Samos hospital in Vathy have been arrested for
issuing 'false' vulnerability certificates, that allowed people to be prioritised for transfer to the mainland, in return for payment.

Cornwall, Friday 6 September
The gloomy predictions were correct: the Greek government has
decided on a variety of measures to reduce 'congestion,' including
removing the right to appeal if your asylum application is rejected,
increased frontier surveillance and increased searches for illegals. At
the end of August, a broad coalition of NGO's and human rights
groups produced a damming report showing:
"Evidence of sweeping human rights violations of displaced people
and refugees on mainland Greece and the islands of Chios, Lesvos and
Samos, violations that could amount to cruel and unusual treatment

and torture. As a result of the so-called Containment Policy, bought into effect following the EU-Turkey Statement in 2016, thousands are currently trapped on the islands without access to shelter, health-care or education, including many women and children. Those living on the islands, often in severely overcrowded camps, face dire living conditions, including unhygienic conditions and inadequate hous-ing and bathing facilities… a lack of access to medical care. There is a lack of legal safeguards, including access to a lawyer. There are also alarming reports of ill-treatment by the police in detention centres, ranging from beatings, standing on people's backs and heads and ag-gressive behaviour… [that] often go un-investigated, and that there is little to no redress available for the victims. There is an alarming rate of gender-based violence against refugee and asylum-seeking women and girls occurring in Greece, and in particular on the is-lands. In addition, the report highlights the concerning treatment of unaccompanied children. Overall, the findings of this report sug-gest that refugees and asylum seekers in Greece continue to confront an extremely hostile environment, one characterized by uncertainty, violence and neglect."[21]

Meanwhile, the Turkish government have threatened to pull out of the EU/Turkey Deal altogether and open the gates to Western Eu-rope, because Europe has not fulfilled its promise of visa free travel for Turkish citizens in the Schengen area. Nor has it helped Turkey in its wish to create a 'safe zone' inside the Syrian border to which it can return some one million of the 3.6 million refugees currently resident in the country.

Last week severe wildfires on Samos turned one thousand holiday makers and residents into refugees, forcing their evacuation by boat from the nearest beaches. A sign of things to come?

2020

Afterword

June 2020

April 4th, 1984. Last night to the flicks. All war films. One very good one of a ship full of refugees being bombed somewhere in the Mediterranean. Audience much amused by shots of a great huge fat man trying to swim away with a helicopter after him, first you saw him wallowing along in the water like a porpoise, then you saw him through the helicopters gunsights, then he was full of holes and the sea round him turned pink and he sank as suddenly as though the holes had let in the water, audience shouting with laughter when he sank.

– George Orwell, *1984*[22]

Cornwall, Monday 22 June

I am watching a video. It was made by the Turkish coast guard in early March of this year and shows Greek Coast Guard vessels harassing migrants in a rubber dinghy. First, a Greek boat cuts across, hitting the small, packed vessel with its wake. You can hear screams. Another boat gets close to the dinghy, and a man appears to strike the migrants with a long rod. Shots are fired into the water. The migrants get close to a Greek Coast Guard boat and try to climb onto it, but a man on the boat pushes them away with grappling hooks and shouts—*Go back!*[23]

Greece has increased illegal pushbacks to Turkey in the last three months. As I write, Alarm Phone, an NGO that provides a hotline for migrants in distress in the Mediterranean, reports on Twitter that twenty people, including women and children, are on a small raft floating in Greek waters near Lesvos:

"The people say that water is still entering the boat and that they fear for their lives. They sent us a photo with a vessel near them. They say that it is a vessel of the Greek Coast Guard and that it has been in the area since hours. Why are they not assisting?"[24]

Greece is not the only country trying to block migrants in the Mediterranean. Crossings from North Africa have increased, possibly because of fighting around Tripoli and the difficulties of finding work during the pandemic. Sixty one people drowned after a boat sank off the coast of Tunisia in early June, including twenty two women and four children. But in spite of the dangers, Malta has refused to rescue migrants or allow private rescue boats to dock. Instead, it has redirected them at gun point to Italy, or returned them to Libya, which both IOM and UNHCR say is not a safe destination. More recently, the Maltese government has quarantined more than 400 migrants for an indeterminate time on cramped cruise boats. The increasing despair and suicidal feelings felt by those currently trapped in these water prisons is made clear in a social media post:

"Anxiety, resentment, and depression have increased… this has made our health condition worse. Also due to lack of full health care, there's been an outbreak of skin diseases… there is lack of care when it comes to food. Hunger strikes have started and we're in a deplorable state. We have no means of communication to reflect our [condition] to the outside world."[25]

Greece and Malta both use the COVID-19 pandemic as their excuse for breaking international law and creating an ever more hostile environment for migrants seeking refuge.[26] They are not the only ones. In the United States, Donald Trump used public health legislation enacted in 1893, to empower immigration agents to summarily expel migrants arriving at the US borders. This contradicts US obligations to asylum seekers under international law, but the pretext was preventing the spread of COVID-19. This May, Trump indefinitely extended the order. He has also taken the opportunity to deport unaccompanied children already in the country, many of whom have been caged in detention for months. So rather than being released to sponsors happy and willing to accommodate them, children are dumped on planes in the middle of the night and sent straight back to the terrors from which they fled.[27]

Hostility to migrants was increasing long before the pandemic. In Ventimiglia, in Northern Italy, Don Rito's church basement shelter was shut down in August 2017. Vulnerable women and children were told to join the men in the Red Cross Camp outside the town. Don

Rito has been moved to a parish in the countryside. At the other end of Italy, Domenico Lucano, Riace's migrant friendly mayor, was arrested in October 2018 on a variety of charges related to the reception and management of migrants, and he was banned from living in the town. Many of those charges have since been annulled by Italy's highest court and Domenico has returned to Riace, but the mood in the town has changed. In June 2019, the anti-migrant Lega party supported the election of an independent mayor from 'Riace Reborn.' Rebirth has included the shuttering of the migrant shops and work projects, the destruction of some of the murals, and changing the sign on the road into town. Where it once said "Riace, a welcoming town" above a picture of a dark-skinned man, there is now a large panel welcoming you to the home of the "saints and martyrs Cosimo and Damiano." The new mayor put up the sign himself. Apparently, this has nothing to do with politics. It commemorates the 350th anniversary of the arrival of the saints' remains in town.[28]

I chatted to Daniel on the phone. He still works in Riace as a garbage collector, and he and his wife were celebrating the arrival of their new baby daughter Miracle. But he told me the town has changed. Although the new mayor continues to allow migrants to live in free housing, the closure of all the projects and the lack of work meant many left and the local school had to close. He now has to pay for Cosimo to take the school bus to the neighbouring town. *The atmosphere is not like before, there was an energy here and we had lots of visitors*—Daniel told me. *Now it's very quiet.*

This January, I went back to Calais for a few days to provide some more mental health training for volunteers. On a cold foggy morning, I watched the police at work along the Route des Gravelines. The school bus and recreational facilities were long gone. The only water points were two taps next to a couple of porta-loos. Spikes had been put up in the shelf-like areas under overpasses and bridges, where migrants had previously found dry sleeping space. Fences had appeared around patches of waste ground. Here on Route des Gravelines, migrants had found a way through and camped anyway. So, every 48 hours the police arrived and systematically 'evicted' the small clusters of soggy tents. Migrants in these situations had an unpleasant choice. Stay away and risk losing all your belongings or stay to guard them and pick them up when the police arrive, while risking arbitrary arrest and possible detention and deportation.

In Dunkirk, some five hundred migrants created a slightly more stable encampment in some old abandoned warehouses. The small crowd of tents was surround by piles of uncollected rubbish. When the French government introduced lockdown in response to the pandemic, they used teargas to permanently evict the site and fence it off. Around three hundred now live in woodland where their only access to clean water is from a tap some twenty minutes' walk away.

Lockdown in both Calais and Dunkirk forced the suspension of services by volunteers. Social spaces were closed, food distributions were limited or ceased altogether. Buses frequently refused to stop for non-white people, and on occasion, people have been forcibly removed by the police, so it became difficult to travel to clinics or supermarkets. And if you did manage to walk to a shop, it might refuse access. Many migrants went hungry for a number of weeks. Meanwhile, the evictions of the thousand or so living in Calais have continued every other day, with the French police herding people together into small crowds with no pretence at distancing.

The French government did offer a limited number of places in accommodation, but the lack of trust on the part of the migrant community is now too great. Many felt as vulnerable, humiliated and unsupported in these centres as they did on the street, and they still feared fingerprinting and deportation. Around three hundred took up the offer. Many others took to the sea. Boat traffic across the channel has actually increased during the pandemic.[29]

In Greece, the Mitsotakis government continued to make life ever more difficult for asylum seekers, narrowing the definition of vulnerability and making it harder to appeal rejected asylum claims. But this did not deter people from coming. This January, as Afghans and Syrians fled from renewed violence in their own countries, 9265 people tried to get to Greece by boat—almost double those trying in the same period in 2019—and 3096 succeeded. The rest were arrested by the Turkish coast guard and sent back.[30]

By February, there were more than 42,000 migrants camped on the Aegean islands, with 20,000 of those living around Moria on Lesvos. But the Government's plans to build large enclosed detention centres were put on hold in the face of local opposition. The Olive Grove which had provided rest and sanctuary four years ago, had deteriorated into a squalid, garbage filled, shanty town where you were lucky if you had a piece of plastic to shelter you at night, and you had to spend hours queuing for food.

– *The conditions in Moria are indescribable*—Ali told the Guardian newspaper in January. He is an English teacher who escaped Idlib in Syria with his four children. *Sometimes there is no water, there is no electricity. When it rains, we fear for our children's lives, that they will die of the rain, the cold, the wind. For Syrians, this is a hell. We are homeless, our town, Idlib is being destroyed. […] Moria is just a place for waiting for death. Life in Moria is impossible—believe me—most of us here have changed psychologically. Some people have lost their minds.*[31]

Meanwhile, both volunteers and refugees were subject to harassment and physical attacks from vigilante groups. Then at the end of February, Turkey fulfilled its threat to open its land and sea borders to Greece, allowing thousands of migrants to head for Europe. Mitsotakis immediately increased 'the level of deterrence..to the maximum.' Extra troops were deployed to the Turkish land border with Greece, where they used tear gas, rubber bullets and water cannons to keep migrants out. Turkish authorities claimed more than a thousand were injured and four killed.

As in the US and France, the COVID-19 pandemic has given the Greek government licence to tighten restrictions even further. It closed asylum offices completely in early March, for two months, and although the government lifted lockdown restrictions for its own population and visiting tourists in late May, it has continued to severely restrict the movement of all asylum seekers living in reception centres and camps.[32] It chose World Refugee Day (June 20th) to announce a further extension of this discriminatory lockdown. This is in spite of the fact that there have been very few reported COVID-19 cases in any camp. Greece as a whole has only experienced 152 CO-VID-related deaths.[33]

So currently, while tourists and locals can go to the beach, migrants attempting to go to a shop or seek healthcare or legal advice are likely to be stopped and subject to a 150 euro fine if found to be moving without a permit. And in addition to the stress of overcrowded, unsanitary living conditions, there is now the anxiety of catching infection in the packed food queues where social distancing is impossible, or in the shower you share with more than 600 others. There is no escape because the social and educational spaces are closed and your internet connection is poor at best, so you cannot access support or entertainment online. And although asylum offices have reopened, if your asylum application was rejected, you now only have ten days to appeal before you are deported. But with a back log of 1400 cases, and restrictions on movement, how do you get the legal advice you need in time?[34]

Not surprisingly, frustration and anger have increased and tensions between camp residents have escalated. There have been outbreaks of lethal violence between rival gangs vying for control of the camp. Doctors report stabbings to chest and major arteries, a rape with a bottle, a deliberate finger amputation. Five people have been killed, including a 23-year-old woman, and fifteen others wounded since the beginning of the year. In June, a Greek resident was stabbed in the chest when he tried to break up a fight between asylum seekers in Mytilene town square.[35]

The government's solution to overcrowding on the islands has been to tell some 9000 refugees living on the mainland, who have already received international protection, that they can only live in reception facilities for one month. After that, they are considered quite capable of finding work and accommodation on their own, even if, like one Iraqi family, a father is in a wheelchair and his 5-year-old daughter requires assisted feeding through a gastric tube. NGOs predict a new wave of homelessness.

And if you are an unaccompanied child, you risk being placed in 'protective custody' either in a police cell or a detention centre, sharing crowded space with other adults and children, vulnerable to physical and sexual abuse, with no access to education or legal, medical or psychological support. More than 200 children are in such a situation, in spite of Greek government promises to provide better protection and EU promises to provide sanctuary.[36] One of the main drivers of the problems in Greece is the unwillingness of other European countries to share the burden.

The situation is no better in Mexico. Trump's anti-immigrant policies and closure of borders, combined with the impact of the pandemic, has completely changed the relaxed attitude to those crossing the river from Tecun Uman in Guatemala. As of July 2019, migrants were no longer allowed to move North from Tapachula.[37] Anti-immigrant hostility in the area has grown as many blame migrants for rising crime and violence. COVID has made the situation much worse. Shelters are now closed so those migrants not trapped in overcrowded detention centres, roam the streets with no access to clean water or food.[38]

As I pull all this information together, it is hard not to despair. And I still have the same questions I had five years ago. How is it possible that those fleeing poverty, violence and disaster should be treated with such inhumanity and discrimination by the richest countries in the world? Note, I do not use the term 'natural disaster,' I learnt many years ago working with the victims of 'natural' disasters in Pakistan, Indonesia and Haiti, that the real disaster is poverty. The rich were both more likely to survive any catastrophe, as they lived in safer houses in safer places, and were more likely to recover quickly, having immediate access to the resources they needed. And today, it is the richer nations who pour yet more carbon into the atmosphere, thus warming the planet, and increasing the frequency and intensity of cyclones, floods, and droughts. But it is the poorer regions and nations who suffer the worst consequences. No wonder people are moving.

When I started these diaries in 2015 there were 65.3 million forcibly displaced people in the world. Today, according to UNHCR, there are 79.5 million—that is 1% of the world's population. Thirty million of those are children. Eighty five percent of those displaced live in developing countries. And while Britain granted asylum to 15,000 people in 2019,[39] Pakistan and Uganda each hosted 1.4 million refugees, Sudan and Germany had 1.1 million each and Turkey 3.6 million.[40]

Perhaps I should not be surprised. George Floyd's slow, painful death in the United States and the Windrush scandal in the United Kingdom, in which we attempted to deport the children of citizens we had invited from the Caribbean to rebuild the country after WWII, have reminded us of the entrenched racism and indifference to the suffering of others 'not like us' within our own countries. But these scandals have also strengthened and globalised the Black Lives Matter movement. We are all now re-examining our histories and beginning to acknowledge that much of the wealth and privilege that the so called 'developed' countries take for granted was built on some four hundred years of theft, murder and exploitation. It touches all of us. I went to medical school in Bristol, one of the major ports in the transatlantic slave trade. I sat exams in the Wills building, built to memorialise a family who made their fortunes off the backs of people enslaved to work in their tobacco plantations, and I went to concerts in Colston hall, named after the famous slave trader and 'philanthropist' of the same name. And there is the catch. Theft funds philanthropy, so how to protest? Pulling down Edward Colston's statue and rolling it into the Docks from which his slave trading ships set sail might be part of an answer. (Although personally, I would like him pulled up again, and stuck in a museum with a detailed explanatory history). But it's not enough.

In Calais, one of the art works that caught my attention was a poster stating:

"Fuck your colonial borders. We are here because you were there."

It was a less subtle formulation of the points Don Rito made to me in the church in Ventimiglia in 2016.

– *The rich countries went there, they stole everything, and then they sold arms to create chaos, and in the meantime, they still reap benefits.*

If we are really serious about addressing some of the fundamental injustices of the last four hundred years: the slavery, colonisation, theft and environmental destruction that have contributed to the global inequity that feeds the migrant crisis—*We have to start to give back what we took away*—Don Rito said.

Nigerian writer, Uzodinma Iweala, makes similar points in a 2017 lecture and essay. He argues that the giving back should not be in the form of humanitarian assistance. "It is as though I were to come to your house, steal your things, kick you onto the street and then proclaim to the world that I will grudgingly take up the burden of caring for your lazy, unwashed self." We should stop charitable giving and start paying reparations.

And how much do we owe? Around 97 trillion dollars according to Iweala. That's the conservative estimate of value of the unpaid labour extracted from Africans in North American colonies between 1619 and 1865. Labour that "was absolutely fundamental in building up the very wealth in Europe and America that now makes private philanthropy possible." He went on to suggest creating:

"A 97-trillion-dollar fund, based on the acknowledgement—This is your wealth, which we have wrongfully appropriated and are privileged to give back—that is invested in massive infrastructure development in Africa […] in a 21st-century way that treats environmental costs as real and recognizes human need as only one of a vast constellation of planetary needs. [In which] entire sections of the continent that have suffered from exploitative extraction return to their natural states, [allowing] depleted rainforests to grow back into massive carbon sinks while we hyper-looped between our reimagined urban centers."[41]

We need such radical solutions and we need them now. As I write, it is 38 degrees in Verkhoyansk, Siberia, the highest temperature ever recorded there, and 2020 is likely to be the hottest year on record. Yet, while governments across the world are focussed on the COVID-19 pandemic, they remain collectively paralysed in the face of the greater emergencies of climate catastrophe and ecological breakdown that continue unabated. Lockdowns in industrial cities might have temporarily cleaned the air while animals roamed our streets, but the pandemic has allowed clearing and cutting to accelerate unchecked in the Amazon rain forest,[42] increasing the likelihood of fires that will convert the world's most significant carbon sink to carbon emitter. Habitat loss contributes to the continuing mass extinction of wildlife. And this destruction, along with the illegal trade in wild species, has increased the possibilities of viruses passing from wild animals to humans, and contributes to the likelihood of more global pandemics.[43]

None of these facts make headline news. We continue to cut off the branches of the tree of life upon which we sit. Meanwhile, David Beasley, head of the World Food Programme warns that "almost a quarter of a billion people are marching towards starvation because of the economic deterioration from COVID, wars, conflicts"… and that there could be…"famines of biblical proportions in multiple countries, and especially in Africa."[44]

Pandemics, habitat destruction, climate catastrophe, conflict, famine. As with slavery and colonisation, it is people of colour, indigenous people, and those in the global south who are disproportionately affected. In 2018, the World Bank predicted that there might be 143 million more climate migrants by 2050, mostly from Latin America, sub-Saharan Africa, and Southeast Asia.[45] The non-binding Global Compact on Migration, adopted by the UN General Assembly in December 2019, does little to address the problem. As the British government made clear: although the compact states that migrants have the same human rights as other people, it "protects every country's right to determine its own immigration policies" and "does not create any new rights for migrants."[46] Even so, the United States, Israel, Hungary, Poland and the Czech Republic all opposed it.

Paradoxically, the pandemic has shone a spotlight on who really sustains society when we are in trouble: the people who grow and harvest our food, the cleaners, garbage collectors, supermarket cashiers, bus drivers, porters, carers, nurses and doctors, are the essential frontline workers. And guess what? thirty three percent of doctors in the British National Health Service are migrants. It was two migrant nurses that helped to save Prime Minister Boris Johnsons' life when he caught Coronavirus. It was Romanians who answered the prime ministers' call to come and pick our vegetables during lockdown so that we would not go hungry. Forty percent of those employed in food manufacturing are migrants, 35% of those who clean our floors... I could go on, you get the picture. It is migrants who have helped keep the country running.[47]

It is working with migrants over the last four years that has given me hope. What Housam, Abool, Solomon, and so many others have taught me is the real meaning of social solidarity. It is not about giving to someone, but standing beside them, and sharing in their struggle for both material, social and psychological wellbeing that benefits us both. I witnessed that solidarity in France, Italy, Greece and Mexico. I have seen it blossom in my own street and village during the pandemic: mutual aid groups providing companionship and sharing resources. Recently, I read about Hampay, a refugee living in Athens who founded a community centre, making and distributing food bags to the homeless and vulnerable.[48] On Lesvos, migrants from different countries set up an awareness team to provide information in their communities about the virus. They also set up wash stations, gave out hygiene products and created a mask making factory. It has distributed masks throughout the camp and to nurses at a local hospital. Local women from Mytilene also help.[49]

I search social media and ring round to find out what has happened to the children who shared their stories. Some old phone numbers no longer work and I cannot reach all of them, but I know that Emily is surviving quarantine in Mexico and has a place at medical school. Majd and his family made it to Germany. Sadiq also appears to be doing well there.

One of the calls I make is to Jamal, a Somali boy whom I met during the eviction of the Jungle in the Autumn of 2016. I last heard from him at an accommodation centre somewhere in Western France. He stayed there until he heard that the United Kingdom were not keeping their promise to take all the unaccompanied children. He did not want to ask for asylum in France, so he left the centre and went back to Calais, where he was arrested straight away and put in jail. He was told he would only be released if he left Calais. He spent the following months living between the streets and different shelters in Caen and Le Havre, sleeping in the day and trying every night to get onto a ferry or lorry but never succeeding. One of his closest friends was killed after being hit by a car. Finally, he met someone in Calais looking for children who had been promised entry back in 2016. He was interviewed again and arrived here by legal means in late 2017. Since then, he has studied for two years at college, while working part time. Now he wants to be a nurse. There are happy endings.

Endnotes

1 Malone, Barry. "Why Al Jazeera Will Not Say 'Mediterranean Migrants.'" *Al Jazeera*, 20 August 2015.

2 "UNHCR Viewpoint: 'Refugee' or 'Migrant' - Which Is Right?" *UNHCR*, 11 July 2016.

3 "Who Is a Migrant?" *IOM UN MIGRATION*, 2019.

4 "Differentiation between Migrants and Refugees." *OHCHR*, 11 July 2016.

5 Carling, Jørgen. "Refugees are Also Migrants. And All Migrants Matter," *University of Oxford, faculty of Law*, 3 September 2015

6 A women's protest encampment outside a nuclear missile base in the eighties.

7 A new ruling by the British courts in January 2016 allowed unaccompanied minors with family in the UK to come to Britain while their asylum applications were processed (McVeigh, Karen and Chris Johnson. "Syrian teenagers brother looking forward to reunion after legal victory," *The Guardian*, 21 January 2016.).

8 Psychological debriefing is one of the most widely implemented interventions after exposure to potentially traumatic events. In 2012, the WHO recommended that psychological debriefing should not be used for people exposed recently to a traumatic event as an intervention to reduce the risk of post-traumatic stress, anxiety or depressive symptoms (*WHO. Psychological Debriefing in People Exposed to a Recent Traumatic Event.* 2012.).

9 "Psychological First Aid: Guide for Field Workers." *World Health Organization*, 2 October 2011.

[10] Piketty, Thomas. *Capital in the Twenty-First Century*. Edited by Arthur Goldhammer, Harvard University Press, 2014.

[11] The Dubs Amendment: In May 2016 Lord Alfred Dubs, who had come to Britain as a Jewish child refugee escaping the Nazis, succeeded in committing the British government to accepting an unspecified number of vulnerable, unaccompanied, child refugees from Europe, even if they did not have family in Britain.

[12] Panter-Brick, Catherine, et al. "Mental Health and Childhood Adversities: A Longitudinal Study in Kabul, Afghanistan." *American Academy of Child and Adolescent Psychiatry*, Vol. 50, No. 4, 2011, pp. 349–63.

[13] Costa, Antonio Maria. "Così dopo secoli di sfruttamento l'Europa chiude le porte all'Africa," *La Stampa*, 24 October 2016.

[14] Kingsley, Patrick. "The small African region with more refugees than all of Europe." *The Guardian*, 26 November 2016.

[15] Shire, Warsan. "Home." *Seekers Guidance*, 2 September 2015.

[16] Meaning they are identified as arriving in Italy under the Dublin process, and if they seek asylum, it must be in Italy.

[17] Jones, Lynne. "Borderlands." Reprinted from *The Lancet,* 390 pp. 22-23, with permission from Elsevier, 7 July 2017.

[18] Coyote is a term for people smugglers in Latin America

[19] Sodium valproate is an effective anticonvulsant, but if taken during pregnancy, it can cause serious harm to an unborn child. It is therefore not recommended for women and girls at risk of conceiving.

[20] "IASC Guidelines on Mental Health and Psychosocial Support in Emergency Settings." *Inter-Agency Standing Committee,* June 2007.

[21] Lucas, A., et al. "No End in Sight: The Mistreatment of Asylum Seekers in Greece." *Refugee Rights,* 2019..

[22] Orwell, George. *1984.* Penguin Books, 2008.

[23] @AJEnglish (Al Jazeera English). "Footage appears to show the Greek coastguard harassing a boat of migrants and refugees, pushing them back and opening fire into the water." *Twitter,* 3 March 2020, 4:15 a.m.

[24] @alarm_phone (Alarm Phone). "BREAKING – 29 people, incl. many children in distress in Greek waters off of Lesvos. We informed all authorities at 06:03 CEST. Their last pos. at 07.21 CEST was 39.387947, 26.453352." *Twitter,* 22 June 2020, 1:46 a.m.

[25] "Malta: Disembark Rescued People." *Human Rights Watch,* 22 May 2020.

[26] "Legal Brief on International Law and Rescue at Sea." *UNHCR and IMO,* 1983.

[27] Bochenek, Michael Garcia. "Trump Administration Uses Pandemic as Excuse to Expel Migrants." *Human Rights Watch,* 20 May 2020

[28] ANSA. "Changes in Riace under New Administration." *INFO MIGRANTS,* 25 September 2019.

[29] Hauswedell, Charlotte. "Migrant Channel Crossings by Boat Surge during Pandemic, Concern over Illegal Returns by UK." *INFO MIGRANTS,* 22 May 2020.

[30] Aegean Boat Report. "Monthly Statistics 2020." *Facebook,* 3 February 2020, 4:49 p.m.

[31] Grant, Harriet. "'Moria Is a Hell': New Arrivals Describe Life in a Greek Refuge Camp." *The Guardian*, 17 January 2020.

[32] Cossé, Eva. "Greece Again Extends COVID-19 Lockdown in Refugee Camps: Authorities Should End Discriminatory Restrictions." *Human Rights Watch*, 12 June 2020.

[33] "Greece: First Cases of Coronavirus among Migrants on Lesbos." *INFO MIGRANTS*, 13 May 2020.

[34] Fallon, Katy. "Greece Ready to Welcome Tourists as Refugees Stay Locked down in Lesbos." *The Guardian*, 27 May 2020.

[35] Hume, Tim. "Violence Is Exploding in Europe's Most Notorious Migrant Camp." *Vice*, 15 June 2020.

[36] Roth, Kenneth. "Detention of Unaccompanied Children in Greece: HRW Letter to Prime Minister Mitsotakis." *Human Rights Watch*, 23 June 2020.

[37] Lawal, Shola. "African Migrants Fall Foul of US, Mexico Policy Changes." *The New Humanitarian*, 17 January 2020.

[38] Kustgarten, Abrahm. "Where Will Everyone Go?" *ProPublica*, 23 July 2020.

[39] Sturge, Georgina. "Migration Statistics: How Many Asylum Seekers and Refugees Are There in the UK?" *House of Commons Library*, 2019.

[40] "Global Trends: Forced Displacement in 2019." *UNHCR*, 2020.

[41] Iweala, Uzodinma. "Reparation as Philanthropy: Radically Rethinking «Giving» in Africa." *Le Monde Afrique*, 10 November 2017.

[42] Paes, Caio de Freitas. "Amazon Fires May Be Worse in 2020 as Deforestation and Land Grabbing Spikes." Translated by Maya Johnson, *Mongabay*, 18 May 2020.

[43] Jeffries, Barney et al. "The loss of nature and the rise of pandemics: Protecting human and planetary health," *WWF Italy*, March 2020.

[44] Perelma, Marc. "World Food Programme Head Warns COVID-19 Pandemic Could Provoke 'Famines of Biblical Proportions.'" *France 24*, 5 August 2020.

[45] Rigaud, Kanta Kumari, et al. "Groundswell: Preparing for Internal Climate Migration." *World Bank Group*, 2018.

[46] Fella, Stefano. "The United Nations Global Compact for Migration." *House of Commons Library*, August 16 2019

[47] "Key Workers: Migrants' Contribution to the COVID-19 Response." *Overseas Development Institute*, 2020.

[48] Campana, Fahrinisa. "In Greece, Refugees and Migrants Turn to Each Other to Get Through Coronavirus Pandemic." *The World*, 23 April 2020.

[49] Bizot, Olivia, et al. "Minority Communities Mobilize." *Are We Europe*, 15 July 2020.

Author Biography

Lynne Jones OBE, FRCPsych., PhD, is a child psychiatrist, relief worker, and writer. She has spent much of the last twenty five years establishing and running mental health programs in areas of conflict or natural disaster including the Balkans, East and West Africa, South East Asia, the Middle East, Haiti and Central America. Most recently she has worked in the migrant crisis in Europe and Central America through which she has established a storytelling project for children: migrantchildstorytelling.org

It is this period of work that is recorded in the diaries alongside some of the children's stories. She is a course director for the annual course on Mental health in Complex Emergencies, run by the Institute of International Humanitarian Affairs at Fordham University, in collaboration with UNHCR. Her other published works include: *Then They Started Shooting:Children of the Bosnian War and the Adults They Become* (Bellevue Literary Press 2013,) and *Outside the Asylum: A Memoir of War, Disaster and Humanitarian Psychiatry* (Orion 2017).

Jones has an MA in human sciences from the University of Oxford. She qualified in medicine before specializing in psychiatry and has a PhD in social psychology and political science. In 2001, she was made an Officer of the British Empire for her work in child psychiatry in conflict-affected areas of Central Europe. She regularly consults for UNICEF and WHO. She is an honorary consultant at the Maudsley Hospital, London, and with Cornwall Partnership NHS Foundation Trust, and is a visiting scientist at the François-Xavier Bagnoud Centre for Health and Human Rights, Harvard University.

CPSIA information can be obtained
at www.ICGtesting.com
Printed in the USA
BVHW080953240421
605735BV00007B/1599

9 780823 296989